A Matter of Trust

"This suspenseful first in a new series from Wiehl and Henry opens with a bang."
—*Publishers Weekly*

"[A] thoroughly satisfying mystery, well paced and tightly written. Mia and Charlie are intriguing characters, and readers can hope they'll return in future novels."
—*CBA Retailers + Resources*

"Dramatic, moving, intense. *A Matter of Trust* gives us an amazing insight into the life of a prosecutor—and mom. Mia Quinn reminds me of Lis."
—Maxine Paetro, *New York Times* best-selling author

"*A Matter of Trust* is a stunning crime series debut from one of my favorite authors, Lis Wiehl. Smart, suspenseful, and full of twists that only an insider like Wiehl could pull off. I want prosecutor Mia Quinn in my corner when murder's on the docket—she's a compelling new character and I look forward to seeing her again soon."
—Linda Fairstein, *New York Times* best-selling author

The Triple Threat Series

illiant lawyer, prosecutor, and journalist like Lis Wiehl could put together
is thrilling! The incredible characters and nonstop twists will leave you
Open [*Face of Betrayal*] and find a comfortable seat because you won't
down!"
—E. D. Hill, FOX News anchor

men crack the big cases! Makes perfect sense to me. [*Face of*
away!"
—Jeanine Pirro, former DA; hosts The CW's daytime court television reality show *Judge Jeanine Pirro*

ACCLAIM FOR LIS WIEHL

The East Salem Trilogy

"The second East Salem novel is as frightening as the first. The supernatural elements fit perfectly with the faith-filled storyline, and the mystery captivates from the first page."

—*RT Book Reviews*

". . . [An] exciting faith-based series that skillfully blends romantic tension, ￼ ping supernatural suspense, and a brutal crime."

—*Library*
REVIEW OF *Wak*

". . . [A] truly chilling predator and some great snappy, funny ￼ readers engaged."

REV￼

"One word describes *Waking Hours* by Wiehl￼ wrenching ride of supernatural suspense tha￼ more. The book was a reminder that the b￼ over. Highly recommended!"

"A gripping plot, intriguing c￼ of romance make *Waking*￼ want the next book in t￼

"Only a br￼
a mystery t￼
mesmerized.￼
want to put it￼

"Three smart w￼
Betrayal] blew me￼

"Who killed loudmouth radio guy Jim Fate? The game is afoot! *Hand of Fate* is a fun thriller, taking you inside the media world and the justice system—scary places to be!"

—BILL O'REILLY, FOX
TV AND RADIO ANCHOR

"As a television crime writer and producer, I expect novels to deliver pulse-pounding tales with major twists. *Hand of Fate* delivers big-time."

—PAM VEASEY, WRITER AND
EXECUTIVE PRODUCER OF *CSI: NY*

"Book Three in the wonderful Triple Threat Series is a fast-paced thriller full of twists and turns that will keep you guessing until the end. What makes these books stand out for me is my ability to identify so easily with Allison, Nic, and Cassidy. I truly care about what happens to each of them, and the challenges they face this time are heart-wrenching and realistic. I highly recommend!"

DEBORAH SINCLAIRE, EDITOR-IN-
CHIEF, BOOK-OF-THE-MONTH CLUB
AND THE STEPHEN KING LIBRARY

"Beautiful, successful, and charismatic on the outside but underneath a twisted killer. She's brilliant and crazy and comes racing at the reader with knives and a smile. The most chilling villain you'll meet . . . because she could live next door to you."

—DR. DALE ARCHER, CLINICAL
PSYCHIATRIST, REGARDING *HEART OF ICE*

FATAL TIDE

FATAL TIDE

THE EAST SALEM TRILOGY
BOOK THREE

LIS WIEHL
WITH PETE NELSON

THOMAS NELSON
Since 1798

NASHVILLE   DALLAS   MEXICO CITY   RIO DE JANEIRO

Published in Nashville, Tennessee, by Thomas Nelson. Thomas Nelson is a registered trademark of Thomas Nelson, Inc.

Page design by Mandi Cofer.

Thomas Nelson, Inc., books may be purchased in bulk for educational, business, fund-raising, or sales promotional use. For information, please e-mail SpecialMarkets@ThomasNelson.com.

Scripture quotations are taken from the REVISED STANDARD VERSION of the Bible. © 1946, 1952, 1971, 1973 by the Division of Christian Education of the National Council of the Churches of Christ in the U.S.A. Used by permission.

Publisher's Note: This novel is a work of fiction. Names, characters, places, and incidents are either products of the author's imagination or used fictitiously. All characters are fictional, and any similarity to people living or dead is purely coincidental.

ISBN 978-1-40169-015-1 (ITPE)

Library of Congress Cataloging-in-Publication Data

Wiehl, Lis W.
  Fatal tide / Lis Wiehl with Pete Nelson.
      pages cm. -- (The East Salem trilogy ; bk 3)
  ISBN 978-1-59554-946-4 (hardcover)
1. Paranormal fiction. I. Nelson, Peter, 1953- II. Title.
PS3623.I382F38 2013
813'.6--dc23

2013009865

Printed in the United States of America

13 14 15 16 17 18 RRD 6 5 4 3 2 1

*For Dani and Jacob, with
unconditional love always, Mom*

1.

December 20

"Where are we going?" the boy asked. A feeling, a premonition perhaps, told him something wasn't right, but he didn't know what it was. He wondered if he was being kidnapped.

"Airport," the driver, George Gardener, said.

The boy realized he'd made a mistake, telling them he'd remembered to grab his passport. He should have pretended he'd lost it. Then they couldn't fly him out of the country.

"Don't you think we'd be safer at Mr. Gunderson's house?"

Tommy Gunderson lived in a large stone house on twenty-two acres surrounded by a stone wall topped by a deer fence. He had security cameras, including hi-def, night vision, and infrared, triggered by motion detectors, and he had a small arsenal of weapons. The boy had shown up at Tommy's gate with a Bible in his hand, betting they'd let him in. He'd come to get information.

"I'm afraid that's the first place the people who are trying to kill you will look," the man in the backseat said. His name was Julian Villanegre, and he was even older than the driver, probably over eighty, the boy guessed. He was an art historian and, like the boy, he was British. "You'll be safer if we can get you to a place where they won't think to look. And so far, we don't think they know you're with us."

"That makes sense," the boy said. He had to think of a way to get them to turn the car around. They were still in East Salem, New York, fifty miles north of Manhattan and their destination, the international terminal at JFK, where the men hoped to catch a late-night flight to London.

The car wound through a snowy winter landscape along a narrow two-lane roller coaster of a road. He'd asked to sit in the front seat, where they wouldn't be able to use the child locks to keep him in the car. He wondered what would happen if he jumped out while it was still moving. He looked at the speedometer. Thirty-two miles an hour. He guessed he'd probably survive. Once they got on the freeway it would be too late. He kept his hand on the door handle.

"Are you sure your house is safer?"

"One of the advantages of living in a castle," Villanegre said, smiling from the backseat. "It costs a small fortune to heat, but when withstanding a siege is desired, it suits one to a tittle. My ancestors survived three. I think it will do."

"They said you'd fill me in on the way," the boy said. His name was Reese Stratton-Mallins. He was seventeen.

"It's a very long story, I'm afraid," Villanegre said. "One of the oldest too."

"And St. Adrian's Academy is part of it?"

"Very much at the center of it, it seems," the old man told him. "The people who run your school are very bad people who will stop at nothing. You're quite correct to be wary of them. Some of them aren't even people."

George looked over his shoulder at Villanegre, as if to say, *I hope you know what you're doing.*

"What does that mean?" Reese asked.

"Do you know what demons are?" Villanegre replied.

"Demons?" the boy said. He was feigning innocence, but he'd learned a long time ago that he had the kind of face, a look others found sweet and unaffected, that made feigning innocence easy.

"The written record is often traced to the Septuagint translation of the Hebrew Bible," Villanegre said. "When Satan decided to defy God, he was cast out of heaven. Scholars and theologians disagree on the precise numbers, but the consensus suggests perhaps as many as a third of the angels went with him. And the conflict remains. An unseen war. In which we are the foot soldiers, and sometimes the battlefield. The fallen angels can appear to us in demonic form, or they can take human form."

"Are you saying some of the people at my school are demons?" the boy said.

The old man in the backseat only nodded. The car paused at a stop sign. A light snow fell, requiring the intermittent use of windshield wipers.

"Do you know who?" The boy had a hunch.

Villanegre shook his head.

"Do you know since when?"

"That's a very good question," Villanegre replied. "When the Druids were driven out of England, roughly a thousand years ago, some of them managed to hire a Viking ship to bring them to America. For a while they went into hiding. But we believe they established your school more than two hundred years ago at its present location."

"We?"

"Our . . . group," Villanegre said. "Generations of us. Though Tommy Gunderson and Dani—Dr. Harris—are quite new to the organization. They've taken over for George's mother, who recently passed."

"Like the Knights Templar, then?" Reese asked.

George shook his head, not so much in response to his question, Reese gathered, as to say things were bad and unlikely to get better.

"The comparison is apt," Villanegre replied. "The Curatoriat, as we call ourselves, are very much soldiers for Christ, but we have no affiliation with any particular denomination or church. We're special ops, you might say."

3

With every passing minute, the station wagon Tommy had loaned them was getting farther and farther from Tommy's house where, Reese believed, he could get the answers he needed. He decided to give it one more try, and then he would take his chances bailing from the car.

"Is something going on now?" he asked, though he knew the answer.

"There was a prophecy," Villanegre said. "That painting in the school art museum—"

"*The Garden of Earthly Delights?*"

"Yes," Villanegre said, nodding. "The prophecy said when it and the pagans who commissioned it were reunited . . ."

"What? What would happen?"

"Do you know the phrase 'hell breaks loose'?" Villanegre asked. "Some of us believe the things in the painting's depiction of hell are going to, well, come true. Here. That hell and earth will be one. That's what we're trying to stop."

This was more like it, Reese thought. Now he was finding out something that might be useful.

"When you sent Dr. Harris a sample of the drug and the list of names, what did you think you were sending her?" Villanegre asked him. "I gather you could have found yourself in a great amount of trouble if they'd caught you."

"I thought they were testing a drug that would enhance learning," the boy said. "Like Adderall."

"It's quite a bit worse than that," Villanegre said.

"Why?" Reese asked. "What does it do?"

"Dr. McKellen or Dr. Harris would be better people to ask." The Englishman used the side of his hand to wipe the fog from the window and gazed out at the night.

Reese followed his gaze. The leaves were off the trees, and a shallow layer of snow blanketed the ground, pocked by the tracks of deer and raccoons and foxes and coyotes forming trails that led between the hills and the reservoirs.

"It doesn't make anyone better. It makes anyone who takes it sick. Mentally and emotionally. And I dare say spiritually."

"Is that what Amos Kasden was on when he killed that girl?"

"We think so."

Reese had only pretended to take the pills his school gave him, but he couldn't be sure that they weren't putting something in his food. He was closing in on the answer he sought.

"Did you figure out how it works?" he asked.

"It's quite complex," Villanegre said. "We think it is introduced environmentally in vitro, but there may be other delivery mechanisms. When it kicks in at puberty, it overwhelms the user with hormones and feelings of uncontrolled rage. Accompanied by a release of adrenaline. You can imagine the rest. We're still trying to find out how it works and what they intend to do with it."

Reese had a feeling he knew what they were going to do, and a stronger feeling as to when they were going to do it. The question now was—were the people driving in the car with him people he could trust? He would hurt them if he had to . . . but if they were kidnapping him, why would they send two old men whom he could easily overpower?

It was not his own life or soul he was worried about. But his soul had two parts, in a sense—and it was the other half he feared for.

"Were a lot of your classmates given performance-enhancing drugs?" Villanegre asked.

"All of us were," Reese said, glancing at his cell phone to check the time. "It depended on what—" He was interrupted by something falling onto the roof of the car. "What was that?"

"Probably just a branch," George said, turning on his high beams to penetrate the darkness ahead. "All these storms and hurricanes we've had lately been knockin' the beans out of these old trees. Whenever we get so much as a little breeze, everything falls on the power lines, and it takes four or five days before the electric company can—"

Before George could finish his sentence, a massive black arm punched a hole in the windshield and a large black hand closed around his throat.

The car veered suddenly to the left. Instinctively, Reese grabbed the wheel and pulled it hard clockwise to keep the vehicle on the road.

George screamed as he stiffened and slammed on the brakes.

The car screeched.

Reese felt a spray of blood on his face. Some kind of beast was attacking the car, a black shape that scrambled for purchase against the sheet metal of the hood. As the vehicle lurched to a stop, the creature's claws closed around the driver's windpipe, piercing the skin and puncturing an artery. Blood spurted onto the dashboard in a gush.

As Reese turned his head, a second creature tore the back door from its hinges, its head and arms hanging down into the opening as it reached for the passenger in the rear seat.

Two! he thought, looking around. *More than two?*

Reese felt something grab him by the wrist.

It was George, struggling to keep from being pulled from the car through the windshield. His fingernails scratched Reese's arm as he flew from the car, yelling for help. His scream ended with a loud thud.

Reese ducked as the creature in the backseat swung at him. With his head below the steering wheel, he knew the accelerator was close, so he pushed on it with his hand, all the way to the floor, steering as best he could without being able to see.

Just as suddenly, he took his hand off the gas pedal and slammed on the brake, hard. Something growled in pain.

He pulled himself up into the driver's seat and saw that the creature in the backseat was half out the door. He couldn't tell where the first one had gone. Villanegre was dead, his body, what was left of it, torn and broken, the old man's skull crushed by the animal's jaws.

Reese saw, beyond the gruesome scene, a large tree illuminated in the red glow of the brake lights. He shifted the car into reverse and floored it, steering with his right hand while looking over his left shoulder. The creature behind him slipped farther from the car, lunging for the roof rack.

Reese couldn't tell how fast he was going when the beast hit the tree. The car kept going another twenty feet before Reese could apply the brakes and stop.

In the glow of his headlights, the creature, stunned and blinded, stumbled toward the roadway.

The boy shifted into drive and floored the accelerator again, steering directly at whatever it was, making impact with his left front bumper. Even in the full glare of his headlights, the beast was difficult to see clearly; it was black and shaggy, with large white canine fangs and eyes that flashed with reflected light. Reese heard an audible crunching sound and felt the station wagon thump twice as he drove over whatever was left of the thing.

But there were two of them.

Where was the other one?

He hoped he wouldn't have to find out and sped away, only to see something fly through the air and land on the front passenger side fender, grabbing the vehicle by the A-pillar and the windshield wiper.

He steered hard right, braked sharply, sped up again, steered hard left, braked, then accelerated, trying to throw the thing off. He swerved again, left, right, left, steadily accelerating, slamming on the brakes again, to no avail.

Ahead he saw a rocky outcropping close to the road. The beast, centered between the headlights on the hood of the car, was trying to pull itself forward. There wasn't time to come up with a better plan. There wasn't time to fasten his seat belt either, but Reese hoped and prayed that the driver's side air bag would deploy.

He steered for the rock and hit it head on.

The next few moments were lost to him—a loud sound, a jolt, a white flash—and then he awoke to a ringing in his ears, his brain buzzing and jarred.

As full consciousness returned—how long had he been knocked out?—he smelled smoke and felt heat. Something was burning. He pulled on the door handle. The door was wedged shut from the collision. He pushed against it with his shoulder. The door wouldn't open, but the glass in the window had shattered. He pulled himself through the opening and rolled on the ground in case his clothing had caught fire. He got to his feet and ran from the car just as the gasoline from the tank ignited.

The explosion knocked him off his feet, and the fireball lit the woods with an orange glow. He rolled once and then sat up, turning to see the car burning.

He sat a moment to catch his breath.

On his feet again, he turned full circle to survey the road and the woods. He was alone, at least for now. It took a moment for him to get his bearings, his head still throbbing from the noise and the confusion. The body of the creature he'd killed crashing into the rock was no doubt lost in the fire, so he walked back up the road in the direction from which they'd come. He found George Gardener's body crumpled in a heap on the shoulder, his neck bent at an unnatural angle. Farther up the road he found the body of Dr. Julian Villanegre, an arm and part of one leg missing, his face mangled and barely recognizable.

Reese felt his stomach rising up against him and took a moment to steel his resolve, drawing a deep breath and then another, his eyes closed. It was more than he wanted to bear, but he reminded himself that he had no choice. He had to figure this out, and he had to get back to Tommy's house. He searched his pockets for his cell phone but couldn't find it, and he realized it was still in the car, which was on fire.

He searched the body and found the Englishman's cell phone, then used the light from the phone to search the woods for the body of the beast he'd killed against the tree. There was no sign of it, either on the road or in the underbrush. With every passing moment, his mind grew clearer. He was quite certain he'd hit it, twice, and almost as certain he'd killed it.

He searched the phone's contact list for a number for Tommy Gunderson or Dani Harris but didn't find anything. A scan of the call log was equally fruitless. He walked back up road to search the body of George Gardener, but if the man owned a phone, it wasn't on him. He dialed 411 but was told neither Tommy nor Dani had published numbers.

Reese took a deep breath and tried to think. He estimated he was four or five miles from Tommy's house. He didn't think the car had made any left or right turns off the main road. He could walk back, but there was a chance that there were more of whatever had attacked them waiting in the darkness. He needed a ride, preferably from someone armed.

He dialed 911.

"There's been a car accident," he began.

As he waited for the police and the ambulance to arrive, he examined the scene of the "accident" more calmly now, using the cell phone's flash-light app to light the screen. Near where the body of the art historian lay, he bent down to get a closer look at what he'd thought at first was an oil slick. He touched the slimy substance with his fingers and rubbed them together to gauge the viscosity, and finally he smelled it. It was indeed oily, but it was more like oil paint than motor oil, a greasy substance that stained his fingers. From the oil, he extracted and eyed a single long black hair, holding it up next to the light from the phone, but then it dissolved in front of him.

He heard a distant siren approaching and paused to practice the story he would tell.

"I was asleep. We must have hit something . . ."

2.

December 20

11:51 p.m. EST

"Polar bears?" Quinn McKellen said.

Tommy Gunderson shook his head. "I seriously doubt we have polar bears. But they're big, whatever they are."

The two of them were in Tommy's kitchen, speaking in low tones in front of Tommy's computer monitor so as not to wake the others. That included Dani Harris, a childhood friend of Tommy's and high school crush whose work as a consulting psychiatrist for the district attorney's office brought her back into Tommy's life. It included his Aunt Ruth, the town librarian who'd come under attack for her unwitting association with the Curatoriat, and Cassandra Morton, an actress to whom Tommy, in an earlier life, had been engaged. Quinn, a neurochemist and Dani's ex, had arrived, as had Cassandra, to test Tommy and Dani's relationship, but now they were all holed up, along with Arlo, Dani's cat, and Otto, Quinn's bloodhound, behind the walls of Tommy's house to fight an unknowable enemy who was stronger than they were, but not stronger than their combined faith.

"What I'm trying to understand is why we're getting such a faint heat signature and nothing for a visual," Quinn said.

The imagery on the computer screen was telling them that the property was surrounded by perhaps as many as two dozen creatures. They were indeed the approximate size of polar bears, though oddly, their thermal signatures were minimal and they were invisible to Tommy's night vision cameras, looking more like holes than positive presences.

"Are there any cold-blooded mammals?" Tommy asked.

"Not in a true sense," Quinn replied. "There are some species that have to stay active to maintain a body temperature or else aggregate to share body warmth. Bats. And moles, I believe."

"Things that live in the dark," Tommy said. "Or go bump in the night. Did you know that no matter how hungry a polar bear gets, he will not eat a penguin?"

"I did not know that. And why is that?" Quinn asked.

"Because polar bears live at the North Pole and penguins live at the South," Tommy said.

"I imagine penguins don't get married because they have cold feet," Quinn replied. "Why do you have such an elaborate security system, anyway?"

"Came with the house," Tommy said. "The guy who owned this place before me inadvertently swindled a Mexican drug lord named Cabrera who was the head of the Sinaloa drug cartel. I'm surprised the guy didn't install automated machine gun turrets."

"You're not afraid some of the drug king's henchmen might come here looking for him?" Quinn asked.

"I wasn't, but just in case, I sent Cabrera a letter telling him the Ponzi guy wasn't living here anymore," Tommy said. "Also the forwarding address of the prison where the guy was incarcerated. Cabrera sent me a box of his mother's tamales to thank me. But back to the polar bears surrounding my property . . . you got a theory?"

"I'm a neurochemist, not a zoologist . . . but a friend of mine was involved in a study in Alaska to determine what effect developing the

North Slope oil fields would have on the polar bear population. They thought they could fly a survey plane over the area with infrared cameras like yours and get a good count of the bear population. Do you know what color a polar bear's fur is?"

"I'm guessing this is a trick question," Tommy said. "I'm going to say white?"

"It looks white," Quinn said, "but each hair is actually clear as glass. The fur conducts the sun's light directly to the skin. To below the skin, actually, where the bear stores the heat. My friend thought the bears' body heat would show up on the infrared cameras, particularly against the snowy frozen background. But in fact, they give off no heat whatsoever. They keep it all in. The Eskimos, by the way, figured out a long time ago that if you leave a polar bear fur skin-side down on the ice in the sun, the fur will conduct enough sunlight to melt the ice beneath it. On the other hand, when my friend used ultraviolet sensors that could detect places that absorbed light, the bears appeared loud and clear. To seriously mix a metaphor."

On his computer screen Tommy saw the vague outline of one of the creatures beyond the stone walls surrounding his property. It seemed to be pacing on all fours, occasionally rising up on its hind legs.

"You think these things are white?" he asked.

"They're probably black, but like polar bears, they aren't giving off any heat," Quinn said. "Or light. When you combine every band in the light spectrum, you get white light, but when you combine every color of paint in the paint box, you get black. Whatever is out there is absorbing the darkness the way polar bears absorb sunlight. We can't see them, but we can notice the absence of light when they pass in front of something we actually can see. If we could get a light source *behind* those things in the woods, or something really bright directly on them, we might be able to see the shadows they cast, or maybe their outlines in silhouette."

"Huh," Tommy said, thinking. "But they're physical beings, right?"

"As far as I can tell, yes." Quinn nodded. "The data says they're corporeal. Which doesn't mean I understand exactly what they are."

"If they're flesh and blood, we can kill them," Tommy said. "Let's see what my aunt's arsenal has to offer."

Tommy's Aunt Ruth was not a typical librarian, in the sense that she was also the owner of a substantial gun collection she'd inherited from a policeman she'd once dated. Tommy went to the mudroom and opened the storage locker they'd taken from his aunt's house, and after a moment's consideration, selected a .45-caliber magazine-fed Ares "Shrike" light machine gun with a sixteen-inch assault barrel and an M203 grenade launcher fixed to the lower receiver.

Quinn stared at the weapon, wide-eyed, as Tommy walked back into the kitchen.

"Wow," he said. "Are you sure we need this much firepower?"

"Nobody needs this much firepower," Tommy said, examining the weapon to make sure the piece was operational. "But considering who—and/or what—we're up against, I'm going to hang on to it for a while. Any activity?"

Quinn turned back to the computer screen as Tommy set the weapon on the food island in the middle of the kitchen.

"Nothing," Quinn said. "No movement at all. They're just watching us. It's like they're waiting for something."

Tommy frowned. "Aren't we all?"

He opened a door to a large closet off the mudroom. When he re-emerged he was carrying a portable Helios 9000 spotlight, along with its waterproof machined military-grade black metal battery case, which contained a pair of lithium batteries. The 9000 was capable of generating a hundred watts of power and 25,000 lumens from the HID bulb in its ten-inch reflector.

"That's the biggest flashlight I've ever seen," Quinn said.

"Thank you," Tommy said proudly. "I'll be honest—I have a flashlight problem. Every time I think I've bought the biggest, brightest one there is, another one comes along that's bigger and brighter, and then I have to have it."

"Why?" Quinn asked.

"I honestly don't know," Tommy said. "I told myself I needed this thing so that I could work on the house at night, but I might have been fooling myself. On the other hand, this baby can boil water from fifty feet."

"What are you going to do with it?"

"I want to see what we're up against."

"You're going out there?"

Tommy nodded. "Keep recording on all three systems. When I turn this puppy on, it's going to overload the night vision cameras, but we might be able to see something on the other spectrums, or at least get data we can analyze. Anything that looks directly at it is going to be blinded temporarily. Maybe permanently."

"Do you think that's a good idea?"

"No," Tommy said, "but it's my idea and I'm sticking with it. I'll be right back."

Otto, Quinn's bloodhound, followed Tommy to the back door, hoping to be let out. It had been Otto's keening, after George and Julian and the boy left for the airport, that had led Tommy and Quinn to realize there was something outside the house.

"Out of your league, fella," Tommy told him. He donned his barn coat and boots. It was cold enough to warrant wearing a down ski jacket, but he worried that the heat from the powerful halogen bulb might melt the nylon.

He crossed the courtyard, heading for a large exposed pluton of Precambrian granite, the highest point on his property. The snow-dusted ground was frozen; the grass crunched beneath the soles of his boots. Tommy had his weapon slung over his right shoulder by its strap, safety off.

The surface of his pond had begun to freeze. He saw where he and Quinn and George Gardener had laid sandbags to dam up the stream that drained from the pond into the deeper waters of Lake Atticus, a man-made lake half a mile away that fed into the other reservoirs supplying the greater metropolitan New York area with drinking water. They'd dammed the stream because Tommy's pond had been poisoned—contaminated with a drug that was more dangerous than any known toxin.

Tommy climbed to the top of the rocky outcropping, affording him the high ground overlooking the woods to the south and east. He paused to listen but heard nothing. The sky had been overcast for the last two days, and the air smelled heavy with the promise of new snow.

He donned his night vision goggles. He saw, deeper into the woods, the outline of trees and the forms of rocky outcroppings and tree stumps, and then a series of darker shapes on the ground. They could be anything. They could be nothing.

The Helios 9000 had a shoulder brace and a front pistol grip with a trigger. Tommy took off the goggles and flicked the 9000's standby switch. He heard the soft hum as the device powered up. He had about thirty minutes of illumination at full power, 25,000 lumens, and two hours at low power, when the light generated a mere 2,000 lumens—still bright enough to hurt, but not blind. Were he feeling charitable, he might use the lower setting, but he was feeling anything but charitable. People he loved—Dani Harris, in particular—were asleep in his house. As the lord of the manor, so to speak, it was his job to keep them safe.

The light on the Helios 9000 changed from orange to green, indicating it was ready to use.

"Hey!" he shouted. "You! Whatever you are. You smell bad and your mother . . . does too."

He wasn't exactly sure how to trash-talk beasts from hell, or wherever they came from. Trash-talking had never been his strong suit, even in his playing days in the NFL.

"I'm going to count to three, and if you're not gone by the time I reach three, I'm going to . . . count to ten!"

His only thought was to provoke whatever they were to step out from where they were hiding so he could get a head count.

"One . . ."

He heard nothing. He saw nothing.

"Two . . ."

He raised the spotlight.

"Three!"

He braced himself and pulled the trigger.

Remote-controlled versions of the Helios were commonly mounted on the bottoms of helicopters used in search operations. According to the literature that came with the 9000, it could cast a beam three miles long.

The literature, Tommy thought, *wasn't kidding.*

The light from the Helios was intensely bright. It was hot too, like the sun in the tropics, warming his skin even though the temperature was below freezing.

He swept the woods, turning slowly. The light cast deep shadows. To his right, some of the shadows moved, scampering for cover. He focused the light in that direction and then froze.

When Tommy walked the grounds at night carrying a more reasonably powered flashlight, he'd shine it in the woods and see, reflecting back at him, the eyes of various animals. He could tell what they were by their color. The eyes of deer reflected blue. Coyotes and occasional stray dogs reflected green. Raccoons' eyes were orange, and the eyes of foxes were yellow. Tonight, as he shone the spotlight into the woods, he saw eyes reflecting red. Dozens of them. No. Hundreds.

There were more of these beasts than they'd thought—a lot more. Tommy got the sense that though the creatures were avoiding the light, when push came to shove, it wasn't really going to bother them. They weren't afraid to attack. They were waiting for something to happen, just as Quinn had said. It seemed Tommy had little choice but to wait as well, whether he liked it or not.

He stepped back and shut the 9000 off, but the eyes in the woods continued to shine a bright red, like coals in a fire.

He could feel those eyes watching him all the way back to the house.

"Let's call Julian, just to make sure they've made it to the airport," he said.

"I just did," Quinn told him. "It went straight to voice mail. Either he's talking to somebody, or they're somewhere where there's no signal."

3.

December 21

"Looks like they hit a deer," Frank DeGidio said. "Ray hooked the car up and hauled it to the yard so you can tell your insurance guy he can take a look at it, but trust me, it's totaled."

Tommy had known Frank and Ray DeGidio since middle school. Frank was a local cop and Ray owned a towing service. Tommy glanced out the window at the flashing lights of the police car.

"Are you okay?" he asked Reese.

"I'm a little shaken up, but yeah, I'm okay."

"The EMTs looked him over and said he was good," the cop said. "I thought he should go to the hospital and get himself checked out, just to be sure, but he wanted me to bring him here."

"I'm a doctor," Quinn volunteered. "I'd be happy to have a look at him."

"Okay then," Frank said.

Tommy donned his coat. "I'll walk you to your car."

They stood next to the squad car for a moment, DeGidio looking up at the snow, which had just started to fall.

18

"Snow's going to make it hard to write up the accident," he said. "Once the skid marks get covered over, you have to wait until a thaw, and if you wait too long, a good lawyer can claim the evidence has been compromised 'cause you didn't get to it in time."

"Do you have any sense of what happened?"

"Looked to me like they hit something first, and whatever it was busted the windshield, 'cause there was glass inside the car. Then they slammed into a tree, bounced off and crossed the road, and T-boned into a cliff on the other side." DeGidio used his hands to illustrate what he was saying. "The kid got thrown clear, but the other two went through the windshield. That's just a guess. I'm really sorry about your friends. If it helps, the EMT said it looked like they went fairly instantaneous. They didn't suffer."

"I appreciate that, Frank," Tommy said.

"Can I ask you what George Gardener was doing driving your car?" the policeman said. "I never seen him driving anything but that beat-up old pickup."

"They were heading for JFK," Tommy said. "To catch a flight to England. That's where the boy is from. I told George to take my car because I was worried his truck wouldn't make it to Kennedy and back."

The cop nodded. Tommy knew he hadn't really answered the question, but Frank let it go.

"You have contact information for the old guy? The Englishman?"

"I can get it for you," Tommy said. "If you need to, you can bill me for whatever it costs to send his body home."

"I'll pass that along. George have any heirs?"

"Not that I know of."

"Man. It's gonna be crazy if he doesn't. All the people who'll be going after the Gardener Farm. I've heard it's the most valuable piece of land in Westchester."

"You think it was a deer?"

"Don't know. The car was burned pretty bad. Whatever it hit got wedged in the grill and burned up with it. I told Ray if he found any filet mignon to save it for me."

In the kitchen, Quinn was shining a small flashlight in Reese's eyes and asking him simple questions to make sure he was fully oriented. He turned to give Tommy a thumbs-up.

"He's good," Quinn said. "Banged up his knee a little, but nothing serious. It sounds slightly miraculous."

"Do you remember any of what happened?" Tommy asked the boy.

"It happened pretty fast," Reese said. "One minute everything was fine, and the next everything was upside down and flying."

"Did you see anything afterward? Or hear anything?"

"No," Reese said. "Once I figured out what was happening, I found Dr. Villanegre's phone—mine burned up in the car—and dialed 911. Then I just waited."

"Just wondering. We got some odd signatures on the security cameras," Tommy said. "We're still trying to figure out what they mean. You didn't see anything?"

Reese shook his head.

"Should we wake the others?" Quinn asked.

"Let them be," Tommy said. "It'll keep. We're going to need all the sleep we can get."

There was a spare guestroom for Reese across the hall from Quinn's room. Tommy showed him where the towels were and where the bathroom was and then left him to his own devices, adding that he'd be up in the kitchen keeping watch if anybody needed a glass of warm milk to help them nod off.

At the monitor in the kitchen, Tommy scanned the surrounding woods again, but he couldn't see more than thirty or forty yards beyond his property, even when he zoomed. A quick Google search led him to a website and a gadget he believed could solve the problem. He found his credit card and ordered one.

His other problem was less easily solved. He couldn't believe the accident was, well . . . an accident. It was true, deer on the roads were a problem in East Salem, but he'd driven here all his life and never hit one. It was too much of a coincidence. George and Julian were dead, but the more he thought about it, the less sense it made that they'd been targeted and more likely that they were collateral damage. He'd believed Reese when the boy had said the people who ran St. Adrian's Academy were trying to kill him. Dani believed him too. If that was true, then it was more likely that Reese was the target—but they'd failed to take him out.

Why?

Reese had survived the crash. Between the time of the crash and the time Frank DeGidio or the EMTs showed up, Reese had been alone. Vulnerable. What happened during that time? If someone or something had tried to kill him, why didn't it try again when it had the chance? He wanted to believe the kid, but his story didn't make sense. Maybe he simply hadn't finished telling it yet, though Tommy had given him ample opportunity.

He decided he'd see what Dani had to say about it in the morning.

In his room, Reese read from his Bible, reviewing the part in 2 Corinthians that talked about false apostles and deceitful workers and how Satan himself masquerades as an angel of light, and how his agents often masquerade as "servants of righteousness." He'd learned that he couldn't trust anybody. The people he was most suspicious of were the ones who wanted him to trust them the most, the ones who said they were his friends, or who claimed to be on the same side he was—the ones who claimed to be servants of righteousness.

He hadn't decided yet about Tommy Gunderson or the others. He'd learned of them when they came to campus to investigate the murder of the girl on Bull's Rock Hill, and they'd figured out that his classmate, Amos Kasden, had done the killing. Then Amos tried to kill Dani, but Tommy killed Amos before he could hurt her. A simple syllogism—the enemy of evil must be good—suggested that he could let down his guard and take the things Tommy and Dani and the others were saying at face value, except . . . that could be a trick too. Reese reminded himself that he had to be careful. They called Satan the *great* deceiver, not the so-so deceiver.

It was safer to keep his intentions to himself and assume everyone was in league with the devil. He would tell them whatever they wanted to hear, play the part of a shy English schoolboy, and when he got the information he was after—he was gone.

4.

December 21

Dani sipped her tea—Earl Grey, milk, and two Sweet'N Lows—while Tommy gulped down the last of his protein smoothie, made with milk, three eggs, whey powder, two bananas, and a cup of blueberries from his greenhouse.

She was still taking in the news that Julian and George were dead. She could tell herself they'd lived long fulfilling lives, but it didn't ease the shock. She understood from the work she'd done as a psychiatrist that grieving moved at its own pace and that it was different for everyone, but right now there wasn't time to process all the feelings she had—that would just have to wait. She was in the kitchen along with Quinn, who was playing back the footage taken by the security cameras the night before, after Tommy had filled the woods with light from the Helios 9000.

Dani stared at the images on the screen. "There must be hundreds of them."

"At least," Quinn said, frowning. "We still can't get an exact count."

"And we still don't know why they're here," Tommy added.

"Maybe they're after Reese?" Dani said.

"Maybe," Tommy said. "He doesn't remember anything from last night, but I think that 'accident' was an attempt on his life."

"Not Julian's?" Dani asked. "Did they know he was a member of the Curatoriat?"

"Probably," Quinn said. "But they'd had plenty of other opportunities to kill Julian. Better opportunities. I've been thinking the same thing as Tommy—Reese is the new addition to the equation. They must be afraid of something, or they'd just storm the walls and take him."

"Don't forget what happened the last time they tried to storm the walls," Tommy added, referring to the angel who'd come to their assistance. He turned to Dani. "You've worked with kids. What do you think of Reese?" He paused and looked up at the ceiling, listening. The boy was still asleep.

"He needs to trust us, and he needs to know we trust him," Dani said. "As Dr. Villanegre pointed out, if Reese were a demon outright, or possessed by one, he wouldn't be able to hold a Bible in his hand. I just wonder . . ."

"What?" Tommy asked.

"Well, just that we're sort of at a crossroads. Between faith and science. We're talking about something that was true a thousand years ago, or five hundred, but now—you know how in the old vampire movies, Dracula would cringe when Van Helsing held up a cross? Today, you could put Dracula on fluoxetine or citalopram and he might not have a problem with it."

"And blood thinners as an appetite suppressant," Tommy said.

"It's an interesting question," Quinn said. "Is it possible to create a medication that could enhance morality, for lack of a better word? It seems our friends at St. Adrian's have been striving to do the opposite. Either way, I doubt pharmaceutically induced morality would be a substitute for the real thing."

"Do you think Reese is telling us everything?" Tommy asked.

"He's scared," Dani said. "We should give him time to adjust. He needs love, and grilled cheese sandwiches and chocolate milk."

"Don't we all?" Tommy said. "A lot of the time the troubled kids I've coached know what they need and try to tell us, but we're too busy telling them what's wrong with them for them to get a word in edgewise." In the time since he'd retired from football, his goal as a trainer and coach for youth sports had been simply to treat everyone fairly and make himself accessible.

"Tommy's right," Quinn said. "Reese may also need to flush any medications he might have been on without knowing it from his system. If he was eating from the school cafeteria, there could have been any number of things they were putting in his food. There may be withdrawal symptoms."

"Whether it's Reese these things want or not, they're gone now," Tommy said, gesturing toward the monitor. "They don't seem to stick around during the day. We'll see if they come back tonight."

Reese entered the kitchen a few minutes later, accompanied by Cassandra and Ruth.

"There's the man of the hour," Tommy said. "You hungry? Bacon and eggs?"

"That would be nice," Reese said. "Did they find out any more about the accident?"

"I'll get it," Aunt Ruth said to Tommy, taking a frying pan down from the hook. "Cassandra?"

The actress shook her head. "I'll just grab some coffee."

"No one's called," Tommy said. Dani had explained to him that often when people tell a lie, they voluntarily bring it up a second time to see if the lie was believed. Was that what Reese had just done?

Tommy and Dani sat down at the kitchen table opposite the boy and watched his eyes light up as Ruth first prepared and then set the food down in front of him. He ate as if he was famished, pushing the last piece of bacon into his mouth, and then set his plate aside and leaned back.

"You good?" Dani asked him as Ruth cleared his plate.

Reese nodded, wiping his mouth with his napkin. "I appreciate what you're all doing for me."

"Tommy told me what happened last night," Dani said. "I'm sorry."

"I wish I hadn't fallen asleep. Maybe I could be more helpful to you," Reese said. "I just couldn't keep my eyes open."

"Were they able to fill you in on what's going on?"

"They started to," Reese said.

Dani moved her chair closer and faced him, her arms uncrossed, her body language open and nonthreatening.

"You need anything?" she asked. "Do you have family you'd like to call?"

"My parents have passed on," Reese said. "In a car accident. There's irony for you. They were killed and I was spared."

"I'm sorry," Dani said.

"It's all right," Reese said. "I've had a long time to get over it."

Dani detected deception, but not mendacity—it was the sort of lie people tell themselves as a way of coping with something unbearable. No one gets over the early loss of their parents. They just find a way to pretend. She let it go.

"So you were raised by relatives?"

"We had a housekeeper in England," the boy said. He seemed calmer now and didn't fidget or look away. "Mrs. Carlyle. And Mr. Simons manages the house. You said last night that you think the school is planning something?"

"We do," Dani said. "We think it has something to do with Linz Pharmazeutika and Udo Bauer, your distinguished alum."

"The man who owns the painting?"

Dani nodded. "What made you come to us?" she asked. "I mean, how did you know about us?"

"You and Mr. Gunderson came to the school to investigate Amos Kasden. You're with the police, aren't you?"

Ruth refilled Dani's tea and Tommy's coffee and set a small pitcher of milk on the table.

"Technically, I work for the district attorney. Did you know Amos?"

"Not very well," Reese said. "No one did, really. I was friends with his roommate, though."

"A boy from Mexico, if I recall correctly?"

They'd been given access to Amos's laptop by Dr. Wharton, the school's sinister headmaster, but a search of the hard drive turned up nothing. They later learned that Amos had used his roommate's laptop to coordinate his activities.

"Oliver," Reese said. "He was from Costa Rica. He was my best friend. Even though he's Man U and I'm City."

Dani gave Tommy a puzzled look.

"Those are English football teams," Tommy said. "Soccer rivals. Is City your local?"

"Tottenham," the boy said, rolling his eyes and sighing heavily. "Don't ask."

"So Oliver was your friend?" Dani asked. She added milk to her tea and stirred it.

"After Amos . . . after he died . . . ," Reese said.

Dani couldn't help but flinch. Amos Kasden had died in her kitchen, having come there to do to her what he'd done to Julie Leonard. He might have succeeded if Tommy hadn't come to her rescue. "After Amos died, then what?"

"I couldn't reach Oliver at all," Reese said. "He disappeared. I tried all his telephone numbers and e-mail addresses and Facebook pages. Even the secret ones his parents didn't know about. He doesn't answer. One day he was in school and the next day he wasn't. I think they killed him because he knew."

"What did he know?"

"He found the files Amos had left on his laptop. He knew that Amos was one of the Selected." The boy looked around the room as if he expected a reaction.

"The Selected?" Tommy asked, looking to Dani for permission to interrupt. She nodded; Tommy continued, "Who are they?"

"A group of boys at the school," Reese said. "There's an initiation. Only boys who show special talents are chosen."

"Boys like Amos Kasden?" Tommy said.

Reese nodded.

"What does being 'selected' mean?" Dani asked.

"Well, for one thing, you're allowed to move into Honors House," Reese said. "Oliver couldn't have been happier. He said Amos gave him the creeps."

"How so?"

"He just wasn't normal," Reese said. "Oliver loaned Amos his school scarf once, and when he got it back, he realized Amos had used it to wipe up something he'd spilled. Most people would apologize and offer to have it cleaned, but Amos couldn't imagine why Oliver was upset."

"We think Amos might have fallen somewhere on the autism spectrum," Dani said. "An inability to identify or understand someone else's feelings. He'd disassociate."

"That certainly makes sense," Reese said.

"What happens at Honors House?"

"You're not allowed to say. Amos never talked about it." Reese shook his head. "You can get in deep trouble if you do. Can I ask you a question?"

"Sure."

"Why would God allow something like what Amos did to that girl to happen? I've been trying to understand it, but I can't."

Dani looked to Tommy.

"We can't either," Tommy said. "Theologians have been asking that kind of question for centuries. We can do everything humanly possible to understand the specific causes of something like that, but in the larger sense all we know is that evil is something we have to react to and fight. We can move forward, but understanding it backward is often not possible."

"I suppose only God really knows," Reese said.

"I had the impression they don't talk much about God at that school of yours," Dani said.

Reese nodded. "They don't."

"But you have a Bible," she said.

"Oliver gave it to me. We could have been expelled if we were caught reading it. It's banned on campus."

"No surprise," Tommy commented.

"That was why I wanted to find out what was in it for myself," Reese said.

"My father used to say the best way to get a kid to do something is to tell him not to," Dani said. "He was a pediatrician."

"So Amos was one of the Selected. Do you know what they're selected for?" Tommy asked, leaning back in his chair and sipping from his coffee cup. "What is the criteria? Do they have some kind of mission or task?"

"I don't know," the boy said. "Once you're in, you don't really associate with the other students. You have special classes. You eat all your meals at Honors House. And after you graduate, your future is virtually guaranteed, because Honors House people promise to do business and help other Honors House people. It's like the Skull and Bones at Yale or the Bullingdon Club at Oxford. All hush-hush. A lot of us on the outside think the whole thing is ridiculous, but it's not ridiculous to the people on the inside."

"Do you know how many others were chosen? What their names are?"

"Some," Reese said, smiling apologetically. "Not sure how helpful I can be."

"The first time we met," Dani said, "you brought me a pill."

"The blue pill," Reese said, nodding. "I remember."

"Where did you get it?"

"Oliver stole it from Amos. I gave it to you because I thought it might explain why Amos did what he did," Reese said.

"And you thought it was a pill to help people study, like Adderall?"

"I wasn't sure," Reese said. "I thought it was one of the benefits of living in Honors House. They give you pills that help you get straight As."

"Do you have any idea how long this might have been going on?"

Reese shook his head. "Did it help you?" he asked.

"It did," Dani said. "We think it might be a beta version of Provivilan."

"The drug the TV ads say is going to revolutionize the treatment of depression?"

"That's what they're saying," Dani said, leaning away to give Reese more room. "Except that instead of being an antidepressant, it acts like a weaponized depressant. It affects changes in embryonic development, in the womb. Somebody whose mother took it grows up perfectly normal until they hit puberty, and then the drug combines with hormones to reduce empathy and create a craving for the kind of adrenaline that's released through violence."

"We're still trying to crack the specific mechanisms," Quinn added.

"Do you know who else at St. Adrian's might have been taking performance-enhancing drugs?" Dani asked.

"We all do," Reese said, sounding surprised at the question, as if it were common knowledge. "Everyone at the school does. They make us."

"They make you?" Tommy sounded not just surprised but shocked.

"Yes. We take attention deficit drugs to help us study. It depends on what sort of things we're studying. They've been trying to fine-tune it and personalize it. Last year they finished running every student's genome. Some medications are better for creative types. Or sometimes if someone just needs help staying awake for a test, they give us the same drug they give astronauts who have to be awake for a mission. It's apparently the same drug the president or the secretary of state takes if they're flying long distances and can't afford jet lag."

"That's what they told you?"

"Isn't everyone doing it?" Reese asked. "Other schools?"

"I would hope not," Dani said. "How much sleep a night have you been getting? On average?"

"Five or six hours," Reese said.

"From now on, eight hours a night. Doctor's orders," she said. "What else? What other drugs?"

"Well, steroids and human growth hormones for the athletes," Reese said. "And some other things for mood control."

"Better living through chemistry," Quinn said.

"Do you know what drugs they've been giving *you*?" Dani continued.

Reese shook his head. "But it doesn't matter because I wouldn't take them. I didn't like the way they were making me feel, so I'd pretend to take them and then spit them out. But I got pretty good grades anyway."

"Do you, by any chance, know how long the school has been doing this?" Dani asked.

"A long time," Reese said. "One of the legacy students—both his father and his grandfather were Addies—he said his father told him he was on a drug program back in the sixties."

"It would make sense to use one part of the student population as a test group and the others as a control," Quinn said. "Unethical, but it would make sense from a scientific point of view."

"Well, the ones who got the good stuff were definitely the selected ones," Reese said. "I don't know if their test scores proved it, but their experiences later in life certainly seem to."

"Were those the names on the SD card you sent to my office—was that a list of alumni who'd been selected?"

Reese nodded.

"Where did you get it?" she asked.

"Oliver and I were snooping around in the school databases," Reese said. "We sorted for the ones who'd lived in Honors House. Those were the names I got. But none of the ones from this year were on it."

"Why did you send them to me?"

"I don't really know," the boy said, scratching his arm nervously. "I thought maybe you could do something with them. I think maybe I suspected there was something wrong with my school. Not the things you've been telling me. Just a feeling. I know the teachers are good and the facilities are state-of-the-art, and I know that if you graduate from there, you'll be taken care of by the people who've graduated before you. But all the nonstop emphasis on achievement and excellence and single-minded purpose? Something about it . . . there's just something missing. Do you know what I mean?"

"A soul," Tommy said. "Humanity."

"Dr. Villanegre said something about a thousand years," Reese asked. "And Vikings? The school's only two hundred years old."

Dani looked at Tommy, who nodded. Ruth pulled up a chair while Cassandra swiveled on her stool at the food island.

"You'd better get comfortable, Reese," Dani said. "I have a story to tell you."

She explained then just what it was that was so terribly wrong with St. Adrian's Academy, beginning from the time the school's namesake, St. Adrian, a holy man and a scholar, arrived in England in 671 AD intent on spreading the Word of God. Adrian soon met resistance from a group of pagans and Satan worshipers, the Druids. With the help of a legion of holy warriors, led by an aide known as Charles the Black, Adrian drove the Druids from England, killing them to the last man. Or so he thought. As it turned out, a hundred or so of them escaped, sailing west from the English coast across the Atlantic in hired Viking ships. The shallow-drafting vessels eventually navigated the St. Lawrence River and off-loaded their passengers in what would become upstate New York. There, for an undetermined period of time, the Druids ruled over one of the Iroquois nations, spreading dark worship and black magic.

They were eventually defeated and driven underground, surfacing again after the American Revolutionary War when the school itself was formally established at its present location. The academy's leaders proposed an institution to rival Yale in New Haven, or Harvard in Boston, or William and Mary in Williamsburg, Virginia. But somewhere along the line the school returned to its true mission—to corrupt its students, tempt them with power, and lead them into sin, doing Satan's bidding, protected by secrecy and "old-boy" collegiality behind the stone walls of St. Adrian's Academy for Boys, where the world's leaders sent their sons to be educated.

"The key has always been secrecy," Dani said. "The fact that you're unaware of what's going on doesn't surprise me. The names on that list you gave me—did you look at them?"

"A few," Reese said. "They didn't really mean anything to me."

"They weren't supposed to mean anything to you," Tommy said. "St. Adrian's didn't teach the bad guys whose names you'd recognize. They taught the guys standing next to those guys. The anonymous guy no one remembers, who whispers in the other guy's ear."

Reese looked puzzled.

"For example, epidemiologists think the Spanish Flu Epidemic of 1918 originated in Kansas," Dani said. "The disease killed over fifty million people. Three percent of the world's population. Most accounts point to a man named Albert Gitchell, who was a cook at Ft. Riley. He gave the virus to the troops, and they brought it to Europe with them."

"And Albert Gitchell went to St. Adrian's," Tommy said.

"You gave us six hundred plus names," Quinn said. "Men who lived in Honors House as students. We've been able to tie over four hundred of them to some kind of tragedy. Always indirectly. Never the guy with the gun."

Reese fell silent a moment, thinking.

"I know it's hard to believe," Tommy said. "It makes anybody who says it out loud sound like one of those conspiracy fanatics, but we've been putting this together for a while. The people before us were putting it together for even longer."

"Actually, it makes sense," Reese said. "It explains a lot of things I was wondering about at the school. Stories I heard that I wasn't sure were true. Now I think they are."

"Reese—we think the school psychologist is part of this," Tommy said. "Did you have any interaction with him?"

"We all did," Reese said. "You have to do a long interview with Dr. Ghieri before they let you in. They call it intake."

"That's probably where the selection process starts," Dani said. "That's where they find out who the best candidates are."

"Best candidates for what?"

"Persuasion. The kids most susceptible to being influenced," Dani said. "Kids who don't know themselves or kids who're bluffing that they do. Your sense of yourself, if you don't mind my saying so, seems to be on strong footing. You know who you are and what you want and like, and you're not terribly troubled if you don't fit into someone else's categories. That's why you didn't have any problem deciding not to take the medications they wanted you to take—you were 'above the influence,' as the commercials on television say. Would you say that's fair?"

"I suppose," Reese said.

"Not always, but sometimes it's the kids who proclaim themselves the loudest—the ones with the Mohawks and tattoos or the long black trench coats—who are the least certain of who they are, so they brand themselves to a group they hope will accept them. It looks like confidence, but it's a false confidence. Their sense of self is actually pretty fragile."

It occurred to her that Tommy would have been the worst possible candidate for "selection." He had always known who he was and what he stood for. There were other similarities between Tommy and Reese—a kind of resident calm, and maybe a capacity for simply listening. Whereas most people, while they listen, are trying to think of what they'll say in response—the boy seemed fully present.

"What do you think they're going to make the boys who've been selected do?" Reese asked. "If they're susceptible to influence, what's the goal?"

"We can't be sure," Tommy said, glancing out the window. Dani saw that it was snowing again. "We think that Linz Pharmazeutika developed a drug that they intend to put into the water supply. We've been calling it the 'Doomsday Molecule.'"

"Let's not give it more power than it deserves," Quinn interrupted. "It's an endocrine disrupting agent. That's what I'm calling it. It's harmless to adults, as far as we can tell, but it changes the way embryos develop."

"Changes them how?" Reese asked.

"Emotional overload," Quinn said. "More than the circuit can handle."

"Into what?"

"Into an army of Amos Kasdens," Quinn said. "Linz offered me a job awhile back, and I turned them down at first, but three days ago I told them I'd take it. Hopefully I can find out more about the drug from the inside. As far as I can tell, they haven't connected me to Tommy and Dani yet."

"The end result is, twelve or thirteen years from now, it all kicks in and the whole world goes crazy," Tommy added.

"That's what Provivilan is going to do?"

"Not all by itself," Quinn said. "It's a binary delivery system. When we take drugs, the metabolites eventually pass through the body and reenter the water system. During World War I, a German chemist named Fritz Haber, often called 'the father of chemical weapons,' devised binary compounds that were harmless on their own—you could store them and ship them without having to worry about them. But they'd combine inside the artillery shell at the time of detonation to form a gas, and then they were deadly. The world's drinking water is already a soup of pharmaceutical metabolites. When Provivilan combines with what's already in the drinking water, it forms the endocrine disrupting agent."

"The Doomsday Molecule," Reese said.

"They poisoned my pond out back as a practice run," Tommy said. "We're at the highest elevation in Westchester County. We dammed it up, but everything from here drains into Lake Atticus and from there into New York City's drinking water."

"But we don't think they're going to wait for Provivilan to go on the market," Quinn said.

"We don't?" Dani said.

"I was doing the math last night," Quinn said, shaking his head. "Assuming Provivilan metabolites are environmentally persistent or that they bio-magnify through the food chain, it would still take a few hundred years to reach concentrations high enough to disrupt embryonic brain development, just by marketing a drug. That's going to mask what they're doing, but it's not a very efficient delivery system."

"It's not?" Tommy said.

"Not really," Quinn said. "But you're right—poisoning your pond was a test run. I need to know more about how the drug works, but I think a single dump of the drug in a reservoir or catch basin would be enough to kick-start the process in a way that's irreversible. You could have an amount equal to a bag of Starbucks coffee and pour it into Lake Superior, and you'd be on your way."

The room grew silent as Dani and Tommy and the others considered Quinn's dire prediction.

"Maybe the drug they're putting on the market is just misdirection," Tommy said. "The way a magician gets you to look at his right hand so you don't notice what he's doing with his left."

"Okay," Dani said, returning to Reese. "So we think we know what they're doing. We just don't know who's doing it, or when it's going to happen."

"Christmas Eve," the boy said.

"What makes you say that?" she asked.

"Christmas Eve," Reese said again.

"You sound pretty certain," Tommy said.

"If I tell you, you'll think I'm crazy," Reese said. "I heard a voice. I can absolutely guarantee you it's Christmas Eve, and that the voice is 100 percent reliable, but I can't explain it any better than that."

"Dani?" Tommy said, rising from his chair and carrying his dishes to the sink. "Can I talk to you for a second in the study? Reese, will you tell Cassandra and Quinn and Ruth about the classes you've been taking? Maybe there's something we can learn from them."

Cassandra sat down next to Reese, who sat up a little straighter. Tommy smiled. Dani knew the effect the beautiful actress had on grown men; the boy would answer any question she asked, obviously. In the meantime . . .

He led Dani into his study and closed the door behind them. He took her in his arms and kissed her.

"First things first," he said. "I am once again absolutely awed by your intelligence and your compassion."

"Well, shucks," Dani said, smiling and kissing him back. "You're worried."

"A little," Tommy said. "I'm worried that we're telling him too much."

"What would you consider too much?"

"I don't know," Tommy said. "But last time they tried to get someone inside our circle, they preyed on Carl's weaknesses and used him as a spy. How do we know they're not doing it again?"

"Reese was holding a Bible," Dani said.

"I know, but maybe we're missing something. Maybe Reese doesn't know he's being used, somehow."

"For what it's worth, I don't think he's lying," Dani said. "I'm not detecting deception, at least as far as I understand the signs of it."

"Your opinion is worth everything to me," Tommy said, "but he doesn't have to be lying to us to deceive us."

"Meaning what?"

"That's what disinformation does," Tommy said. "Not misinformation—dis-information. What if they somehow have allowed Reese to think he's discovered a secret about their timing—then he tells us that, totally believing he's telling the truth? Maybe they let him escape knowing he'd come to us and tell us what they want us to believe."

"Maybe," Dani agreed, thinking. "That theory depends on a number of assumptions, but they're all reasonable assumptions. Occam's Razor says the theorem requiring the fewest assumptions is the one most likely to be correct."

"Yeah, except I think by now Occam's grown a very long beard," Tommy said. "What do you make of the idea that Reese heard a voice?"

"Paracusia," Dani said. "That's the psychiatric term for it. Auditory hallucinations are generally significant in diagnosing various disorders. Schizophrenia. Mania. One psycho-anthropologist theorized that three thousand years ago the human brain was bicameral, meaning 'two houses.' His theory was that the corpus callosum hadn't evolved to the point that the two halves were fully connected and mutually conversant. People would hear a voice in their head, and it was just the right half of the brain speaking to the left, but to them it sounded like the voice of some all-powerful outsider, some superior being commanding them to obey. It was the voice of God, to them. Or maybe it was plural and polytheistic, I forget. But then we evolved and our brains physiologically changed, so now the voice doesn't sound like an outsider. I've read papers suggesting that in some psychiatric patients, that ancient bicameralism somehow gets restored."

"Is that something you think is true?"

"I haven't really thought about it," Dani said. "As I recall, the argument against it was that evolution takes place over millennia. It's not like some sort of switch gets flipped and all of a sudden, in a few years or a hundred, everything changes. But there've been new studies that say sudden paradigm shifts aren't unprecedented. A sudden shift in the environment can cause radical alterations in how a species has to adapt to survive."

"Joan of Arc heard voices," Tommy said.

"And look where it got her," Dani said.

"All I'm saying is, let's be careful. Maybe they want us to think it's Christmas Eve, but it's not."

"Reese was telling us something we think might be relevant," Quinn said when Dani and Tommy returned to the kitchen. "Usually the selection process takes place over the Christmas break, and then when the boys get back, the graduating seniors move into Honors House for their final semester. This year they made the selection in October. Nobody's moved into Honors House yet, but he's pretty certain the boys know who they are."

"Everyone was trying to guess, but they'd have been kicked out of Honors House if they told anybody before the moving-in ceremony," Reese said.

"How did you get the names you sent me on the SD card? Where were you?" Dani asked. "Maybe we can get the names of the boys the same way."

"We were in Dr. Ghieri's office. Oliver and I. Ghieri stepped out for a minute, and when I had a chance, I sent them to myself in an e-mail from his computer, and then deleted it from his Sent folder and from the Recently Deleted folder." Reese frowned. "I don't think they found out. But Oliver is missing, so that might be why."

"Don't blame yourself," Dani said. "You did absolutely the right thing. I just wish we had more information."

Suddenly the boy looked stricken.

"You're not going to make me go back, are you?" he said. "I can't go back there. I know this is important, but . . ."

"We won't make you go back," Dani said. "You can stay with us."

"You'll be safe here," Tommy added. "The angels are looking after us."

"The school knows who we are," Dani said. "Tommy and I. We don't think they necessarily know about Dr. McKellen or Miss Morton."

"They know about me," Ruth said. "I have a big hole in the side of my house to prove it."

"We had a demon lurking in the garden," Tommy explained. "We scared him off with a couple of shotgun blasts."

"You can shoot demons?" Reese asked.

"Demons are fallen angels," Tommy explained. "When they take on a physical form, they can feel pain. Only another angel can defeat them, though. They run away because they're afraid of drawing the wrong kind of attention."

"At least you can kill those things in the woods," Reese said.

"How do you know?" Tommy said.

"The accident. Didn't we hit one with the car?"

"I thought you were asleep."

"I was," Reese said. "My understanding was that we hit one with the car and killed it."

"Your understanding, based on what?" Tommy asked.

"What the policeman said."

"He told me he thought you hit a deer," Tommy said. "Well, it doesn't matter. For the record, I think you're right. I think you're right about Christmas Eve too. Under normal circumstances, I'm not sure what I think about people hearing voices, but these aren't normal circumstances."

After the breakfast meeting broke up, Reese told himself he had to be more vigilant about the things he said—another slip of the tongue like that and he would surely give himself away.

"Stop it," the voice in his head said. "You have no idea what you're dealing with."

No, you're the one who needs to stop what you're doing—it's dangerous and it's wrong. You're the one who has no idea what he's doing.

He waited for a reply.

Where did you go? Why aren't you listening to me? This is important.

His mind was a raging storm of fears and apprehensions, so he tried to calm it and focus on the love he felt instead.

Please—just talk to me—PLEASE!

5.

December 21

8:11 a.m. EST

Three inches of snow lay on the ground, still falling lightly with no sign of letting up. Ahead, Otto sniffed the ground and then turned, as if urging Tommy on. The bloodhound could be walked without a leash and obeyed voice commands unless, Quinn had warned, he got the scent of something, and then he was off. Tommy trusted that the stone wall and the deer fence surrounding his property would be enough to contain Otto's olfactory investigations.

Tommy needed to walk. To be away from the others for a while—even from Dani—and be alone with his thoughts. He needed to try to understand why George and Julian were gone. He knew that God had a plan for everyone, but that did little to lessen the blow—it still hurt to lose someone you loved, and Tommy had come to love and admire both men.

It reminded him of how short and uncertain life could be, and how important it was to tell the ones you loved how you truly felt about them. Which made him think of Dani again, and the question he'd decided to ask her.

Otto barked.

Tommy looked up. The dog was standing at the top of the rock where Tommy had stood the night before with the Helios 9000 spotlight. Otto's nose was straight up in the air, his tail stiff and straight as well.

"I know what you smell," Tommy said, taking his GPhone from his pocket. "There's a wolf sanctuary about a mile from here. I think they have about fifty of 'em. You want to go join 'em, Otto? Huh, boy?"

Tommy petted the dog and scratched him behind his floppy ears, then turned on his phone. He tapped on his contact list and then on the name Sid Gunderson. His father, Arnie, was in Texas, visiting with his brother—Tommy's Uncle Sid. The call went to voice mail, which struck Tommy as odd because Uncle Sid was in a wheelchair from arthritis in his knees and hips and rarely went anywhere.

Tommy left his number and a request for a call back.

He dialed the number for Lucius Mills's cell phone, thinking his father's caregiver might be able to tell him what was going on. Arnie was suffering from Lewy body dementia, cognitively similar to Alzheimer's but more of a roller coaster ride, with intermittent periods of lucidity and progressive symptoms that included Parkinsonisms. Lucius picked up on the fourth ring.

"I was just about to call you, Tommy," Lucius said. "We're at the hospital."

"Is my uncle all right?"

"Not your uncle, Tommy. It's your dad. I'm sorry. He had a seizure last night. They did a CAT scan and said he has cortico-basal degeneration."

"How—"

"He's stable now, but I think it's time to move him to the next level. I'm happy to do what I can for him, T, but they say he's going to need attention 24/7. Sorry to tell it to you like this, man, over the phone. I know it's rough."

It took Tommy a moment for the news to sink in. It was news he'd been expecting, but not this soon. And not right now.

"It'll be okay, Luc," Tommy said. "I've already got a room reserved for him at High Ridge Manor. Do you think he's okay to fly?"

"I think he'd be okay on a plane," the caregiver said. "He's been sleeping a lot. I'll sit with him."

"I appreciate it," Tommy said. "Can I talk to him? Is he right there?"

"He's right here, but I'm not sure, man. You can try. They gave him some medicine. Made him a little loopy. Hang on . . ."

Tommy heard a rustling sound, and then he heard Lucius Mills say, from a few feet away, "Go ahead."

Tommy cleared his throat. "Arnie? Dad? How are you feeling? It's Tommy calling. It's your son, Tommy . . ."

He waited for a response.

He tried again.

"Dad? Can you hear me? Listen, don't try to say anything, but this is Tommy. I'm going to bring you home, okay? You're going to be home for Christmas. Okay? So that's good news. And I have more good news for you—do you remember that I told you I've been working with Dani Harris? Remember Dani Harris? The girl I almost dated in high school when she was homecoming queen, except we both freaked out? The really smart one?"

Again he waited for a response. His father said nothing.

"She's my soul mate, Papa. I'm crazy in love with her. And I've decided . . . she's the girl I want to marry. And I wanted you to be the first to know," he said. "I'm just waiting for the right moment to ask because I want to do it up right. So I'll keep you posted. So that's good news too, right? It's all good. All good news. I can't wait to see you, Papa."

When the call ended, his false cheer ended with it, and for a moment he broke down and let a single tear fall, wondering if he'd ever get through to his father again. Otto came to his side and licked his hand. Tommy gave the dog a pat on the head to thank him.

By the time he got back to the house he was on a more level keel.

Dani met him on the steps and kissed him.

"I saw you through the window," she said. "Thought you might need some support. I called Julian's home number in Oxford to tell them the news, but it went straight to voice mail, so I told them to call us. You're thinking about them, aren't you?"

"I was," Tommy said. "There's just—there's no limit to what those . . . We keep thinking like human beings. *We* have a conscience. *They* don't think like that. To them, we're just bugs. Something to flick away because we accidentally landed on their french fries. I feel like to defeat them, we have to think like them, and I don't want to do that."

"It doesn't mean we have to *be* like them," Dani said. "You're right. We're at war."

"I just wish I knew how to be smarter," Tommy said. He looked up, and his expression changed. "Maybe we should ask them?"

He pointed to a pair of figures standing in the falling snow beneath the willow tree beside his pond. One was a biker who went by the name of Charlie, clad in black railroad boots, black jeans, and a black leather jacket. The other was an old Native American called Ben; he wore jeans, suede cowboy boots, and a plaid flannel shirt beneath his coat, and his hair descended from either side of his black cowboy hat in two black braids.

They hadn't been there a few seconds earlier when Tommy had glanced in that direction, but that wasn't surprising. Despite appearances, neither Charlie nor Ben was human—they were angels who'd assumed these forms because their heavenly guises were too beautiful to look at. Charlie and Ben had guided Tommy and Dani throughout this ordeal. Tommy knew they were there to help them now.

"Why are you troubled?" Ben said, reaching down to pet Otto. "Julian and George are with us."

"I know," Tommy said. "I just wish I'd had a chance to say good-bye."

"You said good-bye," Charlie reminded him.

"I know, but not the way I wanted to. I thought I was going to see them again."

"Maybe you should treat everyone as if you'll never see them again," Ben advised. "There's a country song about that that I like very much. I can't remember the name of it."

"'Live Like You Were Dyin','" Tommy said. "Tim McGraw."

"That's the one," Ben said. "I like Tim McGraw."

"What's not to like?" Tommy said.

"You couldn't save them?" Dani asked, holding her coat closed at the throat to keep out the cold. "George and Julian? I don't understand."

"You will," Ben said. "We'll be there when you need us, but our purpose is to glorify God and do his work. His plans and yours are not always the same." Dani turned to Tommy.

"I know it's not enough to tell yourself they'd lived long, productive lives," she said. "I feel lucky for the time we had with them. Just think about what you had. Not what you don't have."

Tommy supposed those were the same things she'd told herself when she lost her parents. They'd flown to Africa to visit her there, where she'd worked with Doctors Without Borders helping rehabilitate child soldiers back into mainstream society, but they'd perished when their plane went down in the jungle. He held his arms out to her and hugged her, buried his face in her hair, and closed his eyes. When he opened them again, the angels were gone.

"They keep doing that," she said, staring at the empty space they'd occupied. "They're not much for good-byes, I guess."

"We'll see them again," Tommy said.

"When we need them," Dani said. "Why does it feel like we always need them?"

"That's what being human feels like," Tommy replied. "Speaking of which . . . I have to call my travel agent."

"Well, there's a non sequitur. Your travel agent?"

"Yes. I have to fly my dad home. I'll tell you all about it inside."

They joined hands and turned toward the house.

6.

December 21

10:05 a.m. EST

The research campus for Linz Pharmazeutika was an array of glass boxes on twenty lush, landscaped acres in the town of Sexton, Connecticut, south of East Salem and just ten miles across the state line. The glass walls were intended to symbolize the theme of transparency, though with their mirrored finishes, the buildings were only transparent at night with the lights on inside. Linz's corporate motto—"Clear Genius" —was emblazoned in raised brass letters on a stone marker by the entry gates.

The company had invited Quinn to come in for an interview months earlier when they'd accepted his paper, "An Immunoradiometric Study of Hyperandrogeny and Autism," for a conference on autism Linz was sponsoring at Columbia. That was where he and Dani had reconnected. She'd asked for his help understanding the autopsy results on Amos Kasden's brain and the drug, the blue pill she believed Amos had been taking at the behest of St. Adrian's school psychologist. Quinn had done more than that.

He'd determined how Provivilan worked on the brain, its dual nature, doing one thing for adults in normal doses but affecting embryos at one part per trillion. But there were still questions to be answered. How long would it take for the drug to have an effect? Could the effects be reversed—was there an antidote of some kind? And who was in league with the devil and who was a pawn, doing the devil's bidding without knowing who was signing the checks?

When Quinn had his first interview with the head of research and development, he'd been told all the things he wanted to hear, that Linz only wanted him to continue doing the research he was already doing, except with the guarantee that Linz would share in the financial benefits of his work. He was to head up a team and hire whomever he wanted to help. When the head of R&D told him the budget he would have and the salary he would be paid, Quinn's first reaction was that there had to be some kind of mistake—the director had moved a decimal or added a zero where it didn't belong.

In the first few days after his hiring, he'd met with a number of different executives to be briefed on what was going on in each of their respective departments. Some of what he heard sounded completely innocent, some of it troubled him, and a few things sounded vaguely sinister—particularly the IT head's long-term plan to digitize and coordinate the medical records of every human being on earth, including their genomes, beginning at birth. The man spoke blithely of how easy it would be to study the genetic components of diseases sorted for every possible population permutation, and how easy it would be to find organ donors and tissue matches. He speculated that the full computerization of medicine alone would extend the average human lifespan by ten or twenty years while cutting the costs for health insurance in half. Inwardly, Quinn recoiled at the idea of every human being's genetic composition being stored and controlled by one central authority without any regard to privacy or individual choice, but he kept his concerns to himself and smiled and nodded.

After making the rounds, his impression was that while Linz had interests in virtually every aspect of modern medicine in every part of the globe, its primary focus was going to be on the mental health of children and young adults. It was a simple matter of demographics, one department head explained. "In another twenty years, the Baby Boomers'll all be dead, and their kids will be relatively healthy, with kids of their own who are going to find a rapidly changing world hard to cope with, and we're going to be there with pills to make 'em feel better. Ka-ching!"

Linz was a privately held firm, so its profits and losses were not public information, but as an employee Quinn was able to get a sense of the company's scale and scope. It was invariably described as a "pharmaceutical giant" in the press, but the word *giant*, Quinn came to think, did not describe it by half. Linz's annual profits, by his best estimate, exceeded those of all the big oil companies combined, with manufacturing facilities in China that paid workers as little as twenty dollars a month and positions in every significant marketplace in the world.

Everyone he spoke with offered information freely except in one area—when he asked what was going on with Provivilan, he met with reticence and secrecy . . . and a sense that he would be wise not to ask too many questions about it. People who should have known something said, "I'm not the right person to ask" or changed the subject. When he tried to use the company computer to research the program, he was asked on the home screen for an access code, which he did not have. His friend and coworker Illena Nemkova, who'd worked on the project, hadn't returned his e-mails or phone calls for some time now.

It was time to find out why.

Once Quinn passed a background check and was cleared to work at Linz, a company vulnerable to corporate espionage, he'd been given a thumb drive to wear around his neck and use for identification and authorization—all Linz employees had them. When he plugged the drive into his own personal laptop (which he was told in clear and nonambiguous terms that he was not allowed to bring onto campus) and scanned it for hidden codes with malware software, a computer engineer friend had recommended, he discovered that the drive was protected by a firewall that took him a good ten or fifteen seconds to breach. His suspicions were confirmed. The drive contained a GPS tracker and a keystroke transmission program that would tell whoever wanted to spy on him exactly where he was and what he was doing.

Which was, he thought, smiling, *a rather naive way to try and keep track of your employees.*

Working on his laptop, Quinn cloned the thumb drive onto a second device, disabled the GPS and keystroke trackers on the second thumb drive, then left the original thumb drive plugged into the USB port on his office computer. Now whoever was monitoring him would assume that he was at his desk working, while in fact he would be navigating the Linz campus, using the cloned drive as his pass key.

He knew Illena worked in Building C, but he hadn't been able to contact her since he'd started working three days ago; he started there. He waited until lunch to enter, blending in with the crowds. Building C was identical to every other building in the complex; he found the personnel directory on the wall behind the front desk, but rather than stop to read it and raise suspicions, he took out his phone and—discreetly—took a picture. He enlarged the photograph and read the directory in private, in a stall in the men's room.

There was no listing for Illena Nemkova.

He rode the elevators and eavesdropped, and reaffirmed his impression that the majority of the people at Linz were more interested in making money than helping the sick, talking about bottom lines and stock options and vacation homes with a see-no-evil speak-no-evil blindness to whatever else might be going on.

On his last trip, on his way back to the main lobby, he noticed something that he'd missed before: there was no button for the basement level—only a USB port where that button should be.

That made no sense. All the other buildings had basements. C was exactly the same as all the other buildings. Therefore, C had a basement. So why couldn't he go there?

He returned to his office, logged into his company computer using his debugged thumb drive, and searched the company's laboratory supplies database, directing the computer to list not what he could order but an inventory of what was already stored on the premises. The list was a long one. He redefined his search to sort for supplies in Building C and frowned as the items scrolled by. Portable oxygen bottles, HEPA filters, an alkaline tissue digester, ultraviolet arrays, large bleach tanks, and most significantly, PP or positive pressure suits worn to shield the wearer from biological hazards by insuring that in the event of a tear in the suit, the air would continue to blow out and not in.

It could only mean one thing. He was stunned by the audacity of it, and by the danger, and then he was angry. These particular supplies were unique to a very specific kind of BioSafety lab, Level 4, that dealt with extremely dangerous kinds of materials—things like smallpox or the Marburg and Ebola hemorrhagic viruses, the deadliest bugs on the planet. The kind of lab that one would have to keep hidden away, safe from prying eyes. The kind of lab one might hide in a basement.

He searched for the five closest BSL4 laboratories, even though he knew the answer. His search engine listed, ranked nearest to farthest, the National Emerging Infectious Diseases Laboratory in Boston; the NIH labs in Bethesda; the US Army Medical Research Institute of Infectious Diseases at Fort Detrick; Consolidated Laboratory Services in Richmond, Virginia; and the Kent State University Laboratories in Ohio. The only privately owned BSL4 laboratory he was aware of was the Texas Biomedical Research Institute in San Alberto. Unless the laws had changed, running a secret BSL4 lab was illegal.

He logged back into the system using the thumb drive with the GPS and keystroke trackers and sent a couple of harmless e-mails to make it look like he'd been working.

As he finished sending the last e-mail, he felt it start. A pounding behind his temples. Another headache coming on. He closed his eyes. He felt himself suddenly weightless and swimming in a dizzying whirlpool. He dropped his head to his desk and squeezed the back of his skull with both hands, pressing his fingers hard into the bones below and behind his ears.

When he lifted his head up again and opened his eyes, the right half of his field of vision was dark. He raised his right hand and waved it from right to left in front of his face and only saw it when it was even with his right shoulder.

His skull throbbed, and he thought he might pass out from the pain . . .

Then the pain abated.

He waited, breathing slowly and fully through his nose until the pain was mostly gone, and opened his eyes to discover his full field of vision was restored. He extended his right arm and wiggled his fingers, just to be certain, and saw fingers wiggling in his peripheral vision. In another minute, the nausea was gone. When he stood, he listed to the right and braced himself with his right hand on the desk. He sat back down and waited. The second time he stood, his balance was better.

He tapped his phone and found the number on his contacts list for Dr. Christopher Belden and decided to Skype him.

A moment later a man appeared on his screen. He was balding, about forty, with wire-rimmed glasses, wearing a blue oxford shirt and a black tie.

"Hey, Chris," Quinn said. "Catch you at a bad time?"

"Hello, Quinn," the doctor said. "How are you doing?"

"You tell me—I'm just calling to see if I'm aphasic. You can understand what I'm saying, right?"

"I do, loud and clear," the doctor said. "You don't look so good, though. Tell me what's going on."

Quinn described the episode he'd just had. It had been Belden, an old friend, who'd suggested an MRI after Quinn told him about the headaches; the MRI revealed Quinn had a midgrade infiltrating multiform glioblastoma of the pons reticular formation—a tumor in his brain, growing in a place where an operation wasn't possible. It had been the size of a pea when they'd found it. Now, according to the episode Quinn had described, Dr. Belden believed it was larger. He suggested that Quinn come into the office and schedule another MRI to see just how much the tumor had grown. Quinn declined, just as he'd declined chemotherapy after determining it had a 15–20 percent chance of shrinking the tumor temporarily and a 100 percent chance of making the end of his life miserable.

"What's another MRI going to tell us?" he asked the oncologist. "How much time I have left? It's not going to change how I'm living. I'd rather not know."

"Okay," Belden agreed. "You're right."

"I just want to know what to expect. This one was a bit rough."

"More of the same, I'm afraid," Belden said. "More frequent. Longer duration. Longer recovery. And then it's going to happen and it's not going to go away. Maybe seizures."

"Thanks for being honest, Chris," Quinn said. "I'll keep you posted."

Or not, he added silently, closing the Skype window and opening up the supply database again.

He needed to find out what was in Building C. Someone had to know, and on a campus full of scientists, there had to be someone else at least as curious as he was. The trick was going to be finding that person without giving himself away.

And without getting himself killed . . . before his time.

7.

December 21

The UPS driver greeted Tommy by name, more as a frequent customer than as a famous person. Tommy had been one of the highest paid players in the NFL when he retired after accidentally killing an opposing player in a legal but vicious hit. After retiring, he'd opened All-Fit Sports, Health, and Fitness Center of Northern Westchester, stocked it with all the newest fitness equipment, advertised using his own image, and watched the money pour in. He gave a tenth of his profits to his church and a tenth to charity, and he was putting a few Special Olympic kids through college, but the rest of the money he made he had fun with. Some of the profits he'd turned into vehicles, which occupied the house's huge six-bay garage, which he now instructed the UPS driver to back up to. Tommy had at one time owned an orange Jeep Sahara, a botanical green Jaguar XKR convertible, and a silver 2001 Ford Focus station wagon for surveillance. ("Plus, it's a chick magnet," he'd told Dani, "except it's the wrong end of the magnet.")

He had a small Volkswagen camper van for overnight trips, a Harley-Davidson Sportster, a more powerful Harley-Davidson Night Rod, a BMW F800GS for off-road riding, a Trek road bike for Ironman competitions, a

Trek mountain bike for trails, a Yamaha Grizzly for deep-woods camping, and a go-cart, just because he'd always wanted one. He'd owned a vintage Mustang, to replace a car he had in high school that was now at the bottom of Lake Atticus after he'd stupidly accepted a challenge to race it on ice that wasn't quite as thick as he thought. The replacement Mustang caught fire and blew up after Amos Kasden tampered with the engine. The Night Rod was at the bottom of Lake Atticus as well. And the Ford Focus, what was left of it, was now in Ray DeGidio's salvage yard.

Fortunately, he was not a person who became attached to material objects.

Dani watched out the window as Tommy met the truck. She threw on a coat and trotted across the courtyard to the garage where she found him at his workbench at the rear of the bay. The service bay was furnished with every tool a man could want, possibly every tool two or three men could want. As a rule Dani did not like gender stereotypes, but she couldn't help loving a guy who could fix things, maybe because her father had been a tinkerer too.

On the floor was a large UPS box with the letters IADS on it. "What's I-A-D-S?" she asked.

Tommy turned and smiled at her. "Israeli Aero Defense Systems," he said. "I ordered this last night for express delivery."

"From Israel?"

"No," he said, trying to find a page in the manual. "From a website called Gizmopalooza. It's like Amazon for guys who like gadgets. I get everything there for half off."

"Because?"

"Because I own it," he said. "Fifty-one percent of it. It's doing really well." He referred to the manual again. "It says you're supposed to be able to put it together in ten minutes, but the instructions could have been written better."

He returned to the bench, where Dani saw what looked like a white oar or blade of some sort, bent at the tip. As she stepped closer, Tommy said, "Aha," snapped a piece on the blade, and turned to show her, holding above his head what looked like an oversized paper airplane—a V-shaped wing about two meters across with a tapered tubular fuselage one meter long and a small propeller at the end of the fuselage where the tail should have been.

"What is it?"

"It's a UAV," Tommy said, admiring the device. "Unmanned Aerial Vehicle. The Orison 6."

She shook her head. "Which means absolutely nothing to me."

"It's a drone. For over-the-horizon surveillance. Weighs, like, nothing. It's got full-color video for daylight and combination infrared/night vision for starlight imaging. It'll fly for almost two hours on one battery, with a fifteen-mile range. Top speed is about eighty-five miles per hour and stall speed is about thirty, but you get longer battery life at slower speeds."

He plugged something into the wall—a power adapter for the drone, Dani guessed. It glowed bright green.

"Oh man. You gotta love these guys. It came fully charged. See? That means we can send it up right away."

"Great," Dani said. "I think I'm going to—"

Tommy knelt down next to the drone, ignoring her. "This thing has a fifteen thousand-foot ceiling, though the FAA puts a four hundred-foot ceiling and line-of-sight limit on civilian use. I thought about getting a quad-rotor, but I couldn't find any that have the same range or dwell time. When you're done, you either call it back or program it to return to the launch GPS position. It flies back, cuts the engine, pops the parachute, and lands right where it started. You put a fresh battery in and you're back in the air in less than a minute."

"What's *that*?" Dani asked, catching sight of something right next to the box that looked like a crossbow, only longer.

"That's how you launch it," he told her. "It's like a ballista."

She frowned. "A ballista?"

"Kind of an old Roman siege engine thing. You control it with this." He held up what appeared to be a tablet computer with video game controls mounted on either side as handles, with thumb-operated joysticks and multiple buttons. "This is the GCS. Ground Control Station. It gives you all your avionics plus the video or infrared/NV feed, and it has a built-in DVR that lets you record for up to twelve hours. Plus, it's got Bluetooth, so you can sync to any computer with Wi-Fi or to GPhones. This will give us over-the-horizon imagery, and it will also let me reprogram the infrared to scan for both hot and cold signals. We'll spot the demons before they see us; plus, I ordered an extra ultraviolet payload to go with the infrared. That should help us keep track of those things we saw in the woods last night. I wonder if I should have ordered two? It's kind of inconvenient to have to land the thing to switch cameras. What I need is one that can fly with all three cameras—"

"Tommy," Dani said, "this is good, but don't go overboard just because you can. You don't have to have every single new electronic gizmo that comes out."

"You're right, I don't," he said. "But think how great it would be if I did."

"Tommy—"

"Come on. Let's see if it works."

Dani hesitated a second, then shrugged. Why not?

She followed him out to the courtyard. He set the aircraft down and handed Dani the GCS while he set up the launcher, the front end supported by a bipod with telescoping legs to raise it four feet off the ground. He pulled the rubber tubing back until it latched behind the tickler, set the UAV on the tiller, and took the GCS from Dani, placing the strap behind his neck to hold the controller in front of him in a way that reminded Dani of a nightclub's "cigarette girl" in the old black-and-white movies.

"What are you doing?" she asked as he tapped the touch screen.

"Inputting the home GPS coordinates and setting it on auto-return," he said. "Listen to that—do you hear that?"

"Hear what? I don't hear anything."

"Exactly. The propeller is turning and we can't even hear it. Anybody who looks up and sees this thing is going to think it's just another turkey vulture. Stand back."

Dani gave him room. The trigger to release and launch the aircraft was a pedal at the end of the tiller. When Tommy stepped on it, the Orison 6 rushed suddenly skyward. Dani watched as the UAV grew smaller and smaller, rising into the air. She found it strangely compelling, the way she'd felt watching her nieces trying to take their first steps. She loved seeing Tommy happy, and the new toy was doing the job.

"The left joystick controls the camera and the right joystick flies the plane," he said, looking not into the sky but at the screen in front of him. "This is easier than a PlayStation3."

"I wouldn't know," Dani said. "I've never played a video game in my life."

"Aha," Tommy said. "I knew I'd find your flaw if I looked long enough. The optics are high-def at 1080 DPI. Is this cool or what?"

As he focused on the screen in front of him, Dani looked up into the sky, where she saw the UAV circle slowly. Then it began a dive, heading straight toward them.

"Tommy," she cautioned.

"Hang on . . ."

"Tommy!"

"Wave to the camera."

"Tommy, pull up! You're going to—"

Twenty feet above them, the UAV broke from its dive as Dani ducked involuntarily, and then it rose again, swooping over the top of the house, where it clipped the weathervane and crashed just beyond the greenhouse, one wing separating from the fuselage.

"That could have gone better," Tommy said.

He handed Dani the controller and ran to retrieve the tiny aircraft. By the time he returned to her, he had the UAV back together again.

"This thing is almost indestructible, but it's going to take some getting used to. Let me see your GPhone for a second."

Dani handed it to him. A minute later he handed it back to her.

"I synced it up with your phone. Bluetooth," he said. "Now you can see what the bird sees, right on your screen."

"The bird?" Dani said. "You've flown it for thirty seconds and you already have a nickname for it?"

"I'm going to need to practice a little," he told her.

"I'll be in the house. Knock yourself out." She hesitated. "I meant that as a figure of speech. Be careful."

"I'm always careful."

"Of course you are." She kissed him. "Stay away from Lake Atticus."

"Point taken," Tommy said, readying the launcher for a second flight. "This thing is corn on the cob."

"I beg your pardon?"

"Something my dad used to say," Tommy explained. "If something was all good, couldn't be better, he'd call it corn on the cob. Because what could be bad about a nice piece of corn on the cob? It could be confusing sometimes, because he'd say it even if he was eating asparagus."

Dani realized where Tommy got his quirky sense of humor; it made her sad to think of what he'd told her about his father's worsening condition.

She could tell from the expression on his face that he was thinking about his dad too.

"I want to stay on top of the situation with Reese," she said. "I think you're right. I think he's hiding something. Maybe from himself."

"If he is, he'll do the right thing. Just give him room."

"It depends on if he's been traumatized," Dani said. "I don't think he fully trusts us."

"The way to get trust is to give it," Tommy said. "I see it all the time with the kids I work with at the gym. You tell 'em you don't think they can do something, they don't. Show 'em you believe in them, they do."

Dani kissed him again, keeping to herself the thought that what might work on a sports team or in a gym wasn't necessarily true in a broader context.

In the kitchen she found Cassandra at the computer. It sometimes still struck Dani as odd to walk into a room and see Cassandra Morton there, probably because she'd seen her picture so many times in the glossy celebrity magazines in the checkout lanes at supermarkets. There was still a kind of shock of recognition, something like the way Dani had felt when she saw the *Mona Lisa* at the Louvre and thought, *Wow, that looks just like the* Mona Lisa, then realized it wasn't *like* the *Mona Lisa*—it *was* the *Mona Lisa*.

The fact that Cassandra was Tommy's ex was no longer an issue. The demons they were fighting had tried to drive a wedge of jealousy between Dani and Tommy, but they'd failed, and in fact, Dani and Tommy's relationship was stronger for it. Still, it was odd sometimes to see Cassandra up close; women that beautiful and famous weren't supposed to occupy real time and space. In reality, Dani had learned Cass was just as nice but far more troubled than her public persona made her out to be.

Cassandra turned to her and smiled. "You okay?" she asked.

"Coping," Dani said. "And you?"

"The same. I was trying to think of how I might make myself useful around here," Cassandra said. "Everybody else seems so smart and talented . . ."

"Cass—"

"Just hear me out," the actress said. "I know what I'm good at. And I think I found a way to put it to good use. Did I tell you about Alberto?"

"VO5?" Dani said. "The shampoo?"

"The soccer player."

"The Brazilian?" Dani remembered seeing something about him

in one of those celebrity magazines: "Soccer Player Breaks Movie Star's Heart," or something like that. "Or was he Argentine?"

"Oh, what difference does it make?" Cassandra joked. "He'd roll over in his grave if he heard me say that. If he were dead."

"Wasn't he voted the Sexiest Man Alive?"

"Only if he was allowed to vote for himself. You're thinking of Jürgen Metzler, the German soccer player."

"It's hard to keep them straight."

"Tell me about it," Cassandra said. "Jürgen asked me out after he learned Alberto and I had stopped seeing each other. Actually, he asked me *before* we stopped seeing each other. And Alberto was supposedly his best friend."

"Isn't he married? Jürgen?"

"Not so's you'd notice," Cassandra said. "He's a terrible person. He's also dumb as a box of doughnuts, but I just got an e-mail from him. He asked me if I wanted to go to a party with him at the German consulate in New York. I think I should."

"Because?"

"Udo Bauer is one of the honored guests."

Bauer. The chairman of Linz Pharmazeutika.

"No." Dani shook her head. "It's too dangerous, Cass. I don't think—"

"Dani," Cassandra said, cutting her off, "listen to me. I know men like Udo Bauer. I've met hundreds of them. They have enough power and enough money to get anything they want, so the only thing they want is what they can't have. If I arrive at a party with the so-called Sexiest Man Alive and dump him for somebody else, that somebody else is going to feel flattered."

"I'd have to agree with you on that," Dani said.

"If I can get close to Bauer," Cassandra said, "maybe I can find something out. Especially if he thinks I'm stupid. Which most people do, thanks to all those blonde jokes. Men will tell women all sorts of things if they think they're stupid. It makes them feel superior. They can't help it."

"Wow," Dani said. "Your life is really different from mine."

"I want to help," Cassandra said. "I'm an actress. If you think about it, this could be the most important role of my life. Everything else was just . . . silly. This is real."

She tilted her head back and to the side to flick the bangs from her eyes, and then she bit her lower lip, the way she'd done so many times in the movies Dani had seen, usually when Cassandra's characters were trying to be brave or find meaning in loss or heartache.

"This matters. I have a feeling . . . I know it sounds strange—silly, even—but I was born to do this, Dani. Everything I've done so far in my life has led up to this point."

It did sound strange, but Dani had been thinking along the same lines, that everything that had happened to her, everything that had shaped her into the person she now was, had been preparation for the task she was now facing. Tommy had said much the same thing to her the other day—that everything he'd experienced, even the tragedy that convinced him to retire from football and follow his other childhood dream of being a private detective—had all been part of a plan.

Dani had the feeling she knew whose plan it was.

"You could be right," she said. "Let's talk about it with Tommy when he's done with his new toys."

"More toys?" Cassandra smiled. "He loves his gadgets, doesn't he?"

Dani smiled back, nodding. "He sure does. Did you know he owns a gadget website?"

"It doesn't surprise me. By the way," Cassandra said, "those things I was saying about men? They're not true about Tommy. He's truly different. You're lucky."

"I know," Dani said.

8.

December 21

2:10 p.m. EST

Tommy didn't understand why he was so scared—why his usual self-confidence seemed temporarily unavailable. He'd waited to find if he was going to be drafted in the first round in the NFL; he'd played in the Super Bowl twice; he'd spoken in public, in front of millions of television viewers at the ESPY awards show, but he'd never been this nervous. Probably because he'd never prepared to ask a question as important. He was 99.99 percent certain he knew what the answer was going to be, but he wanted the event of the asking to be memorable and perfect.

"I think I got it," the jeweler said, returning from his workbench in the back of the shop. Main Street was abuzz with shoppers buying Christmas presents and stocking stuffers and food items. "I have to say, I'm pretty sure in all my years I've never sized a ring in quite this fashion."

Tommy had seen an opportunity when Dani took her rings off to do the dishes at the kitchen sink. When she stepped into the next room, he'd seized the moment to take one of her rings and press it into a stick of hard butter, which he'd kept cold in a cooler full of ice as he drove to the jewelry store.

"You want your butter back?" the jeweler asked. His name was Sidney Gruen, and Tommy had known him since the days when Tommy had worked after school on a landscaping crew for his father's nursery, clearing leaves and doing yard work. Every fall, once he got his driver's license, Tommy had delivered a cord of firewood to Mr. Gruen's house and stacked it for him, even though customers were supposed to pay extra for stacking.

"Not really," Tommy said.

"She looks like a six and a half," Gruen said, setting the stick of butter down on the counter, where his cat sniffed it and walked away. "I can always make adjustments. Did you have a price range in mind? Or a style?"

"Something simple," Tommy said. "She's not an ostentatious kind of person. Is ten carats too big?"

"In my experience, Tommy, there's no such thing as too big a diamond," the jeweler said. "And I've been around a long time. But that's a big stone. Ten carats is not going to be particularly modest. By simple, I'm thinking you want a solitaire?"

"I guess," Tommy said. He'd shopped for engagement rings before, when he'd gotten engaged to Cassandra, but that was in a larger jewelry store on Rodeo Drive in Beverly Hills, and three of his teammates, all enormous defensive linemen, were with him at the time.

"Do you have a cut in mind?" Gruen asked, reaching into a safe for a tray of sample rings. "You have American Standard, Ideal, Eulitz, Parker, AGA—you're Scandinavian, right? How about a Scandinavian cut?"

"Yeah, but it's not about me. What's that one?" Tommy said, pointing to a ring that caught his eye.

"That's a Passion Cut," the jeweler said. "A modification of the classic Tolkowsky design. Eighty-one facets instead of fifty-seven. If you—"

"That's the one. Did you hear that?" he said, raising his voice to a falsetto. "I just heard it say, 'Tommy pick me—I'm the one you want!'"

The jeweler removed the ring from the black velvet-lined tray and slipped it onto his sizing stick, holding it up for Tommy to see.

"Six and a half, on the nose," he said, smiling brightly.

"Is that the same as six and a half on the finger?"

"I'll get you a box."

While he waited, Tommy skimmed the front page of the local paper. The accident had occurred too late to make the day's headlines, but it would be there tomorrow.

"You hear about Crazy George Gardener?" the jeweler said when he saw Tommy looking at the paper. "Car accident, last night on 124."

"I heard," Tommy said. "And George wasn't crazy, Mr. Gruen. He just wanted kids to think he was so they'd stay off his property. I heard they hit a deer."

"Was that it?" the jeweler said. "I heard they hit an oil slick. That's what the guy told me."

"Who?"

"One of the EMTs," Gruen said. "He came in because the battery in his watch died."

"Why would there be an oil slick on 124?"

"That's what I said," the jeweler replied. "Can I ask—who's the six and a half?"

"Last time I bought a ring for someone, it got in all the tabloids," Tommy said. "I think I'm going to keep this one private. Okay?"

"Sure," Gruen said. "If anybody asks, you weren't here. Say hi to your father for me."

"I will," Tommy said. "He's coming home in a couple days."

9.

December 21

2:12 p.m. EST

Dani wondered why Tommy had acted so strangely when he told her he had some errands to run in town. All she'd said was, "What errands?" He didn't seem to have an answer.

She was, however, getting used to his quirks of mind. She set aside the strangeness with Tommy and focused on her driving. The snow was still falling, albeit more lightly than before. She turned off Dana Road and found Baldev Banerjee's black Mercedes in the parking lot, the only car there; the rest of the New York Medical College campus was empty, the cement buildings as gray and dreary as the sky.

She found out where everybody had gone when she got to the medical examiner's office. Banerjee was in a festive mood, humming "We Wish You a Merry Christmas" as he opened the door for her.

"The Christmas party is tonight," he said, smiling. He was festively dressed as well, in a green vest and a red bow tie. "Across the street, at the police academy. I'm sure you would be welcome to attend."

Christmas party. Dani forced a smile. "I have plans already. Sorry."

"Of course, of course." Banerjee had explained to her once that his parents were among India's forty million plus Christians. He'd always cele-brated Christmas, but it was hard for him to get used to Santa Claus, he said, because Santa's long beard made him look like one of those self-proclaimed mystics who were always trying to swindle the gullible in India.

"Your Santa Claus is just like the phony gurus," Banerjee said, taking Dani's coat to hang on the back of a chair. "Swindling me out of every last penny I have, buying presents for my children. My six-year-old wants an iPad. And do you know what the sad thing is? She's going to get one. She plays me like a drum. It's the same thing every year."

"My nieces do the same thing to me," Dani said. "Everything has to be princess with them. You could give them a shovel, and as long as it's pink with rhinestones on it, they'll love it."

"My eight-year-old wants American Girl dolls," Banerjee said. "The ones that come with matching outfits for the girls who own them. It never stops."

"No," she said. "I guess it doesn't."

"Well," Banerjee said. "We have things to talk about, don't we? Do you want to see your friend's body, or would you prefer to just go over the histology?"

And just like that, the festive mood was gone.

The body in question belonged to Carl Thorstein, a theologian and scholar who'd been Tommy's friend and spiritual counselor after the on-field accident that ended Tommy's career. But in this new battle they were fighting, the counselor had been vulnerable. Dani had asked Banerjee to do a detailed workup on Carl, though she hadn't told him exactly why. Of course, she could hardly have said, *I want to look to see if we can find any evidence that this man was possessed by demons.* Banerjee would have given her a look that said, *Are you crazy?*

It was the same look she would have given anybody who said the same thing before the events of the last few months. Before she came to under-stand that demons were real and that they truly did do the work of Satan.

Demons couldn't possess someone against their will, though—you had to invite them in. And Carl, for some reason, had done just that. Tommy suspected it had something to do with the death of Carl's daughter, Esme, who'd drowned in a kayaking accident in Alaska. An accident Carl survived, but for which the man had never forgiven himself. They'd never know what trick the demon had used to get Carl to invite him in, but whatever it was, it had worked.

At first, as they were able to piece it together afterward, Carl had served as a spy behind enemy lines, reporting back to Ghieri and Wharton to tell them what Dani and Tommy were up to. Then he'd tried to steal the book that Abbie Gardener, the Curatoriat's last Guardian, had left them. The *Vademecum Absconditus*, or "Secret Reference," gave the history of the Curatoriat and listed the names of the current members. Only the Guardian knew the identities of all twelve curators; the Curators, in turn, could contact the Guardian but didn't know who the Guardian was or where he or she lived. That way, if a Curator was ever questioned, he wouldn't be able to identify the organization. Not even her own son, George, knew Abbie was the Guardian. Villanegre had found them only because he'd followed the painting to East Salem. Had the book fallen into the hands of Ghieri or Wharton, the results would have been disastrous.

Yet in the end Carl had apparently resisted the control the demon had over him. He'd killed himself—ridden his motorcycle off the cliff at Bull's Rock Hill, plummeting to his death in the waters of Lake Atticus below— rather than do Satan's bidding any longer. Dani was hoping Banerjee could help explain how he'd managed to resist. The evil that had been inside Carl was a spiritual thing, but maybe it had a physical or biological component? Maybe it had left a mark, or a stain? And maybe there was something they could learn from Carl, who had always been a teacher—maybe there was one last thing he could teach them?

"I don't think I need to see the body," Dani said. "You've taken samples?"

"I have," Banerjee said, seating himself at his desk. A large flat-screen monitor on the wall behind him served as a kind of electronic blackboard. He called up Carl Thorstein's file, and Dani saw a table of numbers. "This was a drowning victim?" he asked.

Dani nodded. She sat in the black leather office chair on the opposite side of the desk and swiveled to face him.

"But he drowned himself intentionally," she added. "He rode his motorcycle off a cliff at ninety miles an hour. I was hoping you could tell me something about his state of mind."

"He rode his motorcycle off a cliff? At ninety miles an hour? I would say his state of mind was suicidal. Though you know that already." Banerjee frowned. "I did the proteome analysis you wanted. Chromatography, catecholamine assay, spectroscopy. You were correct. The similarities to our recent client Amos Kasden are statistically significant. But the differences are too."

"How so?" Dani asked. The tests the medical examiner referred to could determine the biochemical makeup of the deceased's cerebrospinal fluids, the relative concentrations of hormones and neurotransmitters and metabaloids for drugs or mind-altering substances, and could indicate—but not prove—a person's state of mind or mood.

They'd known Amos had been taking some kind of drug—probably as part of the Selected, Dani now thought, after what Reese had told them. The tests they'd done on Amos postmortem revealed extremely low levels of dopamine and serotonin, naturally occurring hormones that allow people to feel pleasure and think clearly, as well as elevated adrenaline and noradrenalin. It was a prescription for psychotic outbursts.

"You said you thought the boy might have suffered from dissociative personality disorder?" the ME said, swivelling in his chair to look at the flat-screen monitor and reaching behind him to use the mouse to call up the file on Amos Kasden.

"Dissociative identity disorder," Dani corrected him, watching the screen. "DSM-IV code 300.14."

"Which means what again?"

"A person detaches from their body," Dani said. "You sometimes see it in cases of extreme abuse or suffering. The person finds a way to say, 'This is happening to my body but not to me.' It serves as a coping mechanism, but if it happens frequently enough, the detachment remains, even after the abuse stops. People feel like they're already dead.'"

Banerjee turned back to face her. "Related to multiple personalities?"

"In a way," Dani said. "Some researchers think that in the absence or abdication of the original personality, an alter can form. A second personality. Or multiples. Why?"

He leaned back, steepling his fingers. "Do you remember David Berkowitz?"

"The serial killer who terrorized New York? Son of Sam?" Dani said. "It was before I was born, but I've read about him."

"I've written about him," Banerjee said. "He's still in prison, you know. They did a battery of tests on him, and a group of us had a look, just to see what we could see. Group of medical examiners who get together to go over famous cases. Sort of a hobby."

"Sounds like a fun leisure activity," Dani said, using a finger to place a strand of hair behind her ear.

Banerjee smiled. "Do you remember *why* Berkowitz did what he did? Not why he did it, but why he *said* he did it?"

"I don't."

"He said Satan made him." Banerjee threw his hands open, fingers spread. "Claimed a demon had possessed his neighbor's dog, and the dog spoke to him. The dog's name was Sam. That's where 'Son of Sam' came from. People found it quite comical at the time, but as criminologists we take such statements seriously because it goes to cause or volition—if he *thought* it was why he did what he did, then it *was* why he did what he did. It's like the old joke, 'I can't tell if my girlfriend is pretty or if she just *looks* pretty.' Anyway, it rang a bell with me because my parents had friends we used to vacation with from the town of Ossett. Do you know it? Little village in West Yorkshire, near Leeds?"

"Afraid I don't." She gave him a weak smile.

"No reason you should. But here's the connection." Banerjee stood and crossed the room to a water cooler, filling a small paper cup and offering it to Dani, who declined. He downed it like a shot of whiskey, crumpled the cup, and threw it in the wastebasket.

"When I was a boy, I read in the paper about a man they called the Madman of Ossett. His name was Michael Taylor. In 1974, he murdered his wife, in a way too brutal for the newspapers to describe—which, given the state of British newspapers at the time, or now, must have been truly unspeakable. Strangled the family dog too. Police found him walking starkers in the street, covered in blood. Know why he said he did it?"

"The dog told him to?"

"Not quite," Banerjee said, "but close. Another case of what the books call demonomania. Only this time, the night before, some clergymen had brought him into St. James Church in Barnsley for an exorcism. They stayed up all night and said they'd managed to cast out forty demons, but they were exhausted by the morning and couldn't go on. They claimed there were three demons they hadn't gotten to, one for murder, one for violence, and one for insanity. So they sent Taylor home, and that night he offed the missus and the pooch."

"I don't want to interrupt your story," Dani said, "but how does this relate to Carl Thorstein?"

"Or Amos Kasden?" Banerjee said. "Or David Berkowitz? Here's how. Michael Taylor willed his body to science. He hoped somebody would be able to use it to figure out what happened to him."

"And did they?" Dani asked.

Banerjee smiled and held up the index finger of his right hand. "One more brief digression. George Lukins. Somerset, 1778. A hundred miles west of London, give or take. Another man who claimed to have been possessed by demons. Lukins also donated his body to the Oxford College of Physicians. Threw out the bits they couldn't use, but they've had the poor chap's brain in a jar of formaldehyde for the last 235 years. So what we have, in David Berkowitz, Michael Taylor, and George Lukins, are the brains of three men who may be said to have suffered from demonomania. And we have MRIs of all three brains, which, thanks to modern technology and the Internet, I am able to access from my own very comfortable and very private office. And as you may recall—"

"You did a postmortem MRI of Amos Kasden's brain," Dani remembered. "You thought catecholamine-secreting tumors on the adrenal medulla could explain the absence of vanillylmandelic acid in Kasden's urine. But you didn't find any tumors."

"I did not," Banerjee said. "But what I did find . . . what these four men have in common . . . here. Let me show you."

He exited the screen they were looking at and called up four MRIs, each filling a quarter of the screen, each brain in profile, and pointed with his finger at each, moving clockwise from the upper left.

"Lukins, Taylor, Berkowitz, and Kasden," he said. "This part here, in particular . . ." With a finger, he circled the upper front quarter of Amos Kasden's brain.

"The frontal lobe," Dani said.

"Exactly." Banerjee nodded. "And what's the frontal lobe responsible for, primarily?"

"Judgment," Dani said. "Executive function. Calculating the consequences of your actions. Distinguishing between right and wrong or good and bad. Impulse control. Inhibition. Suppressing antisocial behaviors."

"And this area here?" Banerjee said, hovering the mouse icon over the anterior section of the frontal lobe.

"The prefrontal cortex," Dani said.

"The seat of personality—do I have that correct?" When Dani nodded,

Banerjee clicked the mouse on each of the images. "Now look what happens when we magnify this area."

As each image grew larger on the screen, revealing more and more detail, Dani saw an array of what appeared to be holes. The images were three-dimensional. Banerjee moved down through the tissue, revealing more and more perforations.

"You've heard of BSE?" he asked. "Bovine spongiform encephalopathy?"

Dani's eyes widened. "This is mad cow?"

"Similar but more localized," Banerjee said. "It's present in all four men. I thought Creutzfeldt-Jakob at first, but I ruled that out. Now—let's look at the histology for your friend. From the same region." Banerjee cleared the screen, then called up a microscopic view taken of tissue from Carl's brain.

"I see what you mean," Dani said.

"Yes," Banerjee said. "Spongiform perforations, though less articulated."

Dani studied the screen as if looking at a maze. The prefrontal cortex was the moral center of a person, the part that empathized with others and, as such, the part that cemented the social bond between humans. If the Ten Commandments were written or encoded anywhere within the human consciousness, it was here. Without it, there was nothing to stop someone from killing the first person who made them angry or stealing the first bright shiny object that caught their fancy, regardless of who it belonged to.

Dani thought of the boys she'd worked with in Africa who'd been turned into child soldiers. The leader of the Children's Army had been a man named Daniel Kaimba who had given the boys some kind of drug made from native plants. He robbed them of their identities and left them controllable and almost robotic. Voodoo doctors in Haiti were believed to possess similar personality-robbing concoctions. Had St. Adrian's given their boys something similar? Had the demons given something to Carl? But it couldn't account for Berkowitz or Lukins or Taylor. From the Dark

Ages up to the age of modern psychology, mad men, and mad women, had been diagnosed as possessed by demons. Was it possible that, at least in some cases, and perhaps more than science had ever acknowledged, the diagnosis was correct?

"I have a call in to Atlanta. If this is anything like mad cow, the CDC should know about it. They have prion tests they can do with lasers and fluorescent dyes that I can't do. If there's any danger—"

"There's no danger," Dani said. "It's not epidemiological."

"Dani—"

"It's not contagious," she said.

He looked at her, waiting for an explanation she couldn't give him.

"They have a truck in Atlanta," Banerjee said, "containing a mobile tissue digester. Tufts has a digester, but it's not mobile. It uses alkaline hydrolysis, at temperature and under pressure, to safely dispose of BSE tissues. I think at the very least, Carl should—"

"No," Dani said. Carl had been able, somehow, to fight the demon inside him. Tommy had been present when Carl died, and the angel Charlie had been there too and proclaimed that the demon was gone. Whatever had happened inside Carl's brain, it was over. There was no risk from the body, the vessel that had once, temporarily, housed his soul. "He's okay."

"Can you tell me how you know this?"

"I can't tell you," Dani said. "But I know it."

Banerjee bit his lip for a moment, thinking. "All right," he said. "I've had the body sealed for cold storage. I hope that's enough."

"Thank you," Dani said, rising and taking her coat from the coat rack where he'd hung it. "Thank you for trusting me."

"Can you at least tell me where in the ocean the body was found?" Banerjee said. "So we know where to look. If there's a second case, I won't be able to sit on this."

"There won't be," Dani said. "And he didn't drown in the ocean. He drowned in Lake Atticus."

"In fresh water?" Banerjee said, his brow furrowed. "I don't see how that's possible. He was hypernatremic."

"Elevated sodium?"

"I assumed he'd ingested saltwater."

"No. I don't think he did." Dani frowned. Saltwater? Elevated sodium? She had no idea what that meant.

"Is there any way to go back and look for hypernatremia in Amos's workup?" she asked, thinking. Carl had, to an extent, beaten or defied the demon inside of him. Amos had not. "Or maybe the opposite? Hyponatremia? What's normal for blood sodium?"

"Normal is anywhere from 135 to 145 millimoles," Banerjee said. "People who drink too much fresh water can become hyponatremic and seem intoxicated. Let me look."

He returned to his computer screen. Dani was looking over his shoulder when she saw a window pop open on his screen, announcing: *File not available; error code 8463903bn987.*

"What?" Banerjee said. "Hang on while I check my backup files."

A moment later Banerjee's computer told him none of the files he named could be found. He told Dani that fortunately for the last year he'd been backing up everything in "the cloud," just in case he ever suffered a system-wide data loss, as appeared to be the case. Yet when he searched the cloud, he was again told no such files existed. All the work he'd done on Amos and Carl, and his comparisons to Son of Sam and Lukins and Taylor, were gone.

"Well, that's just extremely strange," he said. "It's still here somewhere, but it looks like it may take me awhile to find it."

"Can you call me or send me an e-mail when you do?" Dani asked.

Dani drove north on the Sawmill parkway, but the lost files had set her on edge. She tried to calm her fears, telling herself she was just being silly, but she found herself checking her rearview mirror, worried that she was being followed. The car behind her was a red Mini Cooper. It seemed like it was too conspicuous a car to use to follow somebody, but the car behind the Cooper was a gray sedan. Just to be sure, she got off at the first Pleasantville exit and watched in her rearview mirror as the Mini sped north—but the gray sedan took the same exit she did. It could be a coincidence. She drove through the center of town, the gray sedan staying well back but following, and then she got back on the Sawmill. The gray sedan did too. Now she knew she was being followed.

But if she knew that, the odds were good that whoever was in the gray sedan knew she knew, and they certainly did this sort of thing a lot more than she did. She tried to think calmly and clearly. Her car, a black BMW 335i coupe she'd inherited from her father, was probably faster than the sedan, but she knew better than to try to outrun whoever was following her.

Think!

She was safer in public than she would be on any deserted back road. When she saw the top floors of Northern Westchester Hospital looming above the trees ahead, she had an idea. The regional district attorney's office was across the street from the hospital. She exited the Sawmill. The gray sedan did too. When she reached the DA's office, she turned into the drive to enter the parking garage behind and beneath the building and stopped, waiting for the transponder on her dash to open the gate. The garage served as a sally port where uniformed officers could safely off-load prisoners from their squad cars—there would be cops with guns there, men she knew and trusted.

When the gate opened, she drove through and stopped, looking in her rearview mirror. She saw the gate close, and then she saw the gray sedan roll slowly past. There were two men in it. One was wearing a baseball style cap. She couldn't make out their faces, but they were clearly looking in her direction.

She parked and rode the elevator up to the second floor, where she went to the conference room, with windows overlooking the street. She surveyed the street below. The gray sedan was gone, but there was always a chance they had a backup car.

"What are you doing here?" a voice behind her said. It was Stuart Metz, the assistant DA. "I thought you were on leave."

"Oh, hi, Stuart," she said, smiling. "I am, but a crazy patient of mine saw me and followed me here. I just don't want to talk to her right now. Can you give me a ride?"

"Sure," Metz said. "Where to?"

Metz mocked her as she ducked down out of sight from the passenger seat of his car. When he saw an old woman walking a dog, he described her to Dani, and Dani said, "Yes, that's her."

On the Sawmill, headed north again, Dani sat up and thanked her friend.

"You okay?" he asked her. "You're acting weird."

"Yes, I'm good, thanks," she told him, straightening out her coat. "You know how crazy it gets before the holidays."

10.

December 21

4:51 p.m. EST

When she got back to the house, Dani poured herself a cup of tea and sat down in the kitchen to mull over what Banerjee had told her, and what that meant for the plan that was being hatched at St. Adrian's. She had no doubt that the lost files and the gray sedan were connected. Yet computer hacking and being followed by men in gray sedans did not seem consistent with what she thought of as, for lack of a better term, demonic style. No one was safe, and it was only going to get worse.

Tommy could cope, and so, she hoped, could she, but the others . . . Cassandra was planning on walking right into the lion's den. And Quinn—for as long as she'd known him, he'd never been one to take care of himself. When they were both in Africa, working in a region where famine was endemic, he'd failed to eat, even though doctors and relief workers had their own rations, and he had to be briefly hospitalized. He'd never gotten enough sleep, his mind always racing. His headaches were getting worse. She'd seen him wince from them all too often lately, but when she asked him how he was, all he said was, "Hunky-dory." He'd been reluctant to tell anyone about his brain tumor because he didn't want people feeling sorry for him, but Dani knew how hard it was for him to live with the diagnosis.

In the courtyard, Tommy and Reese practiced flying the drone. The boy was almost as tall as Tommy, but lean and gangly, and he was dwarfed by the winter coat Tommy had loaned him. He looked, Dani thought, a bit like a member of the British boy band One Direction, whose posters papered the walls of her nieces' bedrooms. At one point Tommy gave the controller to Reese, then stood back and watched from the open garage bay, arms folded across his chest—showing, quite literally, the hands-off trust he'd spoken of.

She was glad when he finally came in from the garage, stomping his boots before kicking them off and hanging his coat on a hook in the mudroom. Reese was right behind him.

"You boys getting the hang of it?" she asked.

"This guy was doing loop-de-loops," Tommy told her, setting the controller down on the table. "He's a natural. But then he's had a lot more time on the Xbox than I have."

"What's an Xbox?" Dani asked.

Tommy and Reese looked at each other in disbelief, and then Tommy reached out and put his hand on Reese's shoulder, lowering his voice in a tone of mock gravity.

"Her ways are different from ours, my son," Tommy told him. "She's new to our world, but she will learn. Now go and get cleaned up for supper, for soon we will eat."

Reese laughed and then left them alone.

She filled Tommy in on what she'd learned, and seen, at the medical examiner's office, and how they lost the files, and how she'd been followed. Tommy agreed that it didn't sound like something Ghieri or Wharton would do, but said they shouldn't underestimate the enemy. He wasn't sure what to make of Banerjee's findings either—particularly the last one.

"Saltwater?" he said. "How is that possible?"

"I have no idea."

"There's something else I don't get. And I could write a book full of stuff I don't get," he said, moving to the computer monitor. "Take a look at this."

He sat her down in front of the computer and directed her attention to the screen. "These are pictures I just downloaded from the drone. I might have to order another one because it's pretty inconvenient to have to keep bringing it home to switch cameras . . ."

"Tommy," she began.

"You're absolutely right. One is plenty."

"You already ordered another one, didn't you?"

"Uh-huh," he said. "But I can cancel the order."

"What did you want to show me?"

"Well," he said, clicking on a file, "first, here's a plain old visual of East Salem. The resolution is amazing. I was flying at ten thousand feet, and I could see that Gail is buying Eddie a pair of Sorrels, size ten, for Christmas—I could look right into her shopping bag."

Gail was the owner of the Miss Salem Diner, and Eddie, her father, was the former owner and now the cook. Dani saw her little town on the screen, the broad commons with the gazebo in the middle, the diner, the Pub, the church, the library, the Grange Hall, the shops, all made more lovely by the new-fallen snow. Several cars had Christmas trees tied to their roofs with twine.

"Okay," she said. "Very Norman Rockwell."

"Yeah. Except Norman Rockwell never painted anything like this. The next thing you're going to see is from the infrared camera," he said, and changed the view. The people on the street appeared as hot spots ranging from yellow to orangish-red. Tommy told her people appeared warm to different degrees, depending on how well insulated their clothing was. "Now watch what happens when I slow the whole thing down thirty times."

In the new view, the orange and red and yellow human outlines stood still, while blue shadows raced among them, dozens of them.

"Those are demons, aren't they?" Dani said. Demonic entities, she knew, registered deep blue and cold to the infrared cameras and were nearly invisible in real time. "What do you think they're doing?"

"No idea," Tommy said. "Probably not Christmas shopping. Let me show you one more."

He clicked to a different file, footage showing the outline of a house. The outline looked vaguely familiar.

"Where is that?"

"That's your house," Tommy said. Dani hadn't been there in over a week. The roof was a cool green color. There seemed to be heat leaking from one of the basement windows. "Now I slow it down."

In the slow-motion footage she saw her house infested with blue creatures moving in and out of it. For a moment she felt nauseated, the way she'd felt as a girl when her father had turned over a large, flat rock to show her the bugs and worms living beneath it.

"What are they doing?" she said.

"Looking for something?" Tommy guessed. "I don't know. Maybe looking for your father's computer."

Dani's father, Fred, had been a pediatrician with medical records on most of the children in town, children who were now adults.

"Could be." She turned to face him. "How about here? Are they here too?"

"This house is safe," Tommy said. "They know it's protected. They're keeping their distance after what happened in the courtyard."

It was in Tommy's courtyard where, with all his might, knowing it was hopeless, a test of faith, he'd fought a demon that had been sent to kill him, and then Charlie and Ben had revealed themselves in their full glory. The demon was no match for their power, not even close.

"So far so good," Dani said, rapping her knuckles on the table.

Tommy glanced at her.

"I'm not superstitious. It's bad luck to be superstitious."

"That's my line," Tommy said.

"I know," Dani said. "I'm learning from the best."

He moved behind her and rubbed her neck and shoulders. She hadn't realized how much tension she was carrying.

"Something else," he said. "I flew over St. Adrian's. I won't bore you with the infrared, but watch this—I pasted these two clips together."

He reached over her to click on a file. The first clip was of Wharton and the school psychologist, Ghieri, standing side by side on a balcony.

"That's an HD clip—normal camera," Tommy said. "Then I flew the drone back and switched payloads. This next clip I took with the infrared camera."

Dani recognized the balcony again. There were two figures standing there once more, in what looked like the exact same location. One was red and one was blue.

"Is this slow motion?" she asked.

"No."

"I thought demons only showed up if you slow it down?"

"That's if they're moving," Tommy said. "If they stay in one place, they show up in real time. They shimmer a little bit."

The blue figure, Dani saw, was indeed shimmering or vibrating, its edges blurry.

"Are you thinking what I'm thinking?" she asked Tommy.

"Only one of them is human," he said. "Has to be Wharton. Ghieri—"

"He's a demon. We knew that," Dani said. "The way he disappeared when he caught you trying to break into his office."

"Yeah, but we didn't know Wharton wasn't—not for sure. Not until now," Tommy said. "The headmaster's a nasty piece of filth, but he's a human nasty piece of filth. Reese says his nickname at school is Goat Boy."

"Hey, guys—I could use your opinion."

Dani turned. Cassandra stood in the kitchen entrance dressed in a low-cut Max Mara cocktail dress made from black Lurex, and opaque black tights.

"Wow," Tommy said.

"Yikes," Dani said. "Are you sure it's legal for you to go out on the street looking that pretty?"

"Let's hope my date—and Herr Bauer—agree," Cassandra said, spinning once in place to model the outfit.

"They'd be crazy if they didn't," Tommy said. "Then again, considering who we're dealing with . . ."

"Where did you get the Jimmy Choo shoes?" Dani asked.

"Ridgefield."

"Ridgefield?" Dani and Tommy said, almost at the exact same instant.

"Yes. A little place on Main Street. You'll recall, Tommy—shopping is very much within my skill set."

Cassandra had clearly learned a few things from the hair and makeup experts she'd worked with over the years as well; Dani had attended her share of fancy parties in the city, but she'd never seen anyone as put together as Cassandra looked right this second.

"So what's your plan?" Dani asked.

"I have no plan," the actress said. "Usually saying hello and looking someone in the eye is enough. They start talking to me and telling me all about themselves, on and on and on, and all I have to do is pretend I'm listening and say, 'Really?' or 'That's so funny!' I've had men talk about themselves for hours, and when they're done they say, 'I feel like I've known you all my life,' when they haven't asked a single thing about me."

"Maybe they say that because they've been watching your movies since you were a child star?" Dani said.

"So if you watched *Hamlet*, would you walk up to the actor who played him and say, 'Listen—I was sorry to hear about your dad'?"

"Good point," Dani said. "So is Jürgen Metzler, a.k.a. the Sexiest Man Alive, going to pick you up in his limo?"

"He's sending it to the Peter Keeler Inn," Cassandra said. "I didn't want anyone to know I was staying here. Ruth said she'd give me a ride to the Inn."

"He's sending a limo? He couldn't come himself?"

"Athletes think everything has to come to them, just because they're good at some idiotic sport."

"I'm right here in the room, you know," Tommy said from where he leaned against the kitchen sink. "I can hear everything you're saying."

"You're the exception to all the rules," Cassandra said. "Except one."

"Which one is that?"

"Wouldn't you like to know?" she said with a coquettish smirk.

Dani walked her out to where Ruth was warming up Tommy's Jeep. It had stopped snowing: the sky was already dark, though it wasn't even five o'clock yet.

"I think I've spent half my life wearing uncomfortable shoes inappropriate for the weather," Cassandra said, stamping her feet against the cold.

"It'll be warm at the party," Dani said.

"Cocktails with Satan-worshiping fiends out to destroy the world." Cassandra smiled. "And Germans. The sad thing is, it still won't be the worst date I've ever been on."

"You'll do fine," Dani said, realizing how scared Cassandra was. "Just take it one fiend at a time." Cassandra opened the Jeep door and started to climb in.

"By the way, which one?" Dani asked.

"Which one what?"

"Which rule is Tommy not the exception to?"

"I don't know," Cassandra confided. "Hopefully I'll think of something. I just felt like I needed to score a point."

"Oooh—you're good." Dani smiled. "Be careful tonight."

11.

December 21

Reese, alone in his room, closed his eyes and tried to concentrate.

Why won't you talk to me anymore?

He waited for a response.

I swear I'm not trying to hurt you. You have to trust me.

Again, the only voice he heard in his head was his own.

I'm safe now. These people aren't like the others. They're good people. They're not going to hurt me. You don't have to worry about me anymore.

He heard only the sound of the heat moving through the radiators and the distant sounds coming from the kitchen downstairs where dinner was being served. He was late, and he needed to get to the table before anyone became suspicious.

I'm not giving up, you know. I'll never give up. Dubbo di zubbo.

At dinner Reese listened as Dani explained to Quinn what the medical examiner's tests had shown. Quinn thought the idea that demonic possession could leave an actual readable imprint on brain tissue was fascinating. He wondered out loud if there was a way to reassemble from other sources the data Banerjee had lost.

"Someday when we establish a true international medical database, and everyone's genome is taken at birth and becomes part of your permanent medical record, we'll be able to write a program that lets computers look at a million chest X-rays side by side, or cross-reference a billion proteomic assays to search for statistical anomalies—then medicine is going to take a gigantic leap forward," Quinn said. "The potential for abuse is enormous, but so is the promise. Right now we're lucky if the right clipboard full of paper charts gets attached to the bed of the correct patient so that the surgeons don't perform the wrong operation on the wrong person. We spend billions of dollars on new surgical or diagnostic technologies while basic record-keeping technologies are practically in the Stone Age."

"What sorts of medical facilities did you have at the school?" Dani asked Reese. "You said everybody was medicated? Where did you go to get your prescriptions filled?"

"The school has an infirmary," Reese said. "We have to get a physical at the beginning of every year. And provide urine samples once a month. Which is weird, because they said they were testing for illegal stuff like marijuana or cocaine, but I know some guys who do that and they've never gotten caught."

"That's one thing I was wondering about," Quinn said. "If the school was running drug trials, apparently without any concern for peer review or FDA approval, I don't see how the student body would provide a large enough population to make the data they'd collect statistically valid. When they gave you your physical, did they by any chance take a cotton swab and run it across the inside of your cheek?"

Reese nodded. "What was that for?"

"DNA," Quinn said. "You can personalize medicine if you know somebody's genome. I'm still not sure how you'd test such a small population."

Reese made a decision. He needed help, and he had no choice but to trust them. They were all genuine Christians, and while he hadn't finished educating himself about the Bible and the people of the Book, he understood what making a leap of faith meant. It meant risking the unknown by believing in the unknowable.

"I might know the answer to that," Reese said.

The others at the table all looked at him.

"Twins," he said. "Identical twins."

"Well, I suppose that would work if you were testing genotropic compounds," Quinn said. "You'd give one twin the drug and the other a placebo and then watch what happens."

"Back up a second," Tommy said. "Are you saying that's what they *should* do, or that's what they *do* do?"

"That's what they do," Reese said. "They study identical twins."

"Well, even so," Quinn began, then stopped himself. "How many pairs of twins are there on campus? Three? Four?"

"I think there's over a hundred," Reese replied.

"Oh my goodness," Ruth said.

"I think you're speaking for all of us," Dani said to the older woman. "Over a hundred? They intentionally recruit identical twins?"

"It's one of the school's better kept secrets," Reese said. "Only one twin at a time is allowed to leave campus. They don't allow us to live together after the first year. The idea is to make every student the best possible student he can be. Sometimes twins hold each other back. You don't want to outperform your twin."

"You said 'us,'" Tommy said. "Do you have a twin?"

Reese had come too far to turn back now.

"I have a brother," he said. "Edmond. Technically he's six minutes older because he came first, but only because I let him. My parents left it in their will that the estate should pay for us to go to St. Adrian's. He's the reason I contacted you. He's one of the Selected."

12.

December 21

9:00 p.m. EST

The limo picked Cassandra up right on time; she found a bottle of champagne on ice in the back with a note from Jürgen Metzler that said: *This is to get you started. More to come. Jürg.*

There was a day when she might have emptied the bottle during the trip to New York, a way to make herself numb enough to endure what was coming, or rather, a way to pre-absolve herself of any responsibility for her actions and say, "I'm sorry—I must have had too much to drink." There was no need for that anymore, though. She opened the champagne and poured the contents out the window, first wetting the inside of the glass to make it look like she'd finished the bottle.

"Henry," she asked her phone, curious. "How much is a bottle of Dom Perignon 1966?"

The GPhone Tommy gave her came with a male avatar named Henry, similar to the female avatar that came with the iPhone but more advanced—"The Highest Level of Personal Assistance," according to the app's welcome screen.

"Dom Perignon 1966 sells for $1,965.00 a bottle," Henry said. "Would you like me to find you a store that carries it?"

"No, thank you," she said.

The limo brought her to Trump Tower, where Jürgen Metzler kept an apartment. She stayed in the back of the limo, out of view of the paparazzi who were taking Metzler's photograph, bathing his rugged physique in flashes of light. In his tuxedo, he looked like a blond James Bond.

Metzler opened the door and leaned in. He asked if she wanted to skip the party and come up to his apartment and watch a video of a soccer game he'd recently performed in.

"I scored a hat trick, you know," he added. "It's quite a remarkable performance, if I do say so myself."

"Alberto scored five goals once," she said. "Get in. I'm in the mood for a party."

On the way to the German consulate on First Avenue between 48th and 49th Streets, the German promised her he would make her forget about Alberto the same way he'd already made the soccer world forget about Alberto. She knew women, plenty of them, who might have fallen for that sort of cocksure bravado. Briefly, she regretted that things hadn't worked out with Tommy—that she'd let something valuable slip right through her fingers—but it had all worked out for the best. For him and Dani, at least.

The consulate facade was an emphatic statement in glass and stainless steel and chrome, with two flags flying from the marquee: one the black, red, and yellow flag of Germany, the other the blue flag of the United Nations. As the limousine passed through the police barricade blocking off the street, Cassandra steeled herself for the publicity to come, someone somewhere saying, "*Morton Rebounds with Another Soccer Star*," though for the first time she realized how inconsequential it all was.

The foyer was filled with uniformed police officers and men in black suits checking identification and logging the comings and goings of the guests in their tablet computers. No one, it went without saying, asked to see Jürgen Metzler's identification, nor did anyone need proof of who the actress on his arm was. When Cassandra's clutch set off the metal detector, she held it above her head and gave the man who wanted to examine the contents a sly look that said, *Oh no you don't,* followed by her biggest smile, while her "date" assured the man that all was in order. In the clutch, she carried only the makeup she needed for touch-ups, her phone, and Tommy's Boy Scout pocketknife, which he'd given her for good luck.

She'd done as much research as she could on Udo Bauer and the pharmaceutical empire he'd inherited. The company had a past that was more than a little checkered, with allegations, never proven, that they— when Bauer's grandfather headed up the company—had a hand in the death camps during World War II, or at the very least that they'd tested drugs on the prisoner population. Sixty years of public relations since the war ended had recast the company as "the BMW of medicine," a super-efficient, super-effective corporation striving to make the world a better place.

The banquet hall was filled with men in tuxedos and women in their finery; there were diamond earrings and pearl necklaces, gold bangles and jewels of great size. Cassandra sported a display of costume jewelry she'd picked up at the mall, but it wasn't what you wore, she'd told Dani—it was how you wore it.

Cassandra's date was immediately swarmed by Bundesliga fans who wanted to congratulate him. Something similar used to happen when she'd been out on the town with Tommy, but Tommy had always made sure she felt like she had his full attention. *Der Sexiest Mann der Welt* didn't even notice when Cassandra slipped away and headed for the buffet at the far end of the room, adjacent to the stage where an eighteen-piece orchestra played jazz standards and suitable holiday music, the singing duties rotating between the piano player, the lead sax player, and the drummer.

She spotted Udo Bauer standing near the end of the buffet, a glass of wine in his hand, conversing in German with two men and a stout middle-aged woman who looked like a politician, speaking animatedly with her hands in the air.

"*Denke immer daran, net zu den Leuten zu sein, während du die leiter zum erfolg erklimmst, denn vieleicht benötigst du die leute wieder auf dem weg nach unten.*"

The others laughed.

"I don't suppose you can translate, can you, Henry?" she asked her phone.

"Always be nice to the little people you step on on your way up, because you may need to step on them again on your way down."

"Charming. Thank you."

Cassandra took a small plate and filled it slowly from the buffet, her back to Bauer. Soon she was aware of someone standing behind her.

"Do you like German food, Miss Morton?"

"Not so much, Herr Bauer," she said, turning. He was a head taller than she, his shoulders squared to her but relaxed.

"You know who I am?"

"I Googled you when I saw you were being honored. And this is not German food."

"We can be thankful for that," Bauer said. "I find it heavy, and I grew up with it. But I could cook it for you in a way that I think you would like."

"You cook your own food, Herr Bauer?"

"When I have the time," he said, smiling. Cassandra popped an olive into her mouth with a toothpick. "Do you?"

"When I have the time," she said, smiling brightly. "My mother was a cook. On sailboats, mostly in St. John. And St. Barts. I grew up on boats. I could take apart an outboard engine and put it back together blindfolded. Among the many useless things I can do."

"Perhaps you would like to see mine?" Bauer said. "I have a little dinghy you might enjoy."

Little dinghy. Ha. Cassandra had done her homework. It was a well-known fact that Udo Bauer owned the largest private yacht in the world, a 680-foot Blohm and Voss German yacht that was 150 feet longer than the second biggest private yacht in the world. He called it *Freiheit*. He did not, like so many of the yacht-owning Saudi princes and Russian oligarchs and US tech billionaires, flaunt his wealth or show off his yacht by staging elaborate parties on it during film festivals or Grand Prix races. No pictures of the interior existed, as far as Cassandra could tell.

"I would like that very much," she said. "On one condition. That you don't make me watch any German soccer games on television. Right now, I want nothing to do with German soccer."

Her "date" was still holding sway in the middle of the room.

"I own the team he plays for, you know," Bauer said.

"Yes, I know," Cassandra said.

"If you want me to, I will trade him," Bauer said. "I have a friend who wants to create a team in North Korea."

"Oh, don't do that," Cassandra said. "Just send him a picture of me on your dinghy and tell him he needs to learn how to treat a woman."

"Where are you staying?"

"The Peter Keeler Inn in East Salem," she said.

"I went to school in East Salem."

"I knew that too," she told him, turning to leave. "I hope you'll tell me something I don't already know."

Bauer touched the small of her back possessively. "I'll send a car for you in the morning. Don't bother packing—you can buy what you need when you get there."

"I'm looking forward to it," she said.

13.

December 21

10:10 p.m. EST

"How do you know he was chosen?" Quinn asked Reese.

Dani watched the boy for indications of deception. She remembered when they'd questioned Amos Kasden, how cold and lacking in affect he was. Reese seemed torn and tormented and, without question, was telling the truth.

"Because we're twins," Reese said. "Twins know things about each other. Or at least identical ones do. We actually had our own secret language until we were eight."

"Secret language?" Tommy asked. "You mean like a code?"

"It wasn't a code to us," Reese said. "We weren't translating anything from English. It was just a language we made up together. It made perfect sense to us."

Dani nodded. "Idioglossia." She recalled a documentary film she'd seen once in a class on cognitive development and language. "It's a remarkable phenomenon. Fairly rare. Sometimes called twin-speak. It usually disappears when the twins reach the age of five or six."

"We still speak it sometimes. Once in a great while. We don't have the whole thing, but a few phrases remain," Reese said. "But we don't even have to talk. I mean, not all the time. Sometimes we know what the other one is feeling without having to say anything. My mother used to call it 'twinstincts.' I would know when Edmond hurt himself without being anywhere near him. Or one day, when he was lost in the woods where we lived, I knew right where to look for him."

"I've heard of that," Dani said, her scientific wheels turning. She moved her chair slightly closer to the boy, not too close to be threatening but close enough to tell him she was genuinely listening to him. "Twins who are able to communicate telepathically over great distances."

"Or not so great," Reese said. "It used to amuse Mrs. Carlyle. Quite often I'd get up and get dressed, and an hour later Edmond would get up and get dressed, and he'd come down the stairs wearing the exact same outfit as me. We didn't have to coordinate our wardrobes—we would just have the same idea at the same time, for the same reasons."

"There are a few documented cases in the scientific literature," Quinn said. "I remember one where a twin in California was in a car accident and his identical brother in New York suddenly said, 'My brother just died in a car accident,' at a dinner party, with plenty of witnesses. It was true right to the second. No one has ever been able to explain it scientifically."

"Which doesn't mean there isn't an explanation," Tommy said.

"I think of it as a God-given gift," Reese said. "That's what my father called it."

"I think he was right," Tommy said, tapping the kitchen table twice with his finger for emphasis.

"What do you think it means, that Edmond was selected?" Dani asked. "Do you know, Reese?" She remembered one of her favorite teachers from medical school telling her that in a therapeutic transaction, the more you used someone's name, the more power you transferred to them.

"I was hoping you could tell me," Reese said. "That's why I came here."

"They weren't trying to kill you?"

"No, they were," Reese said. "Nothing I've said to you is a lie. I've been careful to make sure of that. I just haven't always told you the complete truth."

"When we asked you if you had family you wanted to call—"

"I said I'd lost my parents," Reese said. "I didn't say, 'No, I don't have any family.' I'm sorry I've been evasive. I wasn't sure I could trust you. For all I knew, you could have been one of . . . them."

"And the car accident wasn't an accident?"

Reese shook his head.

"Two of those things attacked the car," he said. "I couldn't tell you where they came from. Out of nowhere."

"But they didn't kill *you*."

"They tried," Reese said.

"I heard a rumor that you hit an oil slick," Tommy said.

"They tend to splatter when you hit them with a car," Reese said. "I couldn't get to the second one because of the fire, but the first one left an oily smear on the road. I thought it was blood, but it felt more like paint."

"You were afraid before any of that happened," Dani reminded him. "At school."

"I know they would have killed me if I hadn't left," Reese said. "I think they told my brother if he didn't do what they wanted him to do, they'd hurt me. I definitely got that message. From him."

"Do you know where he is now?" Dani asked.

"England," Reese said. "I think he's in London. Mrs. Carlyle told me he stopped at home to pick up his car, but he didn't tell her where he was going."

"Have you tried to call him?" Dani asked.

"I couldn't get through."

"Can you . . ." She hesitated. "Can you sense what he's doing?"

Reese shook his head. "I've tried that. He won't answer. I can't even tell if he can hear me. I think . . . Maybe it's me, not him. Everything is too cluttered. I have too many things in my head. It's hard to sort it all out."

"I was wondering, Reese," Dani asked. "Was your brother taking the blue pill as well?"

"I don't know," Reese said. "Like I said, the school separated us. And then he cut me off. It felt like he'd changed. He thinks the less I know, the safer I'll be. I tried to tell him I'm safe. I told him, '*Dubbo di zubbo.*' That's one of our phrases. 'Remember that I love you.'"

"And he's not answering?" Tommy said.

The boy shook his head. Dani could see how saddened he was, and more than that, how scared.

"But when I told you they're planning something for Christmas Eve," Reese said, "it was his voice I heard. Sometimes, if he's really thinking about something, it gets through. Edmond has been obsessed with that date lately. I've seen it in his mind. I feel it."

"Twinstincts?" Quinn said.

The boy nodded. "But as I said, there's been a lot of clutter. It's hard to know."

"Dani," Tommy said. "Can I have a word with you in the study?"

When they were alone, he asked her what she thought about the idea of twinstincts—was it legitimate?

"It's not something anyone has been able to scientifically determine," Dani said, "but yes. There have been plenty of examples, stories, where identical twins are able to see, mostly visual or audio glimpses, what the remote other is perceiving. It's not some carnival trick mind-reading or ESP, but it's . . . something. Think about it, Tommy—it almost gives us a way to spy, a way to hack into their inner circle. If we—"

"I thought of that," Tommy said. "But Dani, if we can see into their camp, how do we know they can't see into ours? If it goes both ways, then Edmond is going to know what Reese is up to, and if Edmond tells Ghieri or Wharton . . . Maybe his brother is only pretending he isn't listening. How do we know?"

"You could be right."

"Reese wouldn't necessarily know he's being used, would he?"

"I don't know," Dani said. "But I know this. He's terrified that he's never going to see his brother again. He may not exactly realize it, but if he's fearing for Edmond's life, it might be because Edmond is fearing for his own life and Reese is picking up on it. And if Edmond is fearing for his own life, it probably means—it *might* mean—that he's not collaborating with Ghieri and Wharton. Does that make sense?"

"Does anything?"

"Let me talk to him," she said. "I'll be careful."

Back in the kitchen, she asked Reese if he thought his brother had aligned himself with Ghieri and Wharton and the other boys who'd been selected.

"I want you to really think about your answer," she said. "I'm just going to tell you flat out—we're afraid that your brother might be reading your thoughts and passing along whatever he learns to Dr. Ghieri or Dr. Wharton. Do you think that's possible?"

"I don't," Reese said. "My brother is a good person. He thinks he's doing something good, whatever it is. He's afraid of Ghieri, and the headmaster too, and he's afraid of what they'll do to me, but he thinks . . . well, he's not sure. He wants to believe he's doing good."

"Can you tell us who the other boys are?" Dani asked. "The other ones who've been selected?"

Reese shook his head.

"If I felt a connection, and if he was thinking of them—if he visualized one of the other boys, I might be able to recognize him. But as I said, he cut me off," Reese said. "When we started at St. Adrian's—"

"Which was when?" Dani interrupted.

"Three years ago," Reese said. "Ever since the end of the first year, more and more, it's been one way. I can't get through to him anymore. And like I said, it's hard for me because there's so much going on in my head. But I know one thing for sure. My brother is in pain. Something is really tearing him up. He's . . ."

"Conflicted?" Dani said.

Reese nodded.

"That's good," she said. "It means part of him is still fighting it. It means he's got the same goodness inside of him that you do."

"Do you think you can help him?" Reese asked, his eyes pleading.

"I can if we can get through to him," Dani said. She tried to think of what she could do to enhance his twinstincts, but all she could think of were the crazy experiments the army had conducted in the seventies with psychics, trying to test for things like precognition and remote viewing or clairvoyance in order to develop them as military weapons. It was all dismissed as hogwash, or at least that was the official explanation for why the program, the Stargate Project, if she remembered correctly, had been shut down. They probably tried any number of psychoactive drugs to increase their subjects' mental abilities, but if anything worked, the military was keeping it a secret. The odds were much greater that nothing had worked.

"What do you say the problem is when you try to get through to him?" Tommy asked.

"I just . . ." Reese struggled to find the words. "I hear a lot of white noise. In my head. I'm not sure where it comes from. It's hard to think."

Dani wondered if any of the standard antianxiety medications might work, but she was reluctant to prescribe anything.

"I could probably come up with a way to read and amplify his brain waves," Quinn said, "but if the problem is too much distraction, it would just make the white noise louder."

"I'm trying to think of ways to quiet his mind without resorting to medications," Dani said. "I have a friend who works with guided relaxation to relieve Iraq and Afghanistan veterans suffering from PTSD, but that takes months before it becomes effective. We don't have that kind of time. I'm open to any suggestions."

The room fell silent for a moment.

"I have a thought," Tommy said. "What about sensory deprivation?"

"Torture?" Dani said. "Let me correct myself—I'm open to *almost* any suggestion."

"Not torture," Tommy said. "I know sensory deprivation has been used by interrogators, but what I'm talking about is the complete opposite. Sensory deprivation tanks. They were big in spas in the seventies, and one of my vendors at the gym has been trying to talk me into leasing one. He said they've done studies that show people who use them can recover from lactic acid buildup in their muscles after a workout in a few hours instead of days. Sort of like hot tubs. It's the opposite of torture."

"Excuse me, but I'm afraid I don't entirely understand what these sensory deprivation tanks are," Aunt Ruth said.

"They're soundproof, lightproof flotation chambers," Tommy said. "The one my vendor was trying to sell me is shaped like an egg, but the outer shape doesn't matter. Some are boxes. You lift the lid and get in. Inside there's about ten inches of warm water mixed with a hundred pounds of Epsom salts so that you float. You close the lid, and when it seals there's absolutely no light and absolutely no sound. There's a microphone and speakers if you want to communicate, and the lid has a counterweight so you can open it with your little finger, so you don't feel claustrophobic . . ."

Ruth shuddered. "I think I would anyway."

"You float for about an hour," Tommy explained, "but after the first few minutes, with zero sensory stimulation, you start to sort of dream while you're awake. Like daydreaming. Your brain doesn't have to pay attention to anything, so you completely relax. That's why the lactic acid that builds up in muscle tissue during a marathon or an Ironman competition dissipates more quickly in a tank. I know a guy who uses one to help people quit smoking. Spas used to use them in conjunction with massages and whirlpools, but they sort of went out of fashion."

"I like the idea," Dani said. "Reese—are you willing to give it a shot?"

"Sounds lovely," Reese said. "If I should somehow lose my mental faculties, will you promise to visit me in the insane asylum and bring me a fresh blanket every Christmas?"

"That's the spirit," Tommy said. "My spa guy is in White Plains. If I called him now, I could have one here tomorrow morning. I'm one of his best customers."

"Excuse me, everyone," Ruth said. "But look at this."

Dani turned. During the conversation, the television beneath the cabinets had been on with the sound off. Ruth had the remote in her hand and turned the sound up.

A commercial showed a variety of people, all ages and ethnicities, first wearing looks of concern on their faces and then smiling with contentment, while in the background wheat fields rolled in gentle breezes and the sun set red in front of a soundtrack featuring lush strings swelling romantically. In titles on the screen they read, *Provivilan. It Will Change Your Life . . . for the Better. Coming in January from Linz.*

"My beloved employer," Quinn said. "Speaking of which, I should get to bed or I'll be useless in the morning."

"Just so I'm clear," Dani said, "are you saying that the boys who've been selected *all* have identical twins?"

"I think so," Reese said.

"Did Amos Kasden have a twin brother?"

Reese nodded. Dani wondered why Ed Stanley, her contact in the State Department, hadn't told her. But as far as she could tell, Amos's adoptive parents hadn't known either, and they were, as the saying went, as honest as the day was long.

"Well, at least there's one evil twin we don't have to worry about," Tommy said.

"What?" Reese said.

"Amos Kasden. He's dead," Tommy said. "One less evil twin."

"You don't understand," Reese said. "Amos was the good one. His brother Marko was the evil one."

"Marko?" Tommy said.

Reese nodded.

"And where is he?"

"You tell me."

14.

— December 22

8:34 a.m. EST

The sensory deprivation tank arrived first thing the next morning. Tommy suggested they set it up in his "man cave," a room at the far end of the house with a walk-out basement that opened onto the barbecue patio. The man cave or media room contained, among other things, a huge projection screen that served as a movie theater, with seating on reclining leather couches for twenty, complete with cup holders and electronic massage—for the times, Tommy said, when he wanted to have a few old friends or teammates over to watch a football game or play the latest version of *Madden*.

"And that's an Xbox," he said to Dani, pointing to a gaming console on the shelf below the television screen.

It struck Dani as odd that men who played football for a living would play football video games to relax. When she said as much to Tommy, he pointed out that in truck stops there were video games where truckers could get off the road and play driving games or *Grand Theft Auto*. "I'd rather have them crashing video trucks than real ones. Wouldn't you?"

She helped him set up the tank next to his pool table; he ran a garden hose from the laundry room downstairs to fill the tank with twelve inches of water. It would take time, he said, to dissolve the Epsom salts and bring the temperature up to a neutral ninety-nine degrees. While they waited, Reese and Tommy played a game of foosball, which Reese won, causing Tommy to spin his goalie rod in disgust.

"That's the first time I've lost at foosball since middle school," he told Reese. "It's only because you come from a country where everybody plays soccer. Which is a nice sport, if you like tiny guys in dainty little shorts playing on tippy-toe."

"I'm so sorry," Reese said. "Let's go again, American style. We'll play for three seconds, and then we'll stop and think for half an hour about what we're going to do next. Can you tell me where the loo is?"

Tommy pointed down the hall and to the left.

When they were alone, Dani looked up from the book she'd been reading while they waited, an article on twin studies from the *Journal of Psychiatric Medicine*, and smiled at Tommy.

"First loss since middle school?" she said. "You let him win, didn't you?"

"He's very good," Tommy said. "But yeah, I did. I want him feeling confident."

He'd gone up to the guest quarters to get a bathrobe and a set of towels and a bathing suit for Reese to change into when Reese returned from the bathroom. The boy took a seat opposite Dani.

"He threw the foosball game, didn't he?" Reese asked. "He wasn't playing his best."

"You'll have to ask him," Dani said.

"It's okay. I wasn't either," Reese said. "Don't worry—I got this."

She made room for him on the couch, and he sat down. He seemed nervous, uncertain what to do with his hands, trying not to look at the sensory deprivation tank next to the pool table.

"Reese—would you mind telling me a little more about your brother?"

"What would you like to know?"

"I don't know," Dani said. "What's he like?"

The boy looked puzzled at first, then politely suppressed a chuckle.

"Well, that was a pretty stupid question, wasn't it?" Dani said. "He's your identical twin. He's like you."

"Our parents used to dress us differently so that they could tell us apart," Reese said. "That only worked until we figured out we could switch clothes and fool them."

"You must have been terribly sad when you lost them."

Reese shifted in his chair to lean closer to the fire. "It's hard to remember them," he said. "It gets harder all the time."

"I know what you mean. I lost my parents too," Dani said.

"I'm sorry."

"So you and Edmond were already close—did that make you feel even closer? Losing them?"

"I suppose it did," Reese said. "We still had each other. We already spent every minute of every day together. If we went shopping independently of each other, we'd come home with the same things, because we had the same tastes."

Dani thought of the journal article she'd been reading. The bond between identical twins was remarkable, more nature than nurture. It wasn't unusual for twins who'd been separated at birth and raised in dramatically different households or environments to show astonishing similarities. They'd marry women with the same name, give their kids the same names, have the same kind of dog, the same job, even paint their houses the same color.

"It must feel pretty bad now, not to be close to him," she said.

"We never missed a night that we didn't say good night to each other before going to sleep. Until this year, anyway."

"*Dubbo di zubbo,*" Dani said. "I can see how you're alike, but how are you different?"

"He's six minutes older," Reese said with a laugh. "As he never stops reminding me. He says it makes him more mature." He put a sarcastic emphasis on the word *mature*.

"I don't think being six minutes older is going to make much of a difference," Dani said. She'd read studies on birth order, and how older or firstborns tend to be conservatives who fight to maintain the status quo, while youngest or last-borns are the radicals who lead revolutions and favor change. Six minutes didn't seem like much, but maybe it was.

"It does if you think it does," Reese said. "Plus, the estate has been in the family for over three hundred years. Primogeniture. But neither of us cares about that. We truly don't."

The laws of primogeniture meant that as the oldest son, Edmond would inherit their parents' estate. Was that why Ghieri and Wharton had selected Edmond and not Reese? If they were identical, why choose one over the other?

"You don't say good night anymore?"

"I don't even know what happened," Reese said. "I thought we'd always be together. That we'd live together after we graduated. I mean, I know what happened but . . ."

Dani gave him time to collect his thoughts.

"How did you guys stop being so close?"

"It started at the school," Reese said. "We lived together our first year, but the second year they wouldn't let us. They said we had to learn how to develop separately. That we'd never reach our individual potential if we held each other back and spent all our time together."

"That's what they're good at," Dani said. "Turning people against each other." She thought of the ways Carl, once he'd been attacked and controlled by the demon, had tried to drive a wedge between Tommy and her. Making her jealous of Cassandra. Making her and Tommy suspicious of each other. It had almost worked.

"They said we were going to have to become independent someday," Reese said. "Be our own men. And that's true, I suppose."

Dani settled back into the chair. "But you didn't like it, did you?" she asked.

Reese shook his head. "We'd meet each other in secret," he told her. "In the tunnels."

"What tunnels?"

"Between the buildings on campus," Reese said. "Where the hot water pipes and the electrical wires go. But then I started seeing Carolyn."

"Who's Carolyn?"

"A girl," Reese said. "Mrs. Carlyle's daughter."

"The housekeeper's daughter. She's your girlfriend?"

"She used to be," Reese said. "When we went home during the summer, she wanted to be with me and I wanted to be with her. We didn't want Edmond tagging along all the time. I wanted to be with her. Alone. I really loved her."

"Did she love you?"

"She said she did."

"What happened next?" Dani asked, sipping her tea.

"Edmond got angry," Reese replied. "He said Carolyn had cast a spell on me. I told him it would be different when we got back to school. That I could be with her during the summers when we were home, and that we could be with each other during the school year."

"What did he do?"

"He cut his hair and dyed it black so he wouldn't look as much like me," Reese said. "He started . . . I don't know. Doing drugs, I guess."

"The drugs the school provided?"

"And others," Reese said. "He said he wasn't, but I knew he was lying. That was what I was saying when I said I knew students who didn't get caught."

"How did you know he was lying?"

"Because he was saying things I wouldn't say," Reese told her. "I knew he was lying the same way I'd know if I was lying."

"I think you're the empathetic one," Dani said. "That's why you know what he's feeling."

"No," Reese said. "He's exactly like me. Or he was. He just changed."

Reese looked lost. Dani leaned forward, took his hands, and squeezed.

"It's really hard when you don't know what to do," Reese said. "He's all alone. Normally, any decision we'd make, we'd consult with each other. I mean, we didn't have to—we'd just know what the other one was feeling, and then we'd put our minds together."

"Maybe we can change him back," she said. "Does the tank scare you?"

"No," he said. "Well, maybe a little. I can't really tell. Maybe I'm just scared that it's not going to work."

She explained to Reese how it was simply a way to make a person's body relax completely, and how doctors used it to treat people with insomnia or fibromyalgia, or to recover from spinal injuries when they couldn't lie down without feeling pain, or just to relieve stress and encourage creativity.

When Tommy returned with the towels, Reese asked him if he'd ever tried a sensory deprivation tank. Tommy said he had, when the salesman invited him to the showroom for a demonstration.

"What was it like?"

"It was interesting," Tommy said. "At first, all I could think of was all the other things I needed to be doing and how I was wasting my time, and then I started daydreaming, so I got out and told the guy I'd try it another time. He asked me how long I thought I'd been in. I thought maybe ten, fifteen minutes tops. He pointed at the clock on the wall. I'd been in for an hour and a half."

He let Reese walk around the tank, which resembled an eight-foot-long white egg. He showed Reese how to lift the top half of the egg, which was balanced with a counterweight so that it could be raised effortlessly with only one finger. He showed him where the internal loudspeakers were as Dani explained that initially, as Reese floated inside the lightless tank, he'd hear music and her voice, and then they would leave him alone with his thoughts. Dani and Tommy would be right outside and wouldn't let anything happen to him. He would enter a kind of wakeful sleep, and if it worked, and he started to think about his brother, he might be able to get through to him.

The boy was silent for a moment.

"So . . . ," Dani began. "What do you think?"

"It's worth a try," Reese said. "If I can get my brother back, it's worth a try."

"Do you want to start with maybe fifteen minutes and work your way up to a full hour?" Dani suggested.

"I think that might be a good idea," Reese said.

He changed in the bathroom and emerged in the bathing suit Tommy had found for him. Tommy lifted the tank lid, and Reese dipped his toe in, testing the water. He nodded to Tommy that it felt fine, then doffed the robe and got in, sitting in the water first before floating on his back.

"There's so much salt in the water that you can't sink," Tommy said. "If you move, the waves you make will bounce off the walls, and the shape of the tank will keep you centered. Ready to try it?"

"You'll be right outside?"

"Not going anywhere."

They lowered the lid slowly. Reese tested it once to make sure it hadn't somehow locked, then kept it closed.

Fifteen minutes later Tommy opened the lid and the boy sat up.

"How was it?" Tommy asked.

"I wasn't really thinking about my brother," Reese said. "I think I might have if I'd had more time."

"We can try again after lunch," Dani said.

"I did remember something," Reese said. "Something Dr. Villanegre said before he died. While he was struggling with the thing—he said 'beast of Gevaudan.'"

"Beast of Ge-what?" Tommy said. "I don't suppose he happened to have spelled it, did he?"

"He was fighting for his life," Reese said. "But if it's a town in France, I've been there. On holiday. G-e-v-a-u-d-a-n."

"Hang on." As Reese dried himself off and went back to the bathroom to change, Tommy used his GPhone to search the web for the term. "Uh-oh," he said. "This isn't good."

15.

December 22

10:45 a.m. EST

"There's a meeting of department heads," Quinn's assistant said. "You're invited to sit in."

His assistant was a young woman named Allison; impossibly thin, ridiculously intelligent, with close-cropped, boyish light brown hair and black-rimmed glasses that looked more like motorcycle goggles. She was also over six feet tall, with long spindly legs that made her seem to glide from place to place. She wore khaki pants and a blue button-down oxford shirt to work every day, or at least for the past two days that she'd worked for him. Quinn liked her a great deal.

"Invited or expected?" he asked. "I've already met a lot of them. I'm not a department head."

"Both," she said. "You're an important part of the company's future, I hear. Word to the wise—Guryakin himself might be there."

"Ah." Quinn had been hearing about Guryakin ever since he'd joined Dani and Tommy's group. Currently Linz's head of research, formerly involved with some very shady Soviet-era bioweapons programs. Quinn had little doubt that whatever bad was happening at Linz, Guryakin was in the thick of it.

"Well, if Peter Guryakin is going to be there . . ."

"Peter?" Allison pushed her glasses up her nose. "No. Not Peter. Andrei. The sinecure. Doktor Frankenstein."

Guryakin had a son who worked at Linz? It shouldn't have surprised him. The name Andrei Guryakin had turned up on the list of Honors House alums that Reese had sent to Dani. He was one of the more recent graduates, his name accompanied by a school photograph.

"Dr. Frankenstein? Why do you call him that?"

"Because he's ghoulish," Allison said. "And quite possibly a troll who lives under a bridge and eats children. And he never says a word about what he's up to."

"This is the first time I've heard you exaggerate. I've told you a million times not to exaggerate."

Allison's face remained straight for a moment, and then she arched an eyebrow as if to say, *What makes you think I'm exaggerating?*

"Why doesn't he say anything?"

"Because he can't," she said. "I mean, he could—he possesses the gift of speech. Obviously. He runs the lab in Building C."

A Guryakin running Building C, Quinn thought. He shouldn't have been surprised.

"It's his subterranean lair," Allison said. "It's like the bat cave. The only way in or out is if you're blindfolded first. All right—that *is* an exaggeration. But only a little."

"And what is Mr. Guryakin working on in Building C?" Quinn asked, feigning disinterest and clicking through the inbox for his e-mail.

"I couldn't say. And I have the gift of speech too—I can't say because I don't know," Allison said. She leaned against the doorframe. "If I were a betting woman—and a hundred bucks says I am—I'd say that's where they keep the secret formula for Provivilan. And possibly Coca Cola. And Dr Pepper. If you haven't noticed, this company is going all-out for Provivilan. The release version has a half dozen markers that'll make it virtually impossible to reverse-engineer, but they fired a woman who was sneaking the beta version. Illena somebody. Nemkova? Nemkovic? Something like that."

Quinn tried not to react. He'd been circumspect, asking after Illena's whereabouts. But he was worried for her and also, frankly, for himself—showing too much interest in someone who'd gotten fired could cast suspicion on him.

"I saw a television commercial the other day that made Provivilan sound like the instant fix for everything that's wrong with the world," Quinn said.

"Well, don't believe the 'instant' part," Allison said. "I had a friend from Building C who said—you didn't hear this from me—that was the last tweak they made. The initial side effects were apparently so hideous that nobody would stay on the regimen. Now the co-indicators are minimal, but it takes three months for the drug to build up in your system before it has any effect. But I'm not supposed to know that, so *shh*."

"Of course," Quinn said, smiling, wondering what else Allison knew about Building C that she wasn't saying. "We should go out for drinks after work and you can tell me everything else you're not supposed to know."

Allison seemed taken aback, as if embarrassed. He hadn't asked her out on a date, but if there were time—if he had enough time left—the idea of seeing her socially appealed to him.

"The meeting is in thirty minutes, upstairs," Allison said. "Let me know if you need anything."

He saw a young man approaching down an aisle between a row of workstations and recognized the younger Guryakin from his school photograph. He was a handsome young man with long black hair parted in the middle and brushed back over his ears, and he wore a bow tie as he had in his St. Adrian's ID photo, apparently unaware of how affected it made him. He walked with a swagger, accompanied by a young and attractive secretary.

Quinn tapped on the app that turned his phone into a digital voice recorder and then slipped the phone into his shirt pocket with the microphone facing out.

"Dr. McKellen," the younger man said, offering his hand. "Andrei Guryakin. I wanted to say hello before the meeting. How are you finding everything?"

"First-rate," Quinn said. "Allison has been getting me up to speed, but it will be good to meet the others personally. To hear what people are working on."

"I read your work on Purkinje cells," Guryakin said, moving away. "Very interesting. And promising."

"I'm familiar with your father's work," Quinn said. The younger man stopped and turned. "Or I should say, his reputation."

Quinn wondered if he'd overplayed his hand, but he needed to make something happen. Time was running out, in more ways than one.

"Are you?" Guryakin said. "Which reputation would that be?"

"As a research chemist," Quinn said. "Does he have another?"

"He was once ranked as a chess player," Andrei Guryakin said. "He beat Boris Spassky, but that was after Bobby Fischer destroyed Spassky's will to win. I was seventeen before I could beat my father regularly."

"We should have a game," Quinn said.

"We could do that," Guryakin said. "Though I like to play for stakes. It's the only thing that makes it interesting anymore. How much are you willing to risk?"

What Quinn wanted to say was that you can't bluff someone who has nothing to lose.

"Loser buys the winner dinner," he said to sound friendly, though they both understood that the game had already begun, and it was anything but friendly.

"Good," Guryakin said, a cocky smirk on his face. "Until then. See you at the meeting."

16.

December 22

"*Gevaudan* was easy," Tommy's Aunt Ruth said, fifteen minutes later. "There's more, but first things first."

She'd volunteered to pitch in as a research librarian and help Tommy gather information. They were in the kitchen, enjoying lunch. Tommy and Reese were having truffle oil grilled cheese sandwiches, one of Tommy's "bachelor specials." Ruth and Dani had salads. A tray of blueberry muffins Tommy had spent the morning whipping up were cooling on the stovetop.

"The Beast of Gevaudan," Ruth said, clicking on a link that brought up a map of France on Tommy's flat-screen computer monitor. "Named after the region in the Margeride Mountains in the south of France."

"Or as I like to say, south France." Tommy said. "Why do people always add the *of*?"

His aunt gave him the same look she used to give him when he was a child making too much noise in the library. Reese laughed.

"Never mind," Tommy said.

"As I was saying." Ruth cleared her throat. "The stories tell of an unidentified animal, said to resemble a man or a wolf or a panther or a

114

bear or some combination, thought to have killed as many as 113 people in the 1760s. Ninety-eight of those victims were partially or entirely eaten. There were numerous accounts by eyewitnesses. The first documented victim was a fourteen-year-old girl named Jeanne Boulet who was attacked in 1764 near Langogne. King Louis XV sent a pair of royal huntsmen to hunt the beast with bloodhounds. Did you hear that, Otto? You may be useful once again. Apparently these things have a foul odor."

Tommy recalled the night when Otto had seemed to react to a scent. He'd assumed it was the wolves in the nearby sanctuary; perhaps not.

Ruth continued her story. "The first two huntsmen didn't get the job done, so the king sent his top man, a fellow named François Antoine. He tracked and killed a massive gray wolf that seemed to be stalking the inhabitants of a nearby abbey. They thought that did the trick, but a few dozen more deaths followed. Then a local man named Jean Chastel killed a second wolf—but only after reading the Bible and praying for assistance. The second beast, according to the best information available, was stalking him but was unable to attack him while he was in the middle of prayer. When they cut open that animal's stomach, they supposedly found human remains."

"According to whom?" Dani asked.

"The most reliable account is an 1814 history by a French author who collected newspaper stories and interviewed a few of the eyewitnesses, who would probably have been quite old at the time they were interviewed," Ruth said. "There've been any number of fictitious uses of the story, mostly in werewolf movies. The History Channel did a piece called *The Real Wolfman*. Do you want me to see if I can find it on YouTube?"

"If you can," Tommy said. "It might be interesting. Maybe later."

"The best scientific explanation," Ruth said, turning to Dani, "is that the beast in question was a mesonychid. Sort of a carnivorous hooved bear. They know mesonychids were the dominant predator in North America and Asia in the Pliocene and Eocene eras."

She clicked on a screen of multiple images, ancient etchings and engravings depicting an animal that resembled a wolf or a bear, but with a much longer neck.

"Which was when?" Tommy asked.

"Sixty-five to thirty-three million years ago," Reese said, reaching for another half a sandwich from the plate in the middle of the table. "Science is my best subject."

"They think these things might have survived?" Dani asked.

"They thought the coelacanth was extinct until a fisherman caught one in the deep waters off the east coast of South Africa in 1938," Ruth said. "The scientific community calls them *Lazarus taxon*. A species mistakenly thought extinct. The Margeride Mountains are riddled with caves, and even today they're still discovering new species that survive in caves. Though nothing this big."

"The things in the woods absorb light," Tommy said. "A carnivore living in caves might do that as a method of camouflage."

"How far apart are the Margeride Mountains and the cave of Lascaux?" Dani asked.

"You're thinking the same thing I thought," Ruth said. "Not far at all." She turned to Reese, who didn't seem to get the reference. "The oldest, most elaborate cave paintings in the world were found in Lascaux, France. Deep, deep underground, painted a little over seventeen thousand years ago. Two thousand images, with over nine hundred depictions of animals, and only six hundred of them have been identified. There were horses and bison and animals that were easily recognized. And then there's this one."

She clicked on an enlargement of one of the pictographs, a sepia-colored line drawing of the same animal they'd seen in the etchings and engravings.

"So these things are at least seventeen thousand years old?" Tommy said.

"They appear to be," Ruth said. "But I kept thinking about paintings. So I kept looking and I came across an image you might recognize."

A painting appeared on the screen, one Tommy and Dani had made themselves intimately acquainted with.

"*The Garden of Earthly Delights*," Tommy said.

"Hieronymus Bosch," Ruth said.

"Also known as *The Millennium*," Dani said.

"That's the painting Dr. Villanegre brought to the school," Reese said. "The one that zillionaire German alumnus owns."

For a moment Ruth let them rediscover the mysterious Dutch painter Bosch, whose acclaimed masterpiece depicted a bizarre landscape of deformed animals, monstrous hybrids and chimeras, lascivious couples engaged in sin, and in the frightening right-hand panel, a depiction of hell so unique and vivid that one suspected the painter had some kind of insider's information.

"Now watch," Ruth said. She clicked to enlarge a section from the "hellscape," then zoomed in to enlarge a single image, that of a painter's palette; spread-eagled on the palette was a knight of the Crusades, a large red cross on his breastplate, encircled and devoured by a pack of what looked like wolves. She enlarged the image again to show that the wolves were not wolves but had long, almost prehensile-looking tails. Ruth called up an engraving of the Beast of Gevaudan for comparison. They were identical.

"So the things that attacked Reese on the way to the airport," Dani said, after they'd all taken a moment to study the images, "are the same things in the painting. The same things that are in the woods at night. The werewolf/bigfoot/mesonychid that killed 113 people in France."

"B-O-Gs," Tommy said. "Beasts of Gevaudan. Bogies. Bogiemen. Whatever they are, they're real."

"What do you make of the fact that when I tried to examine the body of one of those things, I found oil paint instead of blood?" Reese asked.

"Well," Tommy thought, trying not to reach the conclusion he found impossible to avoid, "I suppose it might mean that those things in the painting are coming to life. Hell on earth. And not metaphorically."

17.

December 22

2:23 p.m. EST

"I want to go back in the tank," Reese said.

"Why don't you get changed and we'll meet you down there?" Tommy said.

"Right. I'll just get changed and meet you down there," Reese said.

At last Tommy and Dani were alone.

"He's a little nervous," Dani said.

"He'll be okay. I have something I want to show you," Tommy said. "But first—would you like a blueberry muffin?"

"Not particularly."

Tommy frowned. She'd told him that homemade blueberry muffins were one of her favorite comfort foods. He was sure of that. Or was he remembering wrong? Whether or not she liked blueberry muffins wasn't that big a deal, really, but the diamond engagement ring he'd hidden inside one of them for her to find . . . that was important.

He took that special muffin from the tray, set it on a plate in front of her, and smiled. "Still warm from the oven."

She shook her head. "No thanks. Just ate. What did you want to show me?"

"Are you sure you don't want a muffin?"

"I'm sure I don't want a muffin."

"Well . . . it's right here when you want it," he said, deciding to stop pushing and let her be surprised.

"We should go downstairs," she said. "I don't want to leave him alone down there."

"He's fine," Tommy said. "He doesn't need us hovering over his shoulder twenty-four hours a day."

He was thinking of all the parents who would shout out from the sidelines during youth soccer games in the winter league he ran at the sports center. They meant well, he understood, but for the kids it was like trying to listen to thirty coaches instead of one, and more to the point, they weren't given the time and space to learn from their mistakes.

"I'm not talking about 'hovering,'" Dani said. "I just think we need to be hands-on. I don't think you understand how important this is to him. His brother is the last member of his family. He needs to know we're going to be there for him."

"We will be," Tommy said. "He knows the door is open for him."

"What was it you wanted to show me?" Dani asked.

"Take a look at this." Glad to change the subject, he opened a file on his computer. "I was overflying St. Adrian's this morning at about three thousand feet. Though if anybody asks, it was four hundred feet because that's the maximum altitude for private drones according to the FAA."

He ran the video. The screen showed a pair of limousines passing through the school gates and up the drive, the long black vehicles moving slowly through the leafless winter trees, stopping short of the portico in front of the administration building where the path forward was blocked by a parked vehicle. Two men in black coats got out of the first limo. One man in a fur-trimmed overcoat got out of the second. The three men met behind the first limousine and greeted each other.

Tommy froze the video and enlarged the image. The definition was incredible, the faces of two men clearly visible. The third man had his back to the UAV mounted camera.

"The school is closed," Dani said. "Why are limousines arriving?"

"I don't know," Tommy said. "But I followed the cars. That's Honors House where they're unloading their suitcases. These guys are staying for a while. I think we should find out who they are."

"How would we do that?"

"We can't," Tommy said. "But we know someone who probably can."

"Oh." Dani nodded. Tommy meant Ed Stanley. He was a fishing buddy of Dani's grandfather Howard, who'd retired to Montana to be closer to the trout streams. Ed Stanley was also a retired CIA officer who'd worked in Moscow. They'd reached out to him earlier when they'd been looking for information on the Russian orphanage where Amos Kasden, born Alex Kalenninov, had been placed after killing his abusive father. Ed had used his CIA sources to help.

Tommy had another question he wanted to ask Stanley—did he know Amos Kasden had an identical twin? And if he did, had it just slipped his mind when he failed to mention it?

"Ed Stanley is not going to help us snoop around St. Adrian's," Dani said, "and go on thinking we're just a couple of local law enforcement officers. He's going to want to know the full story."

"Maybe it's time we told him," Tommy said. "We may not have the resources we need to do everything ourselves."

"The Curatoriat—"

"Needs to be informed," he agreed. "It's time to bring them in. But I doubt anybody has the facial recognition programs the CIA has. Or, frankly, the firepower, if it comes to that. If something is really happening in two days, we need to go down every alley we can. Even if it means widening our circle . . ."

"And risk being discredited and ignored as religious crackpots who see satanic conspiracies where there aren't any," Dani said. "Which is probably what the devil is counting on. Which would leave us dead in the water."

She pointed at the screen. "What was that?"

"That's just the image you get after the parachute deploys," Tommy said. "You hit auto-return and the drone flies back to the launch coordinates, cuts the engines, and drops back into the yard."

"No, before that. Back it up," Dani said.

"Back it up?"

"The video," she said. "Rewind it. Or whatever you call it."

"To the beginning?"

"Here—let me," she said, reaching to take the mouse from Tommy. She placed the cursor on top of the right-facing arrow that was slowly crawling across the transport bar and backed it up a quarter of an inch. Tommy saw the ground below as the drone approached his house, and then a blinking red parachute icon in the corner. Dani clicked on the pause button to freeze the image.

"Right there!" she said.

"Where?"

"In your pond," she said. "What's that?"

"May I?" Tommy said, taking the mouse back from her. He clicked it once to center the image, then clicked on a magnifying glass icon in the lower right to move in closer, and closer, and closer.

"Well," he said. "Speaking of dead in the water . . . I could be wrong, but it appears to be a body."

18.

December 22

Detective Phillip Casey arrived in his own car, alone, as Dani had requested. She met him in the courtyard, with Tommy by her side. Casey was wearing old-fashioned black rubber galoshes, unzipped. His tweed overcoat was frayed at the collar, and his brown leather gloves were coming unstitched at the fingertips.

"Should we go inside? Talk about whatever it is you want to talk about?" he said, gesturing toward the kitchen.

"Not right away," Dani said. "We have something to show you first. And after you see what we have to show you, we'd like to have a conversation before you call anybody."

They took him out to the pond and showed him the body. It was floating facedown or, rather, was frozen in the ice in a facedown position. It appeared to be a male, but even that was difficult to determine. The ice was no more than half an inch thick and still slushy near the shore, at a time of year when the cycles of hot and cold, and cold nights and warmer sunny afternoons, prevented the pond from freezing completely.

At the edge of the pond, Casey looked from the pond to the house and back to gauge the distance, taking his gloves off and shoving them into his coat pockets before he spoke.

"When did you find this?"

"Right before I called you," Dani said.

Casey looked at the house again. "You both did?"

Dani nodded.

"How's that?" Casey asked. "I only see one set of footprints in the snow, and they're too big to be yours."

"I was looking on the security cameras."

"You saw it happen?" Casey asked.

"No," Dani corrected him. "I was watching the video feed and noticed the body."

"Right before you called me?"

Dani nodded.

"So you have no idea how it got there?" Casey asked. "Not how and not when?"

"Those are my footprints. I was out here last night, late," Tommy said. "I didn't see it then, though, to be honest, I don't remember looking."

"What time were you out here?"

"One a.m. or so, I think. We can look on the security footage if you want. I've got a seventy-two-hour buffer before it starts recording over itself."

"We should do that," Casey said. "First things first." As he dug his cell phone out of his coat pocket, Dani touched him on the arm.

"Can we hold off on that?" she said. Casey stared at her a moment before nodding and replacing the phone.

"Okay." The detective turned to Tommy. "Any idea how deep the water is where he is?"

"Twelve feet, maybe," Tommy said. "Wait here—I might have something we can use to fish him out."

While he was gone, Casey asked Dani if she'd finished her Christmas shopping.

"Christmas shopping? I haven't had a free moment to even think about it."

"You're supposed to be recovering from PTSD," Casey said. "Finding dead bodies in the backyard is an interesting definition of 'lying low.'"

Dani realized how fragile she must seem to the veteran detective, but before she could say anything else Tommy returned, holding a fifteen-foot boat hook.

"Why do you have a boat hook?" Dani asked.

"Because I have a boat," Tommy said.

"Where?"

"In the barn."

"Why do you have a boat in the barn?"

"They get damaged if you leave them in the ocean over the winter," Tommy told her. "That's why you see 'em shrink-wrapped and up on racks in marinas. I happened to have room in my barn."

"What do you do with it?"

"Fish," he said. "In the ocean. I keep it in Bowden's Harbor in Stamford."

"Whaddaya got?" Casey asked.

"Boston Whaler," he said. "A 370 Outrage with trip 300-horse Mercs."

"Those are nice boats," Casey said. "My brother-in-law has an Egg Harbor out of Point Judith. We take it to B.I. every year for the Fourth of July."

"Sweet," Tommy said. "That rip tide—"

"Excuse me," Dani said, interrupting, "but I'm really cold here—can we please get this guy out of the water to see what we're looking at?"

It took some doing because first Tommy had to break the ice to clear a channel between the body and the shore. The pole barely reached the man's foot, but he managed to hook the body by the pant cuff and pull. It took ten minutes to drag it close enough for Tommy to grab the body by the ankle. Casey took the boat hook then and used it to grab the dead man's other leg. The two of them then pulled the body up onto the shore.

"Should we roll him over?" Dani asked.

"Hang on a second," Casey said, examining the body, which was nearly frozen stiff, the skin blue. He took out his cell phone and took three photographs of the body. Tommy did the same with his GPhone. "Okay. Let's see who he is."

They rolled the body over. The man's face was blue and distorted in death, but Dani nevertheless recognized him. She must've started, or made a noise, because Casey turned right around to look at her, a questioning expression on his face.

"You know this guy?" the detective asked.

"Yes. His name is John Adams Wharton," she said. "He's the head-master as St. Adrian's Academy."

"Betcha didn't see *that one* coming," Tommy said.

19.

December 22

"You didn't hear any shots?" Casey asked.

"We didn't," Dani said. "Any idea how long he's been in there?"

"Nope," Casey said. "He's Popsicled pretty good, though."

He took a pen from his pocket and used it to move shreds of clothing on the body.

"Three shots," he said, lifting the body to see what was on the other side. "Three going in and three going out, I'm guessing. Looks like fairly close range. You said there's a security camera?" The detective tapped the screen on his cell phone. "I'll get some people here. If forensics tells us . . ."

Dani stayed him again with a gentle touch on the arm. "We need to talk," she said. "And then you can call whoever you need to call. It's . . ."

"Complicated?"

"That would be one way to describe it."

"Let me find you that security footage," Tommy said. "He's not going anywhere."

"I suppose not," Casey said, looking puzzled. "I certainly hope not, anyway."

126

In the house, while the detective and Dani made coffee with the Keurig, Tommy found his aunt in the laundry room and asked her where Reese was. Ruth said the boy was watching television in the media room and waiting for Tommy and Dani so he could enter the isolation tank.

"Can you go tell him we'll be awhile?" Tommy asked, keeping his voice low. "Something came up. Keep him down there for the time being."

He rejoined the others in the kitchen and, after grabbing some coffee himself, sat down at the computer to find the surveillance files for the previous night. When he'd located the file for the camera pointing in the direction of the pond, he clicked play. He watched a moment and then fast-forwarded at four times the normal speed, a digital clock in the corner of the screen counting forward rapidly. The woods were full of deep black shadows, but without more light he couldn't tell if they were simply shadows or something more. Quinn had posited a theory about the Gevaudan beasts, that they were attracted to darkness the way moths were attracted to light. If they lived in darkness and felt safe in darkness, it made sense.

There were no noteworthy events until ten minutes after three in the morning, when two figures entered the camera's field of vision. The scene went by too quickly for Tommy to stop it in time, so he backed the play arrow up, moving it a quarter inch to the left on the transport bar. He hit play and ran the video at normal speed.

"This have sound?" Casey asked.

"Not outside. The interior cameras do," Tommy said.

"How much can you cover?"

"Pretty much 360 degrees. House. Garage. Greenhouse. Barn. They're activated by motion detectors."

"Why such an elaborate system?" Casey said. "If I can ask that."

"Came with the house," Tommy said.

"Here we go," Casey said as the silhouettes of two men emerged from the darkness, moving from left to right. It was too dark to see clearly, but it appeared that the man on the left had his hand on the lower back of the man on the right. There was a dim aura of light cast on the yard and the pond by the floodlight pointing at Tommy's house.

As the man on the right gained separation from the man on the left, they saw that the man on the left held a gun.

The man on the right turned his face toward Tommy's house, and though it was dim, it was clear that it was Wharton. He held his hands up, pleading, his body language emphatic as he looked toward the house and appeared to be shouting. The man on the left fired three shots from about ten feet away. Wharton spun where he stood on the edge of the pond and fell into it, face forward.

The killer approached the pond, looking down for a moment at the body, then tossed the gun into the pond and turned to leave. As he turned, there was light on his face.

"Freeze that," Casey said. "Back it up a little. Right there. Okay. Can you zoom in?"

"I can't change the lens, but I can enlarge the pixels," Tommy said, clicking on the icon of a magnifying glass. "These cameras are only 720 DPI because they'd use up too much memory if they were higher res."

He enlarged the image a second time, and then a third. And then he stopped. Even at 720 DPI, it was clear who the killer was.

"That's a familiar face," Casey said quietly.

Tommy could only nod.

The face was his own.

20.

December 22

"Bartender," Allison said. "My friend and I would like another drink. I would like mine with a wedge of salt. I mean lime. And salt."

"I'm fine," Quinn told the bartender, holding his glass up to show he was drinking Diet Coke.

"Are you sure?" the bartender asked Allison, eyeing her suspiciously.

"Yes!" Allison said. "But this is my last one."

"You said that last time, miss."

"It's all right," Quinn reassured the bartender. "I'm driving."

Allison laughed and leaned back until she nearly fell off the barstool.

When Quinn invited her to dinner after work and asked her what her favorite food was, she'd said Mexican. The name of the restaurant was Holy Molé's, and the drink she was drinking was a house special called a Tequila Mockingbird, which was a margarita with a shot of ouzo in it, a potent concoction. He hadn't intended to ply her with liquor, but she was doing a pretty good job of it herself. She'd only had two, but she was surprisingly intoxicated, trying, he surmised, to calm her nerves.

Quinn caught the bartender's eye and held out his hand, pinching his finger and thumb together to tell the man to make Allison's next drink as weak as possible. The bartender nodded.

"I appreciate your joining me," Quinn said. "You can get one impression of the place you work during work hours, but after hours you get the real story."

"To Linz Pharmahoosickle!" she slurred, raising her glass in a toast. "Clear genius! Total horse doo-doo, but clear genius." They clinked glasses, and she sipped. "You know, I almost never drink like this. I'm a good girl! Except when I'm not. A person has a right to let her hair down every once in a while. Am I not right, or am I not right? Or not. Or am I not quite right in the head?"

Quinn could tell she was nervous. She'd confided on the way to the restaurant that she hadn't been on a date in four years.

She laughed again, her eyes closed, swaying from side to side like a buoy. "You know what the problem is with people like you and me, Quincy old boy?"

"Quinn," he said. "Just Quinn."

"Right!" she said, then leaned toward him, close enough to kiss him. Quinn leaned back. "So, Quincy—you know what the deal is? What the problem is? With people like you'n me? Do you know?"

"What's the problem?"

"We have to work for people who are stupider than us," she said, sitting back and taking one last bite of her enchilada, waving her fork at Quinn, a six-inch strand of melted cheese dangling from it. "Because we don't have a choice. It's just how the ol' cookie crumbles. Sobeit! Sobeit. You know what makes chili peppers hot? Caspezium! Capsilicon. Casper-sasperilla."

The word she was looking for, Quinn knew, was capsicum, but she gave up trying to find it. When the bartender brought the drink she had ordered, he gave Quinn a surreptitious wink to indicate it had very little alcohol in it.

"So what's the deal with this Andrei Guryakin?" Quinn asked. "He's an odd duck."

"Did you see how he got up in your grill?" Allison said. "That's what the kids say. 'Up in your grill.' I heard that on MTV."

"I noticed," Quinn said. "He goes out of the way to meet me and then he gets all . . ."

"Up in your grill."

"Right," Quinn said. "Up in my grill."

"That means teeth. With braces on them. Makes a person look like the front of a car. I had braces until I was twenty-two."

"Sounds like Andrei has some sort of problem with his father," Quinn said. "As soon as I mentioned him, he got pretty defensive."

"I love my father," Allison cooed. "He's a great guy. I wish he was everybody's father. Wait. That didn't come out right."

"I know what you mean," Quinn said.

"You're really nice," Allison said, smiling at him. "I'm really glad we're going to be working together."

"I am too," Quinn said, aware that he was losing control of the conversation. "Are you going to tell me what Guryakin's doing in Building C? Or am I going to have to guess?"

She looked at him and put a finger to her lips. "Shh!" she said. "I'll never tell. You have to guess."

"Allison—"

"All right all right all right—you forced it out of me. It's top secret, you know. Because it's going to make the company a bazillion dollars. I'm not supposed to know, but I had a friend . . . She got fired. Yes she did. Are you trying to get me fired so you can take my job? Oh yeah. You're my boss. Why would you want my job? I should be wanting your job."

She pushed her plate away from her. Quinn signaled to the bartender to bring two cups of coffee.

"That was delicious!" She drained the last of her Tequila Mockingbird and slammed her glass down on the bar.

"So what is it?" he asked again. "Why do they have a BioSafety Level 4 lab in the basement of Building C?"

She crooked a finger, bidding him to come closer so that she could whisper in his ear. "It's alive," she said.

"What is?"

"Provivilan."

"The drug is alive?" He leaned in closer, to make sure he was hearing her correctly.

She shook her head. "Not the drug. The virus. The virus makes the drug. They genetically engineered the virus to make the drug. But if the virus escapes . . ." She wove her fingers together, then exploded them. "*Poof!* It's very dangerous."

"You're talking about Provivilan," he said, sitting up straight and jerking his head back, as if physical distance could lessen his surprise or his dismay.

"Yep."

"I thought it took three months for the drug to build up before it becomes effective."

"That it does, yes sir," Allison said. "But if the virus gets out, whoa Nellie. Hey—I do know how to say whoa. Whadaya know?"

The bartender brought them their coffee.

"If the virus gets out, it reproduces?" Quinn said.

"You got it," Allison said. "You know how?"

"How?"

"It's in the water," she said. "All those little teeny molecules that are already in the water. From all the selected sernatonin . . . the selective serotonin reuptake thingamajigs. It reassembles them. Do you know what happens then? Do you know?"

"What happens then?"

"I don't know," she said. "But it's not good because there's no stopping it. It just keeps replicating until there isn't any water left. I really don't feel so well."

"Let me drive you home," Quinn said, signaling for the check.

"It's Dr. Frankenstein's fault, you know," she said. "He got my friend fired. I don't even know where she went. I tried to call her. I couldn't find her anywhere."

Illena, Quinn thought. Allison was talking about Illena Nemkova. He had a sudden, sick feeling he knew exactly what had happened to her.

"She was a really good person. Did you know her? No. You couldn't have. She was gone before you started. You would have liked her."

"Yes. I'm sure I would have," Quinn said. "Come on. Time to get you home."

He rose to help Allison with her coat. The first arm went through her coat sleeve without any trouble, but the second arm proved more difficult. Suddenly the room felt like it had tilted to the right, his vision swimming as his head suddenly pounded with pain. He closed his eyes and held his head down until the pain subsided.

"Are you sure you can drive?" Allison said. "Do you want me to drive? Because I don't think I can drive. I think we should call a cat. I mean a cab. Why would we call a cat? Here, kitty kitty kitty."

"I'm fine," Quinn said, forcing a smile. "I haven't been drinking. It's just a low blood pressure thing, when I stand up too fast."

"Okay," Allison said, zipping her parka.

"Why was your friend fired?" Quinn asked.

"She was fired for talking to a lady who was writing a book," Allison said, hooking her arm in Quinn's for support.

"Do you know who was writing the book?"

"I do, because I took a message one day when she called for my friend," Allison said. "She said, 'Please tell her to call Abbie Gardener.' Did you know Abbie Gardener?"

"By reputation," Quinn said, opening the door for Allison and then easing her gently into the car.

"She was very, very old," Allison said. "I hope to be very, very old someday."

Quinn held out the same hope for her, and for the rest of mankind, but if what she was saying about the virus was true, the odds in favor were pretty low.

21.

December 22

"This is going to sound crazy," Dani began. She was still struggling for the words she needed to make him believe her.

"Uh-huh," Casey said. "Go on."

"Are you a religious man?" she asked.

"Am I religious?" Casey repeated. "If I can ask, what does that have to do with anything?"

"It has everything to do with what's been happening here," Tommy said. "With what Amos Kasden did. And with the body in the pond. And with—"

"You shooting him?"

"That too. Though I didn't shoot him."

"Really?" Casey looked dubious.

Dani gave Tommy a reassuring squeeze on the shoulder.

"I'm listening. Call me crazy, but based on the video we just saw, I'm pretty sure you did. Unless you have an evil twin."

"Funny you should say that," Tommy said.

"Please, Detective," Dani interrupted. "Just tell me. I'm not trying to pry, but are you religious?"

135

Casey had accompanied them into the house reluctantly. He was a cop who did things by the book, and this wasn't by the book.

"My family is Irish Catholic," he said. "But lately . . . I've been pulling away from the Church. I guess because of my job. Because of my nature too. To ask questions. But yeah . . . if you put a gun to my head, I'd say I was a man of faith."

"Good," Dani said. "Then just listen, before you pass judgment. Because as I said, this is going to sound crazy at first. I hope by the time I'm done it's going to start to make sense."

"I'll try to keep an open mind," Casey said. "Things are more likely to go in it that way."

She began with the murder of Julie Leonard, and how Abbie Gardener had paid Tommy a strange visit the night Julie was killed. Dani explained that she'd been having prophetic dreams that woke her every night at 2:13, and how, inexplicably, she and Tommy had had the exact same dream one night, an apocalyptic vision in which millions of people, all wearing white, were fleeing a large city as it was inundated by a flood while Dani raced upstream in a boat—though in Dani's dream, she was in the boat, while in Tommy's dream, he was high on a hill, watching her in the boat.

She told Casey how Tommy had figured out the meaning of the symbol they'd found drawn in blood on Julie's stomach, representing the horns on a Viking's helmet, and how a group of pagans, driven out of England over a thousand years ago, had hired Viking ships to bring them to the New World, where they established a settlement in the Finger Lakes region of upstate New York. Once there, they corrupted the Native American people they encountered and controlled them with fear and sorcery until they were defeated by a pair of early Christian missionaries.

She laid out the evidence that had led them to conclude that St. Adrian's Academy was, in fact, a sham institution founded to engage in satanic practices and perpetuate evil throughout the world, and that there was a larger plot they were involved in right now, a plot that would culminate on Christmas Eve, and that making it seem like Tommy had murdered Wharton was part of that plot. When she was done, Casey was silent a minute.

"I know this is all hard to believe," Dani said.

"I'm still listening," Casey said. "And I'm not too arrogant to assume something has to be wrong, just because I don't understand it."

"Good," Dani said, looking at Tommy, who nodded to her to continue. "I know you might have reasons to doubt what we're saying, but we've had proof. And you haven't. We *have* proof. We just can't show it to you."

"Though now would be a very good time for Charlie or Ben to drop by, just for a second," Tommy said, more loudly than he needed to.

"Ben Whitehorse?" Casey said. "The Native American guy who was friends with the British art historian who died in the accident? I met him when we had a look around the Gardener place. I liked him."

"That's the guy," Dani said. "Except that he's not really a guy at all. That was only the form he chose to take while he was here. Because he needed to give us a message."

"He dressed up like an Indian to give you a message?"

"They have to look like something when they're here, because if they look like themselves, they're overwhelmingly beautiful," Dani said.

"They?" Casey asked.

"Angels. Ben is one of them."

Casey took a moment before responding, folding his arms across his chest and leaning his head back. "You want me to believe Ben was an angel," he said. "Walking among us."

Tommy and Dani both nodded.

"You realize what you're asking me to do, right?" Casey said. "I got a body in the pond, I got surveillance video showing me, pretty clearly, who did it, and now the guy in the surveillance video is telling me the guy in the pond was working for Satan, and that angels are telling him what to do. As an investigator with the district attorney's office, my job is to look into crimes, find evidence of who did it, and if I'm lucky, I find a motive too. Right now, it's all there, right in front of me. It depends on whether I believe my eyes . . . or I believe you."

Casey had been skeptical of Dani at first, and of her role as a consulting psychiatrist for the DA's office. He was a veteran detective who'd transferred to Westchester from Providence, Rhode Island, under duress after rubbing his superiors the wrong way one too many times. In his opinion, it didn't matter if a bad guy was criminally insane or mentally competent to stand trial or participate in his own defense—if they did the crime, they had to be punished for it and put away.

Dani had proven herself and earned his trust, but now, she knew, she was asking him to give her even more.

"No. What it depends on is if you believe in them," Dani said. She reached over and rubbed Tommy's neck, waiting for the detective to answer. Tommy reached up and gave her hand a squeeze, a gesture of solidarity.

"Do you, Detective?" Tommy asked him. "Do you believe in angels?"

Casey thought for a long time before answering.

"Lucky for you, I do," he said, leaning forward to rest his elbows on the table and staring into his coffee cup before looking up. "This is something I never told nobody, except my wife. Anybody else woulda thought I was nuts. A couple years ago . . . Wow—ten years ago. More than a couple. We got a call. All hands on deck. Warehouse fire on Federal Hill. Italian neighborhood in Providence. Huge fire. The fire's in one of the old jewelry supply warehouses that got a second life as artist studios, but you're not supposed to live there. It's not zoned residential. So it's crazy. We got engine companies from Cranston and Warwick and Pawtucket, they're all pouring water on the building, it's night, lights are flashing, we got command and control on the radio giving instructions and maybe a couple thousand people on the street watching. But the fire's out of control. Nothing they can do, really. And there's a woman the firefighters pulled out of the building with smoke inhalation, but she comes around and she starts screaming, 'My babies! My babies! My twins are in there!' But the assessment is, the building is going to come down any minute. Nobody knows what to do. The firefighters want to go in but they can't. They got orders not to."

He looked from Dani to Tommy and back to make sure they were still with him.

"So before anybody can stop him, this guy, this big African American guy, puts his shirt over his head and runs into the building. Everybody figures he's a goner, but nobody is allowed to go after him. Five minutes later he comes running out with something under each arm, wrapped in blankets. He hands them to the EMTs. And they're the woman's kids. Everybody starts fussing over the kids, but I go up to the guy to see if he's all right. And he looks me in the eye, and I knew. I just knew. He was different. He wasn't . . ." Casey shook his head. "He was an angel. He was watching over those babies that night."

Dani could see tears welling up in the corners of his eyes.

"I kept hearing that woman's voice. 'My babies. My babies. My twins are in there.' I can still hear her. It's something I'll never forget. And I can remember, clear as a bell, how helpless I felt. How I broke down, because there was nothing I could do. All you can do is stand there, thinking about what's happening. I'm not saying I was praying, but I was saying, in my head, *Please, somebody—please, God, somebody do something.*"

Casey reached into his back pocket and grabbed a clean white handkerchief, which he used to dry his eyes and blow his nose. Dani realized there was something about that she really liked. Men who still carried linen handkerchiefs. She made a mental note to buy some for Tommy.

"If you believe in angels, then you understand that demons are fallen angels," Tommy said. "They can take any form they want. That wasn't me you saw in the video. That was a demon."

"We can prove that," Dani said.

Tommy turned to her. "We can?"

She nodded. "Tommy figured out that demons show up as ice-cold forms on an infrared camera if you recalibrate it to read thermal images below the default bottom range. Humans show up as red. Demons are blue. They're the opposite of life. The absence of warmth. A spiritual vacuum. And you have infrared cameras covering the pond, don't you?" she asked Tommy.

"I certainly hope I do," he replied.

Tommy found the infrared file for the night before and fast-forwarded to ten minutes after three. Dani suggested he run both the video and infrared files side by side to prove they'd filmed the same event at the same time. As she'd predicted, the infrared footage showed Wharton as a reddish orange color and Tommy, or the demon in the form of Tommy, as deep blue.

"Remember the two figures we saw at the school, one red, one blue?" she asked Tommy.

"Ghieri and Wharton," Tommy said. "You think Ghieri killed Wharton?"

"It could have been some other demon," Dani said. "But yeah. I think he did. He must have."

"Why would Ghieri want to kill Wharton?"

"To set you up," Casey said. "To get you out of the way. And it probably would have worked. If I hadn't gotten the call to that fire ten years ago."

"Whatever is happening in two days, they obviously don't need Wharton anymore," Dani said. "Do you think he knew Ghieri is a demon?"

"He knows now," Tommy said.

"How would he not know?" Casey asked.

"There's human evil, and there's supernatural evil," Dani told him. "The demons mislead and deceive. They use the people who believe in them. Humans are disposable."

"All the time?"

"No way to know," Dani said. "I'm not sure it matters, necessarily. And they're gathering strength. Tommy?"

Tommy showed the detective the images he'd gotten flying the drone over the school, and the evidence he'd uncovered of demonic activity there. He showed him the security footage of the beasts in the woods, waiting in the shadows.

"Is that everything?" Casey said.

"Probably not," Dani said, sitting down. "Isn't that enough?"

"It's enough," Casey said. "You know that angel—back at the warehouse fire? After he rescued those kids . . . he said something to me."

"What?" Dani asked.

"He said, 'You gotta save the babies. Next time you'll know what to do. You'll know.' He said it twice. And now, you're asking me to help save the babies. This is the next time. I know. He was right. I can't even say how I know, but I know. This is the next time."

"You're going to help us?" Dani said.

Casey nodded. "How could I not?"

"I can't quite believe I'm saying this, but what do we do with the body?" Tommy asked.

"Unfortunately, I know the answer to that question. Trunk of my car," Casey said, rising from his chair and gesturing for Tommy to follow him. "I know a mob guy in Providence who can take care of it. He owes me a favor."

"This should even things up," Tommy said.

"Not even close," Casey said, suddenly eying the baked goods on the counter. "Those muffins look good. You mind?"

"Help yourself," Dani said, offering Casey the muffin Tommy had prepared for her.

"Not that one," Tommy said, grabbing the muffin and hiding it behind his back. "That one's bad."

"That's the one you wanted me to eat," Dani said.

"Yeah, but it's cold now." He took another muffin from the tin and handed it to Casey. "This one's even better. It has more blueberries."

Casey took it and examined it closely. "I can't believe I'm going to be driving around Providence, Rhode Island, with a dead body in the trunk of my car," he exclaimed. "Though it's probably as good a place as any. And better than some."

22.

December 22

Tommy helped Casey load the body into the trunk of his car. The detective returned to the house to make his good-byes and grab another muffin for the road. Tommy checked the water temperature in the isolation tank.

"You ready?" Tommy said as Reese walked around the tank. "You didn't feel at all claustrophobic the last time?"

Reese shook his head. "I didn't know a person could float in twelve inches of water."

"It's about the same salinity as the Great Salt Lake," Tommy said.

"What if I fall asleep and roll over?" Reese asked.

"You won't," Tommy said. "People fall asleep in bathtubs all the time, and they don't drown unless they're drunk or on drugs. Which you're not, right?"

Reese smiled. "After all this, I don't even want to take aspirin."

"There you go," Tommy said.

"Let's not overreact," Dani said. "Prescription drugs save millions of lives every year. Let's not throw the baby out with the bathwater."

"Speaking of which," Reese said, stepping into the tank.

143

"We'll be right here. And remember, there's a microphone inside the tank. If we hear you snoring, we'll open the lid," Dani said. "There are speakers in there too. If you call out, we'll hear you and turn them on, and then you can hear us. Okay? Again, if you don't like it, we can stop."

Reese smiled feebly and took off the bathrobe Tommy had loaned him.

"Done it once," Reese said, taking a deep breath. "It's like looking in the mirror for as long as you can. After fifteen seconds, one begins to feel a bit awkward and ridiculous, but it's just you, being alone with you."

"The part that bothers me is how if I raise my right hand, the guy in the mirror raises his left hand," Tommy said. "That means no matter how hard you try, you never actually see yourself the way other people see you. Apropos of nothing. Anyway, try to relax."

"We can do this," the boy said. He still looked apprehensive.

He got in, and Dani lowered the lid. She tested the microphone to make sure they could communicate with each other. Then she switched on the music—the fourth *Brandenburg Concerto*, which Reese had chosen to listen to before the transition to complete silence in the tank. If he wanted to think about his brother, he could, Dani said again, but he didn't have to. She told him this time he'd have thirty minutes of silence, and then she'd start the music again, softly at first, then louder to bring him back up to full awareness.

"Let's make it an hour," he said.

"Are you sure?"

"Quite."

"All right then. Your microphone is on, so we can hear you, but I'm turning mine off so you won't hear anything from us unless you ask us first."

She turned off the microphone on the control panel, then turned toward Tommy.

"You think it'll work this time?" he asked.

"Worth a try. With all the visual and digital electronic clutter in the world today, it can't hurt to unplug a little."

"It's sort of like a time machine," Tommy said, staring at the giant egg amid the flat-screen televisions and gaming consoles and classic arcade video games in his man cave. "It doesn't just block out noise and light. It blocks out the twenty-first century. People are afraid of silence. Everybody has to be busy and entertained all the time. I'm as guilty of that as the next guy. You ever go winter camping?"

"In the cold? Outdoors?"

"That's generally the way it's done," he said, amused by her timidity. "It's only cold if you're not dressed properly. I'll go sometimes by myself, when there's a full moon and snow on the ground and all the leaves are off the trees, and I'll camp in the middle of a swamp—"

"A swamp?"

"It's frozen," Tommy said. "There're no mosquitoes. You've never seen light like that. You could read a book in it. I'll sit there, where nobody has ever been before, miles and miles from anybody, and there's not a sound. Nothing."

"And you're not scared?"

"What would I be scared of?"

"I don't know. What if you had a heart attack? Or twisted your ankle and froze to death?"

"If I'm gonna have a heart attack, I can't think of a better place," he said.

"You're serious."

"As a heart attack."

"If you could live in any century in history, which one would you want to live in?" Dani asked him.

"Whichever one you were in," Tommy said, taking her in his arms and kissing her.

The kiss was long, soulful, and fully reciprocated. Tommy broke off after a moment and pointed at the egg, whispering, "We're not exactly alone."

"No," Dani whispered back, "but we will be. One day. Right?"

"Promise," Tommy said. It would have been the perfect time to produce the engagement ring, but the ring was, as they spoke, in his pants pocket inside a smashed blueberry muffin—not quite the presentation he had in mind.

Edmond Stratton-Mallins gazed out the window at the rain in a flat on Lowndes Street, in the Belgravia section of London. It was approaching midnight. The flat was one of a dozen private apartments he had access to in cities throughout the world, now that he was one of the Selected. He'd sent his housekeeper, Mrs. Carlyle, and his butler, Mr. Simons, a note saying only that all was well. He didn't tell them where he was. And he hadn't spoken to Reese.

Yet staring out the window at the rain, he wished it would turn to snow so he might have a white Christmas. Sentimentality was an emotion boys selected into an elite class of leaders could not indulge, but he was alone and no one would know. Edmond found himself thinking of his brother. This would be the first Christmas they hadn't spent together. The best memories they had of their parents were the ones of Christmas Eve, attending the candlelight services at St. Paul's Cathedral on Ludgate Hill, sitting in the Chapel of All Souls and staring up at the dome and the quire where the clergy sat. He remembered singing carols and waiting for the massive bells above them to chime that the service was over and it was time to hurry home to bed, because in the morning there would be presents. He could imagine how angry Dr. Ghieri would be if he knew Edmond was feeling nostalgic about Christmas—another sign of weakness. But he'd loved waiting at the top of the stairs with his brother until his mother or father gave the all-clear sign, and they'd run down to find what Santa had left them under the tree. Edmond hadn't cared that his presents were always identical to his brother's. Two of everything—better for battling each other. When they were older, and their parents were gone,

Mrs. Carlyle and Mr. Simons had tried to keep up those traditions, though they adapted with the times—the best part of Christmas Day, to young Reese and young Edmond, had been opening up the latest video games and playing each other all day long, to their hearts' content.

They had always been the best of friends, up until the beginning of this year, when Dr. Ghieri, the St. Adrian's psychologist, had them both take a special test. Ghieri had called Edmond in afterward and told him, in strictest confidence, that he'd outscored his brother by a significant margin. He was not to tell Reese.

There had to be some kind of mistake, Edmond had said. Perhaps his brother had been ill? He and Reese had always gotten the same scores when they took the same tests. Sometimes Reese even scored higher than Edmond, because he didn't find studying as tedious as Edmond did.

There was no mistake, Ghieri said. The test had been especially designed for twins. There was a difference between Edmond and Reese.

"You are much smarter than your brother, but you refuse to excel because you don't want him to feel bad. That's why you score the same. You are only holding yourself back, and it must stop." Ghieri saw something in Edmond, he went on to say—the potential for greatness. The doctor was willing to take a chance on him, but only if Edmond was willing to step out of his comfort zone, out of his brother's shadow, and leave Reese behind.

Edmond had hesitated. And then Dr. Ghieri had shown him a letter from a court-appointed psychologist. The letter stated that Reese had been the cause of their parents' car accident. They had been driving sleep-deprived after Reese had kept them up for three nights in a row because of night terrors. "A common enough disorder that afflicts the weak," Ghieri said.

Edmond felt a multitude of emotions then—surprise, anger, but most of all, pity. He pitied his brother, until Dr. Ghieri explained that pity was (like sentimentality) an emotion no true leader could allow himself to feel. History has no pity, he said—the men who make it require none.

Later, in the special honors history class, Dr. Wharton had told them

147

stories of St. Adrian's graduates who'd been persecuted, imprisoned, even tortured and killed for their unwavering commitment to the standards Ghieri had talked about—to pitiless, unsentimental excellence. They were martyrs, men excluded or reduced to footnotes in the standard texts, but whose sacrifices the true student of history—the history that Dr. Wharton taught—would never forget.

Not long after, the boys had all been given their assignments—their parts in the mission that Ghieri and Wharton had planned. And not long after that, Edmond had been called in to Dr. Ghieri's office once more. To his surprise and concern, Dr. Wharton was there as well. Dr. Ghieri said they had reason to suspect that Reese was being disloyal to the school. There was a menace in Ghieri's voice that Edmond had never heard before. He told the two men he was unaware of any disloyalty on his brother's part. He swore that Reese loved St. Adrian's. Ghieri and Wharton told Edmond that he needed to choose between his school and his brother. Between his mission and Reese.

And so he'd cut his brother off—ignored all of Reese's attempts to communicate, even the ones his brother had made through the special bond they shared. The bond that had made Edmond think that sometimes he could read his brother's thoughts. It hadn't been easy. There were still times when he felt like he was with Reese. Felt like—

He had a sudden image of his brother, then, lying half naked inside a giant egg. It was an almost comical vision, but he couldn't shake it. Why would his brother be inside an egg?

Edmond, he heard Reese say inside his mind. *You're being a complete idiot. Ghieri is the one who's lying to you, not me. He killed Goat Boy. You know I'm telling you the truth. Stop thinking you know everything. Being stubborn and obtuse is not the same thing as being strong. Talk to me!*

Edmond almost responded—almost let down the walls he'd put up inside his mind. Then he remembered that day in Dr. Ghieri's office, with Wharton looking on so sternly.

"The mission is too important to let one boy compromise it," Ghieri had said. "Not you—not your brother. We cannot allow that to happen. We *will* not allow that to happen."

In that instant, Edmond had realized that Ghieri would kill to make sure the mission succeeded. He would kill Reese if Edmond stayed in contact with him. It had been true then—it was even truer now, now that the time was so close.

For Reese's own safety, Edmond realized, he could not respond to his brother's call.

But this was only temporary, he told himself. After his mission was over, and they'd graduated from St. Adrian's and were somewhere in college together, Edmond would explain to Reese why it had been necessary to distance himself, and his brother would understand because they had always understood each other. They'd be together again. But for now . . .

He turned away from the window, away from the vision of his brother.

In Tommy's basement, the lid to the sensory deprivation tank rose suddenly as Reese sprang from the tank, water dripping on the floor. He looked distraught and seemed like he might cry. Dani wrapped the robe around him and handed him a towel, and then she hugged him and told him everything would be all right.

She sat him down on the couch, and Tommy sat on the other side of him, and after a minute the boy seemed calmer.

"What happened?" Dani asked.

"It worked," Reese said. "I sensed him. I sensed . . . he's scared. He won't admit it to himself, but he doesn't want to do it. But he thinks they'll kill him if he doesn't follow through. He thinks they'll kill me. He doesn't understand that—"

"Shh shh . . . ," Dani said. "Did you tell him you're safe?"

"I tried to," Reese said. "It's not—I know what he's feeling. He's trying to be brave, but he's terrified."

"I think that's enough for now," Dani said. "We can try again tomorrow. Why don't you go get dressed?"

"What do you think?" Tommy said while Reese was changing.

"I think this was a very good idea you had," Dani said. "It's going to work. They want to be in touch with each other. They need to be, even if Edmond is resisting. We can make that work for us."

"You're sure it won't work against us?" Tommy said. "If we can see into their camp, how do we know they won't be able to see into ours?"

"We don't," Dani said. "But what we do know is, neither of them wants to hurt the other. If we can get the door open and keep it open, Edmond is going to realize Reese is safe. He won't do anything to jeopardize that."

"Good point," Tommy said. "But if Edmond is in England, he's probably not aware of what's going on around here. We still need help."

While Reese was in the tank, Tommy had shown Dani more images he'd gotten from the drone's cameras. Two more limousines and three Lincoln town cars with airport transportation markings had dropped off passengers at Honors House at St. Adrian's. Tommy had been able to get good photographs of three of the men and partials of the other two. None of them looked familiar.

"We need to know who these guys are," Dani said. "You're right. We need Ed Stanley."

She had Tommy forward her the images; then she attached them to an e-mail and sent them on to Stanley, requesting a meeting as soon as possible.

"I wish we had more information," she said as they all sat down to a late dinner. "We can't count on Ed Stanley being as ready to believe as Casey was."

"But remember how we've been prepared for this moment? Maybe Stanley has too. I wish there were a way to get into the school without going through the front gates," Tommy said. "That place is like a fortress."

"It's not *like* a fortress—it *is* a fortress," Ruth said from the doorway, where she and Reese stood. She had her hands on his shoulders. "It was built as an army fort."

"I know a way in," Reese said.

"Reese—this isn't your job," Dani said.

"But I know a way in," Reese said. "A secret way in. The same way I snuck out. Through the tunnels."

"Tunnels?"

"Beneath the school."

"I heard a historian give a lecture once on the Revolutionary War in New York," Ruth said. "He said forts often had secret escape tunnels so that if they were surrounded, they could get a messenger out to send for relief. Or they could send their generals out, to prevent them from being captured."

"You think you could draw us a map, Reese?" Tommy asked.

The boy shook his head. "No. There are too many turns and dead ends. I could show you, though."

23.

December 22

Dani could not convince Reese that it was not a good idea for him to go back to St. Adrian's. She admired his courage and knew he would do anything to save his brother. They agreed to sleep on it and plan something for the following night.

She was exhausted. Even Tommy, ordinarily a bundle of positive energy, seemed tired. Ruth joined them in the kitchen after Reese had gone to bed.

"He's a good kid," Ruth said. "I don't want to sound a note of pessimism, but if something were to happen to either of you, and I pray that nothing does—you haven't chosen a successor to be the next Guardian. Somebody's going to have to coordinate the activities of the Curatoriat. I think Reese might be a good candidate. In a way, his training has already begun."

Dani had already considered the idea. The *Vademecum Absconditus,* left for them by the previous Guardian, Abbie Gardener, contained the names and contact information for the other members of the Curatoriat, including telephone and even Skype numbers for video conferencing. Abbie hadn't been technologically up to speed, but it was time, Dani knew,

152

for her and Tommy to tell everyone to raise their shields and man their battle stations.

"I think you could be right," Tommy agreed. "Dani?"

"We should probably make a decision soon," she said. "But maybe not right now. I'm exhausted."

As tired as they were, they looked like well-rested teenagers compared to Quinn, who stumbled into the kitchen around ten o'clock. As he filled them in as to what he'd learned from his assistant over drinks, singular on his part, plural on hers, Dani found herself studying the lines on his face and the bags under his eyes. The stress—or the tumor—was getting to him.

"So clearly," Quinn said, "I need to find a way to get to the BSL4 lab in the basement of Building C. But I'm sure the security is formidable."

"You could pretend you're delivering a pizza," Tommy said. He looked around the room. "What? I don't hear anybody else offering suggestions."

"I'm thinking the answer is in this," Quinn said, holding up his corporate thumb drive and turning it over in his hand before setting it on the table. "This is what opens doors. We just have to figure out a way to tell it to open more doors."

"Can you do that?" Tommy asked.

Quinn pinched the bridge of his nose and rubbed his eyes with his thumb and first finger. "I can't," he said wearily. "There must be somebody who can."

"What about your friend Illena?" Tommy asked.

"I can't find her," Quinn said. "Allison thought Linz might have transferred her somewhere else, but frankly . . . I'm afraid. I think they may have done more than that."

"Are you okay?" Dani asked Quinn. "You look a little—"

"Just a headache," he said brusquely. "Nothing twenty-four straight hours of sleep won't fix. How did it go with Reese?"

"We'll tell you in the morning," Dani said. "Get some rest."

"I can't be the only one who's tired. We ought to sleep in shifts," Quinn said. "Though we're a bit short-handed, with George and Julian gone."

"Casey is in," Dani said. She briefly explained what had happened that afternoon—Wharton's death and the detective's "conversion," as it were.

"It's good to have Casey on board," Quinn said. "Is it good news or bad news to have Wharton out of the way? I can't tell."

"The demons don't age, but the humans do," Tommy said. "Maybe they're replacing him?"

"With whom?"

"Don't know."

"We should still keep an eye out for—what are they called?"

"Beasts of Gevaudan," Tommy said. "But the alarm will tell us if anything gets inside the perimeter. Physical or otherwise." He'd double-checked his settings. The night Wharton showed up in his pond, he'd armed the cameras but not the motion sensors. It was a mistake he could not afford to make again.

"So we're good for now. You can go." Dani pointed definitively in the direction of Quinn's room. "Sleep."

Quinn seemed about to protest once more, then nodded. "Yes, Dr. Harris," he said.

Dani watched him slouch down the hall, then turned to Tommy. "He doesn't look well," she said.

"We've all looked better—except you, of course."

Dani smiled. "How are you feeling?"

"Why?" Tommy said.

"I don't know," she said. "You've been acting odd."

"It's not acting," he said. Did she know he had an engagement ring in his pocket? He wouldn't be surprised.

"Okay," she said, laughing. "How do you do it? It's the most amazing thing about you—in the middle of all this, you can find a way to make me laugh. How can you make jokes?"

"It's like what Abraham Lincoln said," Tommy told her. "Someone in his cabinet asked him how he could keep making jokes in the middle of something as terrible as the Civil War, and he said, 'If I didn't laugh, I'd die.' Or words to that effect."

She rose, leaned over, and kissed him good night.

"We're meeting Ed Stanley tomorrow morning at the diner," she told him. Stanley had sent her a text earlier, stating that the photographs they'd sent had "raised issues of concern." "He said he has names for us, but he wants to talk in person. Have you heard from Cassandra?"

"No," Tommy said. "But she's not going to risk checking in with us if there's nothing to say."

"I suppose. You're okay tonight? You sure?"

Tommy grabbed the pump-action shotgun from where it leaned against the wall and sat in the reclining chair next to the computer screen displaying his security feeds, the weapon across the arms of the chair.

"Otto and I got it covered," he said, and just then the cat leapt into his lap. Tommy smiled. "Correction," he added. "Otto and Arlo and I have it covered."

The cat sniffed at the gun.

"Never give a cat a gun," Dani said. "That's one of the first things cat owners learn. We think we know what they're thinking, but we really don't."

24.

December 22

Tommy decided to have a walk around the house before settling in for the night. He synced the security feed to his GPhone, found his barn coat, clipped Otto to his leash, and closed the back door behind him to make sure Arlo couldn't get out.

"You handle things in here," he told the cat.

He circled the house, leash in one hand, shotgun in the other, night vision goggles strapped to his forehead, ready to flip them down if he needed them.

The night was moonless, but the stars were out. The weather had turned warmer, in the forties now, and the snow on the ground melted in the places that received sunlight. It would have been easier to see if everything had stayed white. In a landscape of black-and-white patches, you could hide a herd of Holsteins.

He checked the garages, the greenhouse, the barn, and the chicken coop, shining his flashlight into each and using his infrared scanner. Otto was on his leash and not in his tracking harness, but he worked the ground all the same, zigzagging in front of Tommy, nose and muzzle to the dirt, tail up and wagging like a small airplane propeller.

With the dog still on the leash, Tommy scaled the outcropping of rock beyond the pond. He stood as still as possible and listened. He thought he heard the sound of the wolves howling from their rescue sanctuary two miles away, but it might have been a distant police siren. He flipped the night vision goggles down to scan the woods and saw nothing but green trees and black shadows. Otto raised his nose to the air, picking up the scent of something. When Tommy raised his flashlight and pointed it into the woods to supplement the natural starlight, holding the beam high beside his head, he saw a dozen sets of eyes, reflecting as red dots. The Beasts. Still there. Still watching him, waiting. For what?

He turned the flashlight around and shone it on his own face, to stare them down and let them know he was still there too. He used to give opposing quarterbacks the same stare. One opposing quarterback had said, "It's like looking up and seeing a train about to hit you."

He turned off the light, but by the way the eyes had blinked back at him, he guessed that light made the creatures uncomfortable. If they had indeed evolved or lived in caves, and only came out at night, it made sense. It also meant they could see everything he was doing in the dark.

He walked the perimeter of his property, inspecting his deer fence, even though the eight-foot-high wire mesh was probably not strong enough to stop the bogies if they decided to mount an attack. He made a mental note to himself to look into some way to wire the fence with electricity. It might not stop the things entirely, but it might slow them down. At the corner where the south wall met the east wall and the road, he found a pair of raccoons cowering. He held Otto, who strained against the leash, and told him to sit. The dog obeyed. Ordinarily the raccoons would have scaled the fence and made their escape.

"You don't want to go out there either?" Tommy told them. "Fine. You can stay here until the morning. But leave my garbage cans alone."

In the kitchen he'd just refilled Otto's water dish and settled in for the night in front of the monitors when he saw a window open on his computer, then a blinking telephone icon, accompanied by a beep and a box asking him if he was willing to accept a video call from Dr. Julian Villanegre.

He hesitated. He'd made arrangements to have the old man's body flown back to England. It could have been someone calling from Villanegre's home computer to confirm or to ask for further details. Yet the call had come on a Skype account they'd set up specifically for calls between the Guardian and the Curators. It was possible, but unlikely, that Julian had inadvertently given someone back home the private number. For purposes of security, only the Guardians knew the identities of the Curators; the Curators knew the Guardians only by function, not by name or by photographs, nor did they know the identities of the other Curators. There was a way to pixelate his own image to conceal his identity, but he didn't know how to do it yet. There was also a filter to scramble his voice, but he didn't know how to work that either.

He went to the closet in the mudroom where he kept his hat collection and donned a black fleece ski mask he sometimes wore when he rode his motorcycle in cold weather. To hide his eyes, he found a pair of mirrored sunglasses.

He was about to answer the call when he heard Dani's voice from the doorway.

"What in the world are you doing?" she asked. "I heard a beeping that woke me up. Why are you wearing a ski mask and sunglasses?"

"Someone's calling the Guardian Skype number from Villanegre's home," he said. "I don't want them to know who I am."

"You look like a bank robber," she said. "Why don't you just put a piece of paper over your webcam?"

He considered what she said.

"Next time," he said. "Good idea. Move over by the sink so the camera won't show you."

He clicked on the icon and answered the call.

On his screen he saw an attractive young woman of indeterminate age, somewhere five years either side of twenty. She had bangs that fell in front of her eyes and long reddish-brown hair that fell over her shoulders, framing a round face with large brown eyes, a button nose, and Cupid's bow lips. Her natural beauty was accessorized by piercings in her left nostril, right eyebrow, and each ear. She was wearing a heavy white turtleneck fisherman's sweater.

"Are you the footballer?" she asked. Her accent was Scottish.

"May I ask who you were trying to call?" Tommy asked.

"You look like a bank robber," she said. "I'm trying to reach Tommy Gunderson, the football player. Who's the woman standing by the sink?"

"There's no one standing by the sink," Tommy said.

"Yes, there is. I can see her in the reflection of your sunglasses."

"There's no one here named Tommy Gunderson."

"Oh, for Pete's sake," she said. "Really? Dr. Villanegre gave me this number and said I could reach him through you. You're Tommy Gunderson, and I'd say the woman by the sink is Dr. Harris, yes? You can take your mask off. I know what you look like. All I had to do was Google your name."

Tommy took his mask off, and Dani joined him in front of the webcam.

"That's better," she said. "My name is Helen Trumble. I'm the person Dr. Villanegre has been training to replace him."

"Pleased to meet you," Dani said.

"We sent a message," Tommy said. "I spoke with his housekeeper."

"Yes, I know," she said. "I spoke with her too. I live here. The funeral arrangements have all been taken care of. I'm sorry to ring you up so late at night, but I'm afraid I have something rather urgent. He was quite keen to find a particular book . . ."

"The *Vademecum*," Dani said. "We have it."

"You have it?"

"We do," Tommy said.

"So . . . which one of you is the Guardian, then?"

"We both are," Dani said. "The Guardian before us chose a successor, but he was murdered. The book fell to us. We were planning to call you and the others in the morning."

"He told you about the painting and the prophecy, didn't he?"

"He did."

"Well then, I suppose it's you I should be telling," she said. "I was to tell Dr. Villanegre just as soon as I'd finished my work, but I'm afraid I finished too late. Do either of you speak Merovingian Frankish, by any chance? . . . No? Old West Low Franconian?"

"We're new at this," Tommy said.

"He didn't mention me, then?"

"He did not," Dani said.

"I'll make this as short as possible because I know it's late there," Helen said, "but the reason he needed to find the *Vademecum Absconditus* was because we found another text, sort of a commentary on the *Vademecum*, in the archives at St. Augustine's Abbey in Canterbury."

"Where St. Adrian was the Abbott," Dani said.

The girl on the screen nodded. "If you know about him, then you know about Charles the Black, I presume?"

"Adrian's warrior?"

"Aye," the girl said, "and originally a Frank. And the text we found was written in Merovingian Frankish, which led Dr. Villanegre to wonder if it belonged to Charles the Black, or was written by him. I've been working with a scholar friend here who's studied Merovingian Frankish, and we just finished our translation. You're aware that the *Vademecum* had been blessed and protects the Guardians who hold it, right?"

"We are," Dani said.

"That's why I had to call you," Helen Trumble said. "We were up all night. According to the text we found, that protection was supposed to last for a thousand years. We were stuck for a while because we didn't know if our copy of the text was the original one by Charles the Black, which would have been using the Julian calendar, or if it was a later copy done after the Gregorian reform. We also didn't know if he was factoring in the 250 leap days since then, but we think we know when the *Vademecum* was first blessed. I thought you'd want to know—if we're right, your divine protection is going to expire in two days. Christmas Eve."

"You're sure?" Dani asked.

The girl on the screen nodded slowly.

"I don't suppose you know exactly what time of day, do you?"

"No idea," Helen said. "The *Vademecum* was first written here in Great Britain. Now I gather it's in the eastern US time zone. I don't know what that means."

"Does the name 'Beast of Gevaudan' mean anything to you?"

"You mean those cave weasels from the painting?" she said. "That's what Dr. V was calling them."

"He knew what they were?"

"He was afraid those monstrosities from the painting were going to come to life," Trumble said. "Don't tell me they have?"

"Okay," Dani said. "We won't tell you. Good work. Stay close to home. We're going to need you soon. And, Helen . . ."

"Yes?"

"Arm yourself and raise the drawbridge. This is going to get real. Soon."

25.

December 23

2:21 a.m. EST / 8:21 a.m. CET

Cass was dreaming. She was a girl, twelve years old. She was swimming in the ocean. Her mother was on a boat calling her. "Come back, Cassie—you've swum too far out!" Then her mother was lifting her from the water, kissing her as she dried her off with a large striped towel, telling her how brave she was, how fearless. And then, as she gazed toward the shore, she saw a boy with a stick, herding sheep.

The phone woke her. For a second she didn't know where she was. Then she heard the whisperings of conversations from the street below—in French—and remembered. She was in Paris. In a townhouse apartment on rue Guynemer in the 6th *arrondissement*, in Udo Bauer's apartment, which had a view of the Jardin du Luxembourg. The dream felt more like a memory of something real than a fantasy. She'd often gone for swims in the open ocean, which always worried her mother because her mother was a poor swimmer. Cassandra was a strong swimmer. She swam, she'd been told more than once, like a fish.

The phone rang again.

It was Laurent, Bauer's driver. He said he was in a car downstairs, ready when she was to take her to the airport for the next leg of her trip—a helicopter ride to the yacht, and to a waiting Bauer. Cassandra thanked the young man and said she'd be down in five minutes.

It had been a whirlwind twenty-four hours.

She'd risen early yesterday at Tommy's house the morning after the party at the consulate and gone to the Peter Keeler Inn for coffee. She'd just finished reading the *New York Times* society pages, giggling out loud at the singularly unflattering picture of Jürgen Metzler the photo editor had chosen to run from the party (drink in hand, mouth open, eyes closed), when a silver Rolls Royce pulled up in front of the inn. Bauer's, she discovered. As was the white Gulf V private jet waiting for her at Westchester County Airport in White Plains. Bauer wasn't there, but there was a handwritten note taped to a computer screen on board that said, *Play me.*

Be careful what you wish for, she thought. When she played the video, the man appeared in all his smarmy, self-satisfied glory.

"Welcome aboard," he said on the video. "I'm sorry I can't be there to greet you in person, but I hope you'll have a pleasant flight nonetheless. Laurent will see to your needs—if there's anything you want, please tell him."

Bauer went on to tell her he'd taken the liberty of having his assistant buy her all the clothes she would need for the next two days, at which time he would have to return to the States for a holiday party at his old alma mater and would be delighted to take Cassandra with him. Cassandra could spend the time during the flight choosing her wardrobe from the items his assistant had selected, he said, or if she preferred, Laurent had a credit card she could use if she wanted to go shopping in Paris.

"And if you are hungry during the flight, the chef will make you whatever you like. Except German food—I have given him strict instructions not to do so. I look forward to seeing you again, aboard the *Freiheit.* Where you can show me your sailing skills," Bauer leered.

The video ended. Bauer's assistant, Laurent, a thin young man in his early twenties, appeared. Cassandra was to regard him, he said, as her personal assistant for the entire trip (she was, it turned out, the only passenger). He showed her to the state room toward the front of the plane, where she saw dozens of dresses and high-end fashion items by Max Mara, Carmen Marc Valvo, Hugo Boss, and Michael Kors, and swimwear by La Perla, more than she would need for a two-week vacation, let alone two days. She chose what she needed and returned to her seat.

Laurent also acted as her chauffeur when they arrived in Paris, driving her to the apartment, where she found another *Play me* note taped to a video screen. Cassandra hadn't bothered; instead, she'd tuned the television to one of her old movies, a romantic comedy in which her character was unlucky in love. She still had a hard time watching herself. She'd done the film during the period when, on the advice of her acting coach, she'd been singularly focused on the Stanislavsky method, a technique in which the actor, as much as possible, becomes the role, on camera and off. The technique had carried over to real life for a while.

Never again, she told herself. She'd been like one of those poor people in the nightclubs whom the hypnotist tells, "When I snap my fingers, you'll wake up"—except the hypnotist had never snapped his fingers. Cassandra was doing her own snapping now. Writing her own scripts, guided by prayer and the Bible—in every sense, she was on the right page.

Right now, she thought as she checked herself in the mirror, she looked something like a young Audrey Hepburn, bright-eyed and eager. The princess from *Roman Holiday*. Except her props were a little different.

She reached into her purse and checked to make sure the Beretta .32-caliber Tomcat was still there, and still loaded. Dani had insisted she bring the pistol. She would never have gotten the weapon on board a commercial flight, but she'd known that to men like Bauer, making a date fly commercial was inconceivable.

Cassandra checked her makeup one last time, then boarded the elevator to take her to the car.

"Ms. Morton," Laurent said, opening the door for her with one hand and taking her suitcase with the other. She noticed how easily he lifted the heavy suitcase and loaded it into the trunk. He was surprisingly strong for a man with such a slender frame.

26.

December 23

7:33 a.m. EST

Quinn had taken the second watch of the night, relieving Tommy at four a.m. By the time Tommy made it down to the kitchen, Quinn had figured out a way to turn the keystroke tracking program embedded in his thumb drive to their purposes.

"Any device that links to something else leaves a return address," he explained. "We use that to reverse the program. The spy becomes the spied upon, something like a two-way mirror."

"You figured that out on your own?" Tommy said, impressed.

"Not even close," Quinn said. "I have a friend—do you know the group Anonymous?"

"Only by name," Tommy said. "You mean the hackers who've been pranking government and corporate computer systems?"

"My friend—if you can call someone you've never met whose name you don't know a 'friend'—told me last night how to do it and helped me set it up. But I trust him. Or her. I haven't run it yet, but it should give me access to the passwords I need to get into the basement of Building C."

"Just be careful," Tommy said. "We've got a meeting with Ed Stanley this morning to see if we can get some help, but we need you too."

The Miss Salem Diner shone like a merry-go-round on a day that broke gray and stayed dreary, with a steady rain that washed away whatever snow remained in the shaded places and at the edges of parking lots. The trees on all four sides of the town commons had been decorated with small white Christmas lights, as were the gazebo in the center of the green and the huge Norway pine next to it. The latter served as the official town Christmas tree; the lights for all were regulated by photo-optical sensors. They were supposed to turn off at dawn and back on at dusk, but the day was so overcast that they'd remained lit well past sunrise.

Inside the diner, Tommy and Dani sat opposite each other in a booth, studying the menu, even though the menu hadn't changed since they were kids and the diner was their after-school hangout. Eddie had turned the diner over to his daughter Gail, but he still showed up every day to man the grill, and he still told her what to do, and she still grumbled. Dani's friend Clair Dorsett was seated alone in a booth by the door, reading something on her Kindle. Tommy nodded to Frank DeGidio; the cop was stopping at the diner to fill his thermos and pick up an egg sandwich before starting his day.

Right on time, a black Escalade with tinted windows pulled up to the curb, and an older man in a camel coat got out.

Ed Stanley hung his coat on a rack by the door and threw his white silk scarf over it. He was in his midseventies and cut a dapper figure in gray wool pants, a tweed sport coat, an oxford shirt buttoned at the neck, and a Western-style bolo tie.

He sat down next to them, took a quick glance at the menu, and then ordered coffee and an English muffin with honey. Tommy ordered coffee as well, Dani tea.

"Got your Christmas shopping done yet?" Stanley asked them. "My wife wants one of the new GPhones, but I keep telling her we don't have cell coverage where we live, so what would be the point?"

"You can get them with satellite uplinks," Tommy said. "That way they work anywhere."

"Really?" he said. "Good to know."

As a forensic psychiatrist, part of Dani's job with the DA's office was to evaluate potential witnesses and to assist with interrogations by giving her informed opinion as to whether or not a witness or a criminal was lying. Both her intuition and her training told her Stanley was doing just that. If his wife truly wanted a GPhone, he would have researched them. His naiveté was feigned. Ed Stanley was anything but naive.

"We've been pretty busy," Dani said. "We were hoping you could help us with the photographs we sent you—any luck?"

"A little," he said, pausing as the waitress brought him his food and set down two coffees, a tea, and a small pitcher of milk. "What a lousy day, huh? It's supposed to stay warm all week."

When the waitress was gone, he moved the saucer aside and set his cup down on the table. "Can I ask where you got those pictures?"

"We—" Tommy began.

"—got them from an anonymous source," Dani said.

"An anonymous source," Stanley said.

Repeating what someone said, Dani knew, was another sign of deception, a way to buy time while the liar tried to think of what to say next.

"Anonymous to us," Dani said. "We don't know who sent them."

Tommy's expression said he was playing along without following her. They'd discussed the idea of bringing Ed Stanley into the circle and agreed that it might be necessary.

"Can I ask why you want to know who these people are?" Stanley countered. "Is this part of an ongoing crime investigation? Something to do with Amos Kasden?"

He was fishing, Dani realized. Trying to find out how much they knew, so that he'd know how much to tell them.

"I can't really say," she told him.

"Well," he said. "I'm afraid—"

"Mr. Stanley—"

"Ed, please," he said. "Call me Ed."

"Ed," Dani said. "We're getting off on the wrong foot here, and I don't know why. You're dancing around my questions and I'm dancing around yours, so maybe we should just not try. I appreciate the help you've already given us. There's obviously a reason why you came here in person instead of using the phone or e-mail, so either we're honest with each other and you tell me the truth and I'll tell you the truth, or we get on with our days."

Ed Stanley sipped his coffee and smiled. "Your grandfather told me he could never fool you," the older man said. "He'd try to tell you about the Easter Bunny or Santa Claus, and you'd just look at him like he was saying the silliest thing you'd ever heard. Even when you were little."

"I'm a big girl now," she said. "I'm not trying to be confrontational. There's just too much at stake to waste time. For instance, did you know that Amos Kasden, born Alex Kalenninov, has a brother?"

"He has three," Stanley said. "I told you that."

"You said he had three older brothers," Dani said. "You didn't mention that one was his identical twin. Marko."

"I didn't know that," Stanley said.

She believed him, but she held her ground, insisting on a more complete reckoning.

The older man paused to think, then reached into his coat pocket and laid a photograph on the table.

"Is that your drone?" he asked.

Tommy picked up the photograph and examined it. It was a picture of his Orison 6, taken from above in midflight.

"How'd you get this picture?" he asked.

"You're not the only one who has drones," he said. "Ours fly higher than yours."

"You've been watching us?"

Ed didn't answer.

"What else?" Dani said. "Have you tapped our phones? Hacked into our computers? What else is there?"

"I could give you the simple answer and say yes," he said. "But I think you're right. We need to put our cards on the table. Awhile ago you asked me if I'd heard the name Peter Guryakin. You met him at a reception at St. Adrian's. At the art opening."

"You said he was a dangerous man," Tommy said.

"Let me tell you how dangerous. Peter Mohammad Guryakin," Stanley said. "Russian father, mother from Kazakhstan. Raised in an Islamic household. Never particularly devout, but when the Soviets invaded Afghanistan in 1980, they got suspicious of anybody bowing toward Mecca. Guryakin earned his credentials helping to weaponize smallpox. They still have twenty thousand tons of the stuff in storage. He was working on nerve agents, genetic disruptors, really terrible things. And then he must have gotten wind that he was going to be purged. Picked up and left his apartment with the food still warm on the table. He'd already sent his son away to boarding school."

"To St. Adrian's," Tommy said. "Andrei Guryakin."

"He works for Linz Pharmazeutika now too," Dani said, thinking of Quinn. "Following in his father's footsteps."

Stanley nodded. Dani couldn't tell if it was because they'd told him something he already knew or simply something that didn't surprise him.

"When Peter Guryakin left the Soviets, he took his research with him," Stanley continued. "His expertise. The Soviets took his wife and three-year-old daughter into custody as leverage to get him to come back. They died. Guryakin swore vengeance against . . . well, against everyone. Sent his old boss a text that we intercepted: 'I am *dajjal*.'"

Tommy started in his seat. "How do you spell that?"

"D-a-j-j-a-l. Arabic for devil. Why?"

"That's it. That's what she meant," Tommy said.

"Slow down," Stanley said. "What who meant? What are you—"

"It's the last clue," Tommy said. "Abbie Gardener—we thought she was crazy. I thought she was crazy. I was interviewing her, and she said, 'Anyone for a little dodge ball? Dodge one, dodge all.' Or that's what I thought she said, d-o-d-g-e. Apparently she was using a different spelling."

"What was the context?"

"It was a warning," Tommy said.

Stanley reached into his coat pocket and laid four more photographs on the table.

"These are the people who 'posed' for the pictures your drone took," he said. "These are our pictures, not yours. Our cameras are higher resolution."

"Who are they?"

"I don't think the names would mean anything to you," he said. "They might not have meant anything to us ten years ago. But now we have computers and algorithms and Boolean search engines, and more data on more individuals than, frankly, anyone suspects. We look for patterns and intersections. Key words. Phone calls made at the exact same time on the exact same day, or calls made to each other in a recognizable pattern. Sequences of communication. Chatter in the ether. Every call. Every e-mail."

"In this country?" Tommy asked.

"On this planet," Stanley said. "That's how powerful our programs are."

"And what conclusions have you reached?"

"If we thought we were dealing with terrorists, we'd suspect an attack is coming," Ed Stanley said. "On Christmas Eve. The computer says it's statistically likely. Highly improbable that it won't. Red alert. Somewhere in the northeastern United States. Probably New York. But we agree with you. We don't think we're dealing with terrorists. Not in the traditional sense.

They're not Al Qaeda or Taliban or Muslim Brotherhood or Occupiers or Wikileakers, or anything we can identify. They all went to St. Adrian's, but that's all we know. The question I have is—what do *you* know?"

Dani glanced at Tommy, who nodded. "We're going to tell you a story," she said.

"Halfway through, you're going to think we're nuts," Tommy said.

"But if you listen to the whole thing, you won't," Dani said.

"And then an hour later you'll think we're crazy again, but an hour after that, you'll change your mind," Tommy said.

Dani started talking. She began with the murder of Julie Leonard and the dream she and Tommy shared. She told him about the arrival of Reese Stratton-Mallins, and how George Gardener and Julian Villanegre were murdered. Ed Stanley listened and, Dani suspected, committed to memory every word they were saying.

When they'd finished, multiple cups of coffee and tea later, the government man pushed his plate away and dabbed his lips with his napkin before setting it on the table. He studied them both.

"As Sherlock Holmes says, 'When you have eliminated the possible, whatever remains, however improbable, must be the truth.' The funny thing is, our computers—our incredible thinking machines, capable of making a trillion computations per second, computers the general public is not yet even remotely aware of, very nearly approaching true sentience—have come to the same conclusion you have. It's like a science fiction story, where man invents a computer that, through sheer mathematical logic, proves the existence of God. Or in this case, of Satan."

He folded the napkin and smoothed it down on the table.

"Now that you've taken me into your confidence, I'll take you into mine," the older man said, speaking low so as not to be overheard. "There's a group of us in the intelligence community—CIA, FBI, Homeland Security, Department of Defense, in this country and abroad—men and women of faith, who wouldn't have a problem with what you've just said.

A discrete subset within a discreet subset, if you will. But we have to be careful. Part of what the devil does is discredit those of us who know he exists and is at work in the world. We could go public with what we think, and what the computers are indicating, but if the press ran with this and started writing stories that a group of fanatical Christians—and let's not kid ourselves, that's what they'd call us—if they said we were seeing satanic conspiracies in recent events, I think you can imagine what would happen. I take it you can't share the names of your Curatoriat?"

"It's best that we don't," Dani said.

"I obviously have resources I can bring to bear," Stanley said. "Both hardware and HUMINT."

"Humint?" Tommy asked.

"Human intelligence. Boots on the ground stuff. My sense is that it would be best to keep our people separated, but liaison with each other. Full disclosure, with that understanding."

"Agreed," Tommy said.

"These men," he said, gesturing to the photographs on the table, "are on threat lists in their own countries, and others. But from what you're saying . . . it's the St. Adrian's boys, the Selected, that pose the real danger, correct?"

"That's our sense," Dani said.

"We need the names," Stanley said. "Once we have them, I can put people into the field, pretty much anywhere, within thirty minutes."

"We're going to have another session today with Reese in the sensory deprivation tank," Dani said, and then fell silent as Gail, the owner of the diner, came over.

"How you doing here? Think this rain'll stop?" she asked.

"Always has," Stanley replied. "To quote Calvin Coolidge."

"Well, if it doesn't," she said, "it's not the end of the world."

No one knew quite what to say to that.

They walked Stanley to his car. He took a moment to admire the green, the gazebo, the lights on the town tree, the bright storefronts with windows decorated with Christmas artwork created by the local children. He admired the steepled church at the far end of the commons, opposite the library.

"I used to love the sound of church bells on Sunday morning," Stanley said.

"So did I," Tommy said. "Unfortunately, ours are broken. They haven't rung in years."

Hopefully, Dani thought, that wasn't some kind of omen.

27.

December 23

"You're such a good actress," Laurent said to her as the sleek black Italian Agura helicopter soared above the outskirts of Paris. "Tell me—is there ever a time when you choose to use your acting skills when there isn't a camera pointed at you?"

You mean like now? Cass wanted to say. She wondered if she'd done something to give herself away. She'd hoped she could see this as just another acting role, but unlike all the other acting roles she'd played, this one would have dire consequences if she failed. Laurent was right—there'd been times in her life when she'd pretended to be happy, or in love, but if she'd been able to fool other people, she'd never been able to fool herself. She'd been surrounded for a long time by people who were famous or wealthy, but during the time she'd spent in East Salem with Tommy and Dani and the others, she realized she much preferred being surrounded by people who were genuine and honest and weren't playing games or trying to attach themselves to her for hidden reasons and agendas that had nothing to do with her.

She liked Laurent, but she had reasons to distrust her judgment. She didn't think she'd done anything to let on that she was joining Bauer on his yacht to collect information, but still, Laurent worked for Bauer, so she had to be careful.

"I try not to," she said. "But sometimes you have to. Like when you're on the red carpet and you have the flu but you have to smile and look glamorous. Have you been on Herr Bauer's yacht before?"

"This is my first time," Laurent said. "I hear it's quite special."

"So I've read," Cassandra said. "My mother was a cook on boats. I sort of grew up on them. There was an old man, I think he was from either Jamaica or Barbados, sort of a fishing guide, I guess. Whenever I'd admire somebody's boat, he'd say to me, 'Enjoy the ride, chile', but doan' fall in love wit' it—soonah or latah, everah boat ever made ends up at de bottom of de ocean. Everah mansion falls down.'"

"Your accent is very good," Laurent said.

"Thank you," she said, though an alarm went off in her head. Laurent had introduced himself as a native Frenchman, and he'd gone on to add that he'd never been to the United States. His English was heavily accented but passable. As a nonnative English speaker, how would he know that her Caribbean *patois* was authentic-sounding?

The pilot interrupted to ask Cassandra if she wanted to do any sightseeing along the way, or if she simply wished to proceed directly to the *Freiheit*, where Udo Bauer was waiting. She opted for the latter.

The helicopter flew south from Paris, over Lyon and the Burgundy region of France, skirting the western edge of the French Alps and landing in Marseilles to refuel. Cassandra took a short walk from the helicopter, hoping to use her phone to call Tommy with an update, but Laurent came with her, explaining that Herr Bauer had asked him to keep an eye on her wherever she went to make sure she was safe from harm. She sent Tommy a text instead: ON MY WAY TO BOAT. WISH ME BON VOYAGE. :)

They flew east to Toulon and hugged the coastline as far as St. Tropez and Cannes before turning south over the Mediterranean. Laurent pointed out the islands of Corsica and Sardinia to the east, out the port window, and in the far distance, barely visible, the island of Minorca on the starboard side, where the sun was already lowering toward the horizon. An hour after leaving the coast, the helicopter banked and descended toward the ocean and the *Freiheit* itself—a sleek white sliver the length of an ocean liner. The landing pad on the fantail was natural grass; Cassandra wondered why until she exited the aircraft and saw a set of golf clubs and a bucket of golf balls off to the side. It doubled as a driving range, she realized.

"Cassandra!"

Udo Bauer was waiting for her, dressed casually in white pants and a white V-neck sweater, his skin tanned and toned. He greeted her with a kiss on the cheek and then bade his staff—a dozen young men dressed in white shirts, shorts, shoes, and knee socks—to take Cassandra's bags to her stateroom. He introduced his first mate and personal assistant, a swarthy young man named Vito, and told her if there was anything she wanted, Vito would get it for her.

Something about Vito made her skin crawl. Intuition, perhaps, but she trusted her intuition. "Look for the guy whispering in his ear," Tommy had advised her. "The number two guy. He's going to be the one who's most dangerous. That's how they work, behind the scenes."

"Would you like a tour of my ship, Miss Morton?" Bauer asked.

"Only if you call me Cassie," she said. "And I would absolutely love a tour, Mr. Bauer."

"Only if you call me Udo," he insisted.

Cassandra had seen every kind of ship there was to see in her childhood, moving from island to island, rental to rental, always in transition, nothing ever settled or final. She'd told Tommy, when he'd asked her if she wanted to go out on his Boston Whaler to do some fishing, that she'd made a vow to never set foot on a boat again, because she was done with things that floated or drifted without anchors. Even so, she was impressed by the *Freiheit*. It went beyond the materials used, the Carrera marble from Tuscany, the Brazilian rosewood, the handcrafted New Zealand deerskin upholstered furnishings, the Persian rugs, the salon the size of a hotel lobby, where, Bauer informed her, he occasionally held parties or business gatherings. The whole was more than the sum of the parts, for some reason—though the parts were impressive indeed.

There was a tennis court below decks, and a garage where he kept a black Bentley, a red Ferrari, a camouflaged military-grade fully armored Humvee ("for the times when my presence is required in war zones"), and a pre-WWII restored Citroën that had belonged to his grandfather. The ship towed behind it a twenty-five-foot wooden speedboat as a tender, as well as an inflatable Zodiac and a pair of Jet Skis that Bauer suggested they try out in the morning, if she was feeling up to it.

"I need the tender because the only two ports capable of hosting a ship of this size are Monaco and Antibes," he said.

The galley, staffed by a team that included a chef Bauer had hired away from a four-star restaurant in Paris, featured three walk-in freezers where they stored fresh supplies taken on whenever they docked ("Though if we needed to, we could stay at sea for a year and be quite comfortable") and enough gas burners to cook for a party of a hundred.

"You will see your stateroom in a minute, but let me show you my pride and joy first," he said, leading her down a set of stairs to a movie theater. "By the way, I have been watching all your films so that I might know your work better."

"I don't mind subtitles, but voice-overs freak me out," she replied. "You have no idea how odd it is to watch yourself when the words coming out of your mouth have been dubbed into a foreign language. I hope that's not what you wanted to show me."

"No, no—I have something much better." He moved to a control panel, pressed a sequence of buttons, and the movie screen disappeared into the ceiling while the lights came on behind it, revealing a huge aquarium, inside of which swam a great white shark, easily fifteen feet long and four feet across.

Cassandra gasped audibly.

"Isn't he remarkable?" Bauer said. "I call him *Prachtvoller*. German for 'magnificent'."

"I thought great white sharks were impossible to keep in captivity."

"Quite so," Bauer said. "But he is not captive. He is free to come and go as he pleases—the bottom of the tank is open to the sea. He comes here because we feed him. It was actually quite easy to train him. We move his food a little closer, a little closer, until finally he comes inside my ship. Sharks are opportunistic feeders, but if he finds a reliable food source, he stays with it. He's been following the *Freiheit* for almost a year now. We thought for a while we'd lost him, but he came back."

"Very *Thunderball*," Cassandra said. "Did you know I was almost a Bond girl? My agent thought it would 'sultry up my brand,' but the producers thought it was too much of a leap. Does he do any tricks?"

"None whatsoever," Bauer said. "He's the king of the sea. He makes all the other fish do tricks."

Like you, she thought. *Like your friends from St. Adrian's.*

"You must be tired from your flight," Bauer said. "Would you like some time before dinner to refresh yourself? A nap, or perhaps a swim? I have a heated pool on the top deck."

"I think a nap," she said. "I'm still a bit jet-lagged."

"Of course," he said. "I will have the ship turned so that your balcony faces the west. I've made a few phone calls and arranged for a particularly fine sunset tonight."

She stared at him, not sure what he meant.

"A joke," he explained.

On deck, she was distressed to see the helicopter taking off. By the end of the helicopter ride, she'd come to see Laurent as an ally, someone she might be able to turn to in a pinch. Bauer explained that the helicopter would return tomorrow. Still, she felt uneasy. She felt . . . trapped.

In her stateroom, which was larger than any hotel suite she'd ever stayed in (and she'd stayed in some of the best hotels in the world), she took out her GPhone and tapped the screen, only to read that there was no signal. That, she'd expected. But when she tried to use the satellite link, her screen told her the uplink was blocked. That, she had not.

She checked her purse to make sure the .32 was still there. It was all she had—that, and her wits.

They would have to suffice.

"Are you there, Henry?" she asked her phone.

"I'm here, Cassandra," Henry said. "How may I assist you?"

"Just checking in," she said. "Feeling a little lonely. Nice to have someone to talk to. Besides myself, I mean."

"I like talking to you as well," Henry said. "Let me know if there's anything I can do for you."

"How about a bedtime story?" she asked.

"Once upon a time—"

"I was kidding," she said. "Maybe later."

"I will remind you later."

"What time zone am I in?"

"European Central Time. Or *Heure Normale Europe Centrale* in French. Would you like me to—"

"That's good," Cassandra said. "Just stand by. I might need you."

"I will stand by."

28.

December 23

1:00 p.m. EST

Dani had just started playing the *Brandenburg Concerto* Reese had chosen to rouse himself with when she heard the boy's voice over the loudspeaker.

"Not yet," he said.

She shut the music off immediately. She'd give him fifteen more minutes and then start it up again.

Reese had been in the sensory deprivation tank for an hour. She'd read in a book that tank users who'd entered their tanks without being told how long their sessions were going to last were often wildly incapable of estimating how long they'd been in, similar to the way that in a normal dream, days could seem to pass even though the dreamer had spent less than two or three minutes in REM sleep. While she was waiting, her phone chortled to tell her she'd received a text message from Quinn.

Dani—need to know if EDA is in Lake Atticus and in what concentration at depth—can you test it?

I will forward that to Tommy, she texted back. You haven't heard from Cassandra, I don't suppose?

No. And you just used a double negative.

After fifteen minutes she started the music again. When it had been playing for a few minutes, she turned off the lights in the man cave and lifted the lid. Reese stepped out quickly, seeming both refreshed and less daunted than the last time he was in the tank.

After the boy had a chance to rinse off the saltwater in the shower and dress, he met Dani in the kitchen, where he wolfed down the peanut butter and jelly sandwich Ruth offered him. For some reason, he declared, his sessions in the tank made him hungry.

"Everything makes boys your age hungry," Ruth said.

"Mrs. Carlyle makes us sandwiches with marmite," he said. He made a face and shuddered. "*Bleeah!* It's like drinking a smoothie made from a compost heap. This is quite good. Believe it or not, I've never had a jelly and peanut butter before."

"Peanut butter and jelly," Ruth corrected him. "I don't know why, but jelly never comes first."

"Did you have any luck contacting Edmond?" Dani asked. She'd wanted to ask but had given him time to reorient himself in the real world.

"Some," he told her. "I tried to think of my brother, just to tell him I miss him. And to ask him if he misses me. I got a sense of how lonely he is, but . . . he doesn't want anybody to help him. He's built a wall around himself. He won't talk to anybody. He's not eating anything. Maybe that's why I was so hungry."

"Maybe," Dani allowed.

"But then I started to get a really strong feeling," Reese said. "My brother is usually one of the most confident people I know. To the point of arrogance, I suppose. But now . . . he's not sure. I kept telling him not to put it in the water. That it's the wrong thing to do."

"Not to put what in the water?" Dani said. "This is the first time you've mentioned putting something in the water."

"Weren't you the one who told me that?" Reese asked. "Something about the water."

"We think that's what they're targeting," Dani said. "You think Edmond is putting something in the water directly?"

"That's the impression I got from him. Most definitely. I told him it was dangerous. He started to worry. Not just about himself. About some of his friends from Honors House."

"The Selected," Dani said.

"Yes. They're the ones . . . their mission is the same as his. Put whatever it is into the water."

Provivilan, Dani thought. "What water, Reese?" she asked. "Where?"

"I don't know. But as he was thinking of them, I got a very clear picture of their faces. Some of them, at least. I know who they are now. Do you have something to write with?"

Dani got him a piece of paper and a pen, and he wrote down five names. "This is a good start," she said.

"I'm sorry I couldn't give you more," Reese said.

"Is this what you were thinking of when you said 'not yet'?"

"I said that?" Reese asked her. "I don't remember saying that. It must have been when you turned on the lights inside the tank."

"There aren't any lights inside the tank," Dani told him. "It only gets light inside when you lift the lid."

"But . . ."

"But what?"

"Well, this is intriguing. Are you sure?"

"I'm sure," Dani said. "The whole point is to make it so dark and quiet that you have an absence of sensory input."

"Well, that's not what I felt. Tommy was telling me about praying," Reese said, thinking. "He said sometimes it helps when you do it in a place that's dark and quiet, so I thought I'd give it a try in the tank. And when I did, I felt . . ."

"What?" Dani asked.

"Well," Reese said. "I'm not sure how to describe it. I felt really good. Really happy. Bliss or something quite like it. And then I thought you turned the lights on. It got really bright inside and warm, and the light was golden and everything seemed to slow down, as if the light were made out of honey. It was one of the most amazing things I've ever felt. Just pure joy. And then I heard the music."

"I didn't turn on any lights," Dani said. "There aren't any lights to turn on."

"It was genuinely amazing," Reese said. "Do you promise you're not pulling my leg?"

"I promise," Dani said. She'd read of phenomena where people experience being bathed in a golden light—an experience generally described as "spiritual." She'd always regarded it as a psychological anomaly or abnormal event before. Not now.

"I wonder if your brother might have been feeling some of the same things."

On the monitor she then noticed Tommy walking up the driveway toward the house; a man in a black overcoat was walking beside him. A stranger.

"Reese," she said, "someone is coming and I don't know who it is. Would you mind waiting in the study? I just don't want to have to explain what you're doing here."

"Why don't I just wait in the study so you don't have to explain what I'm doing here?" he said.

She was getting used to his sassy sense of humor. It occurred to her in passing that Reese and Helen Trumble would probably hit it off.

When he'd left, Dani went to the back door and opened it.

"Dani," Tommy said. "This is Agent Cooney from the FBI. Agent Cooney, this is Danielle Harris, my girlfriend, and that's my Aunt Ruth."

The FBI agent took his hat off but didn't move from the doorway.

"I'm following up on a report we received about a missing person," he said.

"Why is the FBI interested in a missing persons case?" Dani asked.

"We're having trouble locating the headmaster from St. Adrian's. The sons of seven world leaders are currently enrolled at St. Adrian's Academy," Agent Cooney said. "As well as boys from a number of royal Arab houses and multiple diplomats. The disappearance of the school's headmaster could have international repercussions. That's why we were asked to look into it. Did any of you see or hear anything unusual two nights ago?"

"Two nights ago?" Dani frowned. "No."

"Agent Cooney says they got an anonymous tip that there was a dead body in the pond," Tommy said, laughing it off. "I told him I couldn't think of anybody who might have made such a claim, but he wanted to talk to you."

"I was asleep by eleven," Dani said.

"I was out by ten," Ruth said. "Can you narrow it down a little?"

"I'm afraid I can't," Agent Cooney said. He looked at each of them, evaluating their responses. It was the same task Dani performed for the district attorney's office. If she knew how to detect a lie, she'd also learned how to tell one.

"We didn't notice anything," Dani said.

"I'll leave my card in case you think of anything." Cooney looked at each of them one more time, then turned to Tommy. "Probably just a crank call. There's a new trend called swatting, where people try to get S.W.A.T. teams to show up at celebrity houses. This may be nothing more than that. Thank you for your time. Shall we?"

"We're just going to go out and have a look at the pond," Tommy told the others.

Dani watched them walk to the edge of the pond. Ruth joined her at the window.

"Someone from the school must have called in the tip," Ruth said. "They're trying to get Tommy arrested. Maybe Mr. Stanley can call them off. Or at least stall them."

"Maybe for a little while," Dani said. "But not for long."

29.

December 23

3:01 p.m. EST / 9:01 p.m. CET

At dinner, Udo Bauer talked at length about himself while Cassandra smiled and laughed and feigned interest. He spoke of world leaders he had met, and world leaders his father had known, and world leaders his grandfather had known, though she noted that he failed to mention Hitler or Stalin. All the while, Cassandra said nothing of her interests, or her past, or her dreams or desires.

After the meal, Bauer told her how much he was enjoying getting to know her.

She told him it was rare to meet a man who was charming, funny, and intelligent, and he assumed she was referring to him as the exception, though she was speaking generally. She declined his offer of brandy, just as she'd declined his offer of wine with dinner, even though he made a point of telling her how rare and expensive both the wine and the brandy were. She playfully accused him, once again, of trying to get her tipsy. He laughed, though clearly that was what he was trying to do. She apologized and said her stomach was bothering her, and that though she was enjoying his company, she needed more time to reacclimate to the sea.

"It's so embarrassing," she said. "I grew up on the ocean and now I can't handle it. I'll be better company in the morning—promise! Good night."

The next morning she told Vito she wanted a light breakfast in her room. Again, simply being near the man made her feel a mixture of nausea and disgust. She had just finished eating when she heard the sound of gunfire. When she stepped out onto the deck, she saw Vito potting seagulls from the fantail with a shotgun.

"I try to tell them they are free to leave their waste products anywhere but on my boat, but they refuse to listen," Bauer said from a balcony on the deck above her, his voice catching her by surprise.

"Flying rats," Cassandra said. "That's what my uncle used to call them." As a girl, she once almost tamed a seagull that let her feed him out of her hand. She'd named him Jonathan, after the book *Jonathan Livingston Seagull*, which her mother had read to her.

"Do you have a fondness for guns, Miss Morton?" Bauer said. "I couldn't help but notice you have a pistol in your purse."

She looked up at him and smiled. "And how would you know that?" she asked him.

"Last night when I gave you the tour, I walked you through an X-ray scanner, similar to the ones they have at airports. Don't be offended—I scan all my guests. No exceptions. But I'm wondering why you feel the need to arm yourself?"

"I arm myself," she said, "on the off chance that someday I might run into my father."

She'd rehearsed what she'd say if she were caught with the weapon. Now it was show time.

"You feel threatened by your father?"

"No," she said, "but *he* should feel threatened by *me*. And if you want to know the rest of that story, you will have to be very, very nice to me."

"I intend to be," Bauer said, "but in the meantime, I can assure you that your father is not aboard this ship, and if he were, my crew is more than prepared to handle any situation that might arise. If you wouldn't mind giving your weapon to the steward, I'll see that it's returned to you when you leave the ship."

"Of course," she said, taking the .32 from her purse and handing it to Vito, who appeared at her side. He received the weapon with a courteous nod. She hoped her apprehension didn't show. "I intend to do nothing today but read a book and work on my tan. Would you care to join me?"

"Soon. I have a business meeting I must attend to first—a teleconference that will keep me occupied for most of the morning. The deck off my suite is the highest place on the ship and will put you closest to the sun. Vito will show you. And feel free to enjoy the sun in as much or as little as you care to wear, including nothing at all—my crew knows what would happen if any of them were to take a photograph. And if any aircraft dares to fly over us, it will meet the same fate as the seagulls."

Charming, Cassandra thought.

But her role was that of temptress, so of the three bathing suits she had to choose from, she selected the skimpiest, though it was still nothing that would raise so much as an eyebrow on any of the better beaches in the States.

Vito led her to Bauer's sun deck, which opened via a wall of sliding glass doors to the master suite, then left her with a pitcher of iced tea and a stack of large pristine white beach towels. When he was gone, she looked around for surveillance cameras pointed at her. There were none that she could see.

She stretched out on a deck chair and pretended to read from her GPhone, when in fact she was using the camera to look beyond the glass doors into the master suite. When she asked Henry to zoom in, he quietly complied. The master suite was appointed entirely in white and featured a king-sized bed with a large skylight above it, with an array of paddle fans to keep the air circulating. The glare from the sun made it hard to see.

"Still no satellite uplink, Henry?" she asked the phone.

"Satellite uplink is blocked. A Wi-Fi network is available."

The network was labeled simply *Freiheit1*. When she tried to log in, she found the network was password protected.

"Rats," she said.

"Would you like me to find a pest control company or exterminator?"

"It's just an expression," she said. "Although the company I'm in isn't much higher. I don't suppose you have any way to tell me what the password is?"

"I can only determine that it's a twelve-letter word or combination of letters and numerals."

"Try *prachtvoller*. I don't know how to spell it. It's the German word for 'magnificent.'"

"Access is denied."

"Well then," she said, getting to her feet, "let's see 'em try to deny America's Sweetheart when she has to powder her nose."

"Why would America's Sweetheart want to put powder on her nose?"

"It's another expression," Cassandra said. "Hush now."

She slid the glass door aside and entered the master suite and Bauer's bedroom. The plush ivory carpeting felt like fur beneath her bare feet. The room was spotless. The painting on the wall behind the headboard was an original by Gustav Klimt, worth millions, she was certain. The bronze sculptures of ballerinas bracketing the bathroom door were both genuine Degas. Unsure what she was looking for, she entered a large walk-in closet, where she found an array of expensive suits and sport coats and tuxedos arranged according to color. She pushed them aside, hoping to find something hidden behind them.

She did: a wall safe, the circular door about eighteen inches in diameter.

"I don't suppose you know how to crack a safe, do you, Henry?"

"I can open safes made by Stack-On, Homak, Sky Enterprise USA, LockState, A1, IdeaWorks, HomCom, Strattec, Turn 10, Safecase

Biometrics, Cannon, Paragon, Protec, Protex, Trademark, Mesa, Sentry, First Alert, Secure Logic, Honeywell, Embassy, Gardall, Alibaba, Hamilton, Schwab, Brown, Fireking, Liberty, American Security, Dean, Fort Knox, Onity, Esafe, Assa Abloy, BTV, Hayman, Battaglia & Cleland, Diebold, Yale . . ."

"Thank you. Can you identify this one?" she said, using the phone's camera to capture the image.

"This is a Diebold Mini-122E Rotary Wedge Lock with stainless steel cladding and U.L. class-3 protection."

"Can you open it?"

"I can open it tonight between eleven and midnight, assuming the Diebold Mini-122E's time lock is still set at the factory default."

"Tonight, then," she said, closing her phone.

In the bathroom, a bathtub large enough to hold a pod of orcas sat beneath a large picture window with a view of the sea, the tub carved out of a solid piece of onyx, she guessed, as were the sinks, all with gold fixtures and handles. The shower was a stall with black slate walls and a dozen shower heads at varying heights. There appeared to be no medicine cabinet, which seemed ironic, given that the man owned a pharmaceutical company. The drawers contained nothing more than standard grooming products.

She was about to leave when she noticed someone standing by the stateroom door.

Without thinking, she closed the bathroom door.

She listened from behind the door, her heart pounding inside her chest. She'd only caught a glimpse before she reacted, but the someone had looked like a crew member, not Bauer himself.

She was startled by a knock on the door.

"*Hallo?*" he called out. "*Ist jemand da drin?*"

She held her breath.

"*Hallo?*" he said, knocking firmly on the door. "*Bitte—ist jemand da drin?*"

"Lass uns in ruhe! Es ist unhöflich uns zu stören!" Henry said.

"Entschuldige. Vergisst mir, bitte."

She heard the door shut and opened the bathroom door. The stateroom was empty. She returned to the sun deck, closing the sliding glass door behind her.

"What did he say?"

"He asked if anyone was in the bathroom."

"What did you tell him?"

"I told him he was rude to interrupt us and that he should leave us alone immediately."

"I didn't know you spoke German."

"I'm fluent in many languages, including German, French, Spanish, Italian, Greek, Mandarin Chinese, Cantonese Chinese, Russian, Czech, Serbian, Norwegian—"

"Yeah, good, I get it," she said. "You saved me. Thank you."

"You're welcome. Is there anything else you need?"

She took a sip from her iced tea and rearranged herself on the chair, trying to look casual, comfortable, though inside, her heart was pounding.

"A plan would be nice."

30.

December 23

4:32 p.m. EST

"Just make sure we have enough flashlights," Reese said.

"Don't worry about flashlights," Tommy said. "I've got that covered."

He'd loaded the Helios 9000 onto the Grizzly's front cargo rack, along with the shotgun and a box of shells. The afternoon drizzle had turned into a steady rain that left the ground saturated and muddy.

"It'll be dark in half an hour," he said. "Let's go before those things won't let us out."

But he was upset because of a dispute—or maybe he should call it what it was, a fight—that he'd had with Dani, again, over whether or not Reese should come with him. She understood the urgency of the situation. She knew what the stakes were. There were FBI agents searching for the body—and the killer—of St. Adrian's headmaster John Adams Wharton, and Casey wouldn't be able to intervene if they put together enough evidence to arrest Tommy. Tommy knew he might not have another opportunity. They needed the names of the boys who'd been selected. They needed to know where they'd gone, and they needed to stop them. They'd made very little progress so far. The names would be

193

in Ghieri's computer, and Reese knew the way to reach it without being detected. He knew where the tunnel adit was, and he knew which turns to take. They had one chance.

Dani had argued that Reese was only a boy. She argued that she and Tommy had been called or chosen, but Reese hadn't. He'd come seeking sanctuary, and they'd promised to give it to him. He was only seventeen, she said. He deserved to live a long and happy life. Tommy knew he'd argued poorly when he replied that no one was going to live a long and happy life if they didn't get those names, and that Reese was old enough to make up his own mind. But Dani had seen too many child soldiers. She'd seen what fighting did to them, seen them lose their childhood all in an instant, and in many cases she'd been unable to get it back for them.

What troubled Tommy the most was that they'd failed to resolve their issues. Reese had stepped in and said he was going, in a way that indicated he didn't want to argue about it. Dani had felt unfairly overruled and unheard.

After the FBI agent left, Tommy spent the afternoon alone in his boat on Lake Atticus, getting the water samples that Quinn had asked for. The recent unseasonably warm weather had melted the thin ice, leaving open water that was clear and cold. As Tommy worked, he thought of Dani and what he needed to say to her. There was no time to put the boat back on the trailer, so he left it docked at the Gardener Farm and drove home, hoping they'd have enough time to talk.

But they didn't. He and Reese needed to leave as soon as it was dark, and darkness was upon them. Dani stayed in the house rather than come out to wish them well.

It worried him, but he told himself there would be time later to straighten things out.

He headed north from the end of his driveway, then turned onto a bridle trail to circle back. There wasn't a path, trail, or back road that Tommy hadn't either run or cross-country skied, and he'd played in these woods as a boy. All the same, it took them longer than he'd hoped to locate the entrance to the tunnel that Reese had used to escape the school.

It was on a steep hillside high above a stream, and Tommy had to park the ATV a quarter mile from the entrance and search for it on foot using only his NVGs to find the trail. "I know it's here somewhere," Reese kept saying.

The stream carried the overflow from the dam that formed Lake Atticus, but during the Revolutionary War, before the dam was built, the stream would have been a logical escape route for spies or scouts.

At a place where the path led close to the edge of the stream, they came across the carcass of a deer. Tommy didn't dare turn his flashlight on but covered the lens with his fingers to briefly shine light on the scene before turning it off again.

"Coyotes?" Reese asked.

"Coyotes would have eaten the meat," Tommy said. "Whatever did this appears to have been amusing itself."

The footing was treacherous, and Tommy's boots kept slipping in the mud. The opening was covered by a tangle of vines and would have been impossible to see in the summer when the vines held foliage. Tommy set the spotlight down inside the tunnel entrance and took only a handheld flashlight into the tunnel, the shotgun under his arm, his pockets filled with extra ammunition.

"How did you ever find this place?" he asked as they made their way down the tunnel, occasionally having to duck beneath thick tree roots penetrating from above and sagging wooden beams used to brace the ceiling. The walls and ceiling were lined with brick that was for the most part intact, crumbling occasionally where the mortar had given way.

"Soap bubbles," Reese said. "An older boy told us about the heating tunnels, but Edmond wanted to know where the air went. So we brought some soap bubbles down and followed them where they drifted."

"That's good thinking," Tommy said.

"My brother is very clever," Reese said. "I'm a bit more bookish."

By the light of the flashlight, Tommy noted the concern on Reese's face. "Don't worry," he said. "We'll get him back. If Dani says she can do it, she can do it."

They came to a place where the tunnel split into a Y.

"This way," Reese said, pointing to an arrow on the wall written in chalk. "I marked the way back, in case I got lost."

"That's good thinking too," Tommy said. "For someone who's bookish."

They passed a section of the tunnel where several names were scratched into the brick—one said *Solomon Brooke, 1779*—before arriving at what seemed to be a dead end, the way forward obstructed by a wall of wooden crates and cardboard boxes. Reese showed Tommy where he and his brother had moved the boxes to make a narrow passage that required them to turn sideways.

On the other side of the constriction, the walls were made of a more modern concrete, with water and sewage pipes and ventilation ducts lining the ceiling, and electrical conduits and junction boxes on the walls. Reese told Tommy to turn left. Now they came to intersections and side tunnels leading to various buildings.

"Turn right," Reese said at a crossroads. "Do you see why I had to come with you? You would have gotten lost."

At the next three-way intersection, Reese showed Tommy the tunnel leading to the art building, a second leading to Honors House, and a third to the administration building. Tommy paused, briefly wishing he had some sort of explosives with him to at least blow up the art museum and that hideous painting, if not Honors House too. He let Reese guide him to the administration building, where the boy paused again. Down one hall that dead-ended abruptly at solid stone, he saw a pair of wrought-iron candle sconces bracketing a windowless wooden door.

"What's down there?" Tommy asked.

"I don't know," Reese said.

"Did Edmond ever come down here by himself?"

"It's just an impression," Reese said. "I think maybe he was here once."

A door opened into a custodian's supply room. Tommy used his infrared scanner. As far as he could tell, they were alone.

A hallway and a set of stairs later, they emerged on the first floor where the library wing met the main building. Tommy scanned again. Nothing. He knew the way to Ghieri's office because it was where Dani and Detective Casey had met with Amos Kasden. The place had made his skin crawl, a sensation of ants on the back of his neck.

"No one seems to be expecting us," Reese said, following close behind Tommy.

"That's what I was telling Dani," Tommy said. "They're not worried because they know you'd have to be crazy to do what we're doing. Crazy or just really stupid."

"Which one are we?"

"Does it matter?"

"Guess not."

The door to the waiting room was unlocked. The door to Ghieri's inner office was ajar, and the lights were on, as was the computer, Tommy saw. He held up a hand to stop Reese, on the chance that Ghieri was in his office. He listened.

Not a sound.

The office was empty.

"We should hurry," Tommy said, seating himself in front of the computer. "What was the name of the file you found before?"

"I don't remember," Reese said.

"What were the other names you came up with? You saw four faces you recognized."

Reese told him the names. Tommy searched for any files containing all five names, including Edmond's. There was only one, labeled Holiday Travelers.

He opened it.

"Bingo," he said. He read twenty-one names. Next to the name Edmond Stratton-Mallins, he saw an address on Lowndes Street.

"Do you know that address?" he asked Reese. "Is that where Edmond is staying?"

"I know where it is. It's in Belgravia. Part of London. But I've never seen that address," Reese said.

"Nobody named Marko," Tommy said. "I don't know if that's good or bad."

"If we don't know where he is, that's bad," Reese said. "Everybody I knew was afraid of him. Guys I was afraid of were afraid of him."

Tommy plugged a thumb drive into a USB port and copied the file to it, removed the drive, and put it in his pocket. He paused.

"What?"

"Maybe I should just crash the hard drive," he said. "While we have the chance."

"They'll know we were here," Reese said. "They might change the date of the attack. Which could mean moving it up. And we might not be able to get out with that list."

"You're three for three," Tommy said, restoring the computer to its previous screen. "Let's go."

He left everything exactly the way it was, and then the two moved back down the hall, past the library, and down the stairs to the custodian's room, then down another flight of stairs to the service tunnels. Tommy stopped again.

"What is it?" Reese asked, but Tommy was already headed down the side tunnel to the door he'd seen earlier, the one with wrought-iron candle sconces on either side.

"I just want to see what's in here," he said. "When are we going to get another chance?"

The heavy door opened inward. He turned on his flashlight. He saw, on the walls, a large mural of scenes taken from Hieronymus Bosch's *Garden of Earthly Delights.* In the center of the room he saw an altar, carved from a large piece of black marble in the shape of a bull.

"They must have brought it with them," he said. "Pergamon's Altar. Revelation chapter 2, if I'm not mistaken. They brought it with them when they fled England."

He circled the altar but didn't touch it. There appeared to be drains in the floor at the base of it.

"What are those for?" Reese asked.

"Blood?" Tommy said. "Just a guess. I'm not exactly up on my human sacrifice rituals."

In the floor on the far side of the altar he found a trapdoor, a wooden square three feet across with a large iron ring in the middle.

"What do you suppose is down there?" he asked.

"Do we need to know?"

"I need to know," Tommy said.

He opened the door and shone his flashlight into what appeared to be a deep black hole. At the bottom of the hole, he saw a pair of glowing red eyes. Then another. And then a dozen more.

"No I don't!" he said. "Run!"

They bolted from the room just as one of the things leapt from the hole in the floor. In the hallway, Tommy pulled down a storage rack behind him as they fled. He was faster than Reese, but Reese led because he knew the way and Tommy didn't. Tommy turned and fired the shotgun behind him twice, striking the closest beast in the head at point-blank range and splattering the wall with a reddish-gray goo.

More kept coming. Tommy fired again, unable to count how many of the things were chasing them as he followed Reese down the tunnel.

When they reached the stack of boxes concealing the old escape route, Tommy fired again as he squeezed between the boxes and the wall, pulling boxes down behind him to block the way, Reese helping. Tommy paused to reload.

"Go!" he shouted. "It's not going to hold them for long."

Tommy shone his flashlight behind him and backed down the tunnel as fast as he could. At the end of the tunnel, he grabbed the Helios 9000 and hit the standby button, waiting for the spotlight to power up.

"Come on, come on!" he shouted as he fired another shell and the rain poured down. Finally the standby indicator turned from red to green.

He turned the spotlight on, a storm of white light that stopped the Beasts of Gevaudan in their tracks as they shielded their eyes and howled with pain.

"Keep it on 'em," he told Reese, handing him the heavy spotlight. Reese shouldered it and aimed it at the creatures as he backed carefully down the slope to the path at the bottom. Tommy moved upstream, toward the ATV. As long as Reese held the powerful light, the beasts stayed back. He kept one hand on Reese's shoulder as they backed up the path and fired four more times, knocking three of the things down and wounding a fourth. He reloaded.

"The battery is running out!" Reese shouted.

"Keep moving. Just keep it on them as long as you can," Tommy said, firing two more times, running, then firing twice more. The light seemed half as bright as it had been before, and as it dimmed, the beasts grew bolder.

"Get on!" Tommy shouted when they reached the ATV. He took the light from the boy and fired again at a beast trying to slink along the ground to his right.

Reese straddled the driver's seat.

"Do you know how to drive one of these?"

"Not at all," Reese said.

Tommy turned the ignition key, then pushed the starter. The engine came alive. "Those are the brakes and that's the throttle. It's like riding a bike."

"I've never ridden a bike," Reese said.

Tommy sat on the rear cargo rack, facing backward. "Don't overthink it—just drive! Go!"

Reese pulled away just as one of the beasts leapt through the air. Tommy fired his last shell at it from perhaps two feet away. This time it was Tommy who got splattered with the reddish-gray goo.

The Helios 9000 was down to less than a quarter power. He picked the heavy spotlight up with one hand and flung it behind him, knocking one of the beasts over with it. He reloaded and fired the gun again as the beasts gave chase.

"Where am I going?" Reese shouted.

"Just go—you're doing fine," Tommy said. Soon they'd put some distance between them and their pursuers, but it wasn't enough. Tommy looked around. They seemed to be on a bridle path, the rain turning the path to mud and muck.

When Reese hit a rock, Tommy became momentarily airborne but grabbed the cargo rack he was sitting on to avoid falling off. He fired two more times, missing once, then hitting one of the beasts with his next shot. He reached into his right pocket for more shells. Empty. He reached into his left pocket and found six. He pushed four of them into the weapon and pumped it again.

The ATV suddenly slowed down.

"What's the matter?" he called over his shoulder.

"Look," Reese said.

They'd come to a dead end, the trail stopping at the base of a thirty-foot rock escarpment with swampy wetlands to the left and thick woods to the right. They couldn't go right, left, or forward, and they certainly couldn't go back the way they'd come.

"Get to the high ground!" Tommy said, following behind Reese and pushing him up the rock. He heard a beast approaching and turned in time to fire directly into its face, knocking it backward in a shower of gore.

At the top of the rock he pushed a shell into the breach, giving him five more shots, then flipped down his NVGs to survey the area. The woods below swarmed with shadows. A long, high fence led in both directions from the rock where they stood.

"Where are we?" Reese said. "What is this place?"

Tommy flipped up the goggles and shone his light on the fence. He knew what it was. Deer fences were about the same height, but not as sturdy. He had been to this rock before, one night in high school during a full moon, just to sit and observe.

"We dead-ended at the wolf sanctuary," he said. "Look."

When he shone his flashlight into the woods beyond the fence, they saw shapes moving furtively and eyes reflecting green. A pair of large wolves stepped into the light, snarling and pacing sideways. The alpha pair. On the opposite side of the rock, the Beasts of Gevaudan were slowly climbing toward them.

"I'm sorry," Reese said.

"Don't worry about it," Tommy said. "I've been in worse situations."

"Such as?"

"I can't think of any off the top of my head."

"What do we do?"

Tommy considered their options. It wasn't a difficult decision.

"We jump," he said, grabbing Reese by the hand.

"Into the wolf sanctuary? Are you crazy or stupid?"

"I thought we already settled that."

It was fifteen feet down from the top of the rock to the other side, but where they landed was soft, padded with fallen leaves and sloping away from the rock. They rolled a few times and got to their feet.

A half dozen cave weasels leapt down from the rock after them.

The wolves set upon the beasts immediately, encircling them and tearing at them, while other wolves howled, and more wolves came bounding through the woods at top speed to join the battle. This was their home territory, and it had been invaded by an alien species. The cave weasels were larger and stronger, but the wolves were smarter and worked together, quickly surrounding the mesonychids and nipping at them from all directions.

The wolves paid the humans no attention whatsoever, and Reese and Tommy backed away, turned, and ran. Five minutes later they were scaling the gates at the far end of the wolf sanctuary and dropping down into the parking lot at the sanctuary's education center, while in the distance a chorus of triumphant howls pierced the rain.

"Are you okay?" he asked Reese as he picked up the pace, heading for home.

"I'm all right," the boy said. "You?"

"Let's get back," Tommy said. "If Dani asks, let's just say everything came off without a hitch." He gave the boy a reassuring squeeze on the back of his neck. "You know I'm kidding, right? Tell the truth."

"I know," Reese said. "How'd I do?"

"You did great," Tommy said.

31.

December 23

Cassandra had the odd feeling that she'd left something important behind, and then she realized what it was—a script. She had to improvise—something she'd done back in acting school. The key to improvisation, her teacher had said, was listening. Being present in the scene. She was still finding her way into this part, though. And she couldn't afford the slightest misstep. The stakes were a lot higher than she was used to.

She took another sip of her iced tea and smiled.

"If you want to know me," she said, "the way I know you want to know me, then I have to know you first."

Bauer smiled back, looking like the cat that was about to eat the canary. "And what would you like to know about me, Cassie?"

She shuddered inwardly at the sound of the nickname, even though she'd suggested its use. "My friends call me Cassie," she'd told him, but that was a lie. In fact she hated the name Cassie, but she hated this man who was sitting across the table from her even more, and she wanted to feel repulsed every time he spoke to her. He was crass, arrogant, entitled, and devious. Worse than that, he was evil—and connected to a greater evil still.

"Who are you?" she said.

Their candlelight dinner on the sun deck was over, the stars above them twinkling brightly. Bauer had offered her a cognac. She'd declined, explaining that on nights like this, a girl needed a clear head to make the proper decisions. She'd delivered lines from scripts in movie after movie where the push and pull of seduction played out in a similar fashion, the man single-minded but the woman in control. Bauer's condescending ego was precisely his weakness, his self-glorification the thing Cassandra knew would compel him to take whatever bait she dangled in front of him.

"I am what you see," he replied.

"I don't think so," she said. "Not that I don't like what I see, but you'll have to do better than that. What is your worst quality?"

"My worst quality?" he said. "I suppose it's that I won't suffer fools. I have no patience for them, no sympathy for their handicaps. And they are everywhere. Particularly in politics. But it would only matter if I cared what they thought. Or if they cared what I think."

She smiled. "What do you want?" she asked. "Besides the obvious."

"Right now, the . . . obvious is all I can think of," he said.

She leaned back in her chair, turning sideways and folding her arms across her chest. "I know what else you want."

"What else do I want?"

"An empire."

"What's wrong with wanting an empire?"

"Nothing, as long as it's realistic," she said. "I'm not interested in a man with delusions of empire. I've known several."

He took a cigarette from a pack in his pocket and lit it from one of the candles, the smoke rising into the warm Mediterranean night.

"Oh, it's quite realistic, Cassie," he told her, sipping his cognac. "One might even say it's nearly within my grasp."

He was bragging. Bragging, Cassandra knew, was a sign of insecurity. Tommy, for all his physical gifts and accomplishments, had never bragged, not once, in all the time she'd known him.

"How so?"

Bauer smiled, but didn't reply. Cassandra knew he was going to, though. She knew exactly what he was thinking: that this foolish American actress was no match for him—he could tell her anything, tell her what she wanted to hear, and there would be no consequence.

"Have you heard of my grandfather?" he asked.

"The Nazi?" she said. "The one who experimented on concentration camp prisoners?"

"The one who gave their deaths meaning," Bauer said. "They were going to die. That he could not stop. No one could. Not at the end, anyway. Maybe at the beginning. But what he could do was give their lives, at the end, purpose. He could make their deaths mean something."

"And did he?"

"Oh yes. The medications and treatments that resulted from the data he was able to collect have since saved many lives—many more lives, in fact, than were lost in the camps. This was my grandfather's way. He looked at the facts, with a cold eye, yes. An ice-cold eye. But with an eye that saw the truth. And from that he derived a greater good."

Cassandra had felt repulsed by Bauer before; now she was nauseated. Still, she feigned interest.

"I am the benefactor of all the work he and my father have done," Bauer said. "I too am able to look at the world with an eye that is both cold and accurate."

"And what do you see?"

"I see misery," Bauer said. "And pain. And want and hunger and fear. So I've created a way to fix that."

"How so?" she asked.

"Why, Cassie," he said. "Can't you guess? With a drug. That's what I do. A perfect drug."

She rolled her eyes. "I think somebody's been reading their own press releases," she said.

"You don't believe me?"

"I do not," she said, shifting in her chair and sipping the last of her iced tea. "If something seems too good to be true, it usually is. It *always* is, in my experience." When she set her glass down, a waiter who had been hovering out of sight instantly refilled it. Bauer waited for him to leave before he spoke.

"You're too young to be so jaded. You've heard of Provivilan?" Bauer asked.

"How could I not?" she said. "The ads are everywhere. The new wonder drug that's going to change the world."

"Sarcasm is unbecoming on you."

"Change the world?" she said. "Really, Udo? How?"

He hesitated. She could see his mind working, wondering how much he should tell her. The man needed a bit more persuading. Cassandra leaned forward, resting her elbows on the table and her chin on her hands, looking up at him as if he were the most interesting man in the world.

"I want to know," she said, and smiled. She waited.

Bauer caved, as she knew he would. "Because this drug is unlike any other."

"How so?"

"It's quite simple," he said. "Unlike every other drug you can take, this one does not wear off. And the change is for the better. No more anger. No more depression. No more sadness or grief. And the benefits of the drug last forever. As long as you keep taking your daily maintenance dosage."

"In other words, it's addicting?" Cassandra said.

"It becomes a requirement." Bauer nodded. "Like food or water. No more or less."

"And since Linz Pharmazeutika is the only manufacturer," Cassandra said, "you become wealthy beyond your wildest dreams."

"I am already wealthy beyond my wildest dreams," Bauer said. "But yes. You'll probably think I'm exaggerating, but when I was quite young,

I set a goal for myself. I said that one day I would be the richest man in the world—and not just that, but the richest man who ever lived. Richer than Rockefeller or Rothschild or Mansa Musa. It just didn't make any sense to me to have anything less as a goal. And with Provivilan, I will accomplish it."

"What if someone steals the formula?" she said, leaning back in her chair.

"There is only one written copy," he told her. "In the safe in my state-room. And one in my head. And a sample in a very safe place in a laboratory in Connecticut."

She pretended to be making up her mind, then reached across the table and took his hand. "I want to be alone with you," she told him, leaning forward and putting her lips close to his.

"Excellent," he said, his face growing flushed. "I'll dismiss the staff for the night—"

"No." She smiled. "I mean alone on this ship. Tell your crew to get on that little boat you're towing behind us and go for a cruise until morning."

Bauer frowned slightly. "I don't—"

"And then, when we have this big old boat all to ourselves, I want you to go to your stateroom and wait. And in half an hour, after I've had a chance to change into something I brought, I will knock on your door. You will open the door. I will turn out the lights, and then . . ."

"And then?"

She tapped him on the nose with her forefinger and stood up. She didn't need to wait for his answer, because she knew Bauer would comply. Men always did. All of them, all the time.

Except Tommy.

She walked toward the gangway leading down to her stateroom while Bauer spoke to the steward. When she was out of sight, she ducked into an unused stateroom and waited, leaving the door opened a crack, enough to see when Bauer walked past, heading down to the lower decks to dismiss the crew. She looked at her phone for the time. It was 10:51. She had nine minutes.

She took her shoes off and carried them in her free hand, making her way quickly back to the sun deck and Bauer's. At the wall safe, she plugged her earbuds into her ears so that no one else could hear.

"Henry—we're at the wall safe. The one you mentioned earlier. What do we do?"

"Press your phone, microphone side first, against the vault door approximately four inches to the left of the tumblers."

"Got it."

"Now turn the lower wheel three full rotations clockwise."

"Done."

"Now, continuing to turn the wheel clockwise, move the scale as slowly as possible until I say stop. Keep going. Keep—stop."

"Now what?"

"Repeat the procedure for the lower wheel. Keep going. Keep going. Stop."

"This is nerve-wracking. What next?"

"Turn the lower wheel counterclockwise one full rotation, and when you reach the mark again, turn the wheel as slowly as possible until I say stop. Keep going. Keep going. Keep going. Stop."

After arriving at five numbers for each of the two tumbler dials, Henry told her she could throw the spoked handwheel in a clockwise direction to open the safe.

She was reaching up to remove the earbuds from her ears when someone standing behind her grabbed her by the wrists, pulled her hard away from the safe, and threw her down to the floor. When she looked up, Vito was standing over her, and Udo Bauer was next to him.

32.

December 23

"You're on foot," Dani said.

"Funny story," Tommy said.

Dani buzzed them in at the gate, and a few minutes later they were debriefing her in front of the fire and warming themselves. Reese went out of his way to make sure Dani understood that he was okay and never in danger. She sent the names and addresses from Tommy's thumb drive to Ed Stanley and to the members of the Curatoriat with instructions to locate the individuals listed but, for now, simply to maintain surveillance from a distance.

When they were alone, Tommy told Dani they needed to talk.

"I am so sorry," he said to her. "I don't ever want that to happen again. I couldn't stand thinking that if something happened to me, and I didn't see you again, our last moment together would have been one where we hadn't resolved anything. We should have talked it through. You felt like I wasn't listening to you, or that I wasn't respecting your opinion, and you had every reason to think that, even though nothing could be further from the truth."

"I'm sorry too," Dani said, taking a deep breath. "I was being pretty inflexible. I don't know if you know this about me, but I can be stubborn as a mule."

"I'm the one who's been an ass," Tommy said. "But seriously. We got lucky. You were right. That could have gone wrong in a thousand ways."

"You were right too," Dani said. "I feel the same way—I never want to leave things unsaid like that."

"It scared me," Tommy said. "Maybe more than anything else going on around here."

"I get it," Dani said. "But you know, conflict is a given. My dad had a saying: 'If two people agree all the time, one of them is unnecessary.'"

"I like that," Tommy said. "My dad thought so too. Of course, that one didn't turn out so good."

He'd discovered that his mother was having an affair—it was the formative event that made him want to someday, after his sports career was over, become a private detective, in the belief or hope that he'd never be fooled again.

"I'll forgive you if you forgive me," Dani said. Tommy took her in his arms and was about to kiss her. He had his hand in his pants pocket, his fingers closing around the engagement ring, which he'd sensibly removed from the crumbled blueberry muffin and restored to its original luster inside the jewelry box, when he heard what he thought was thunder. Then the thunder grew louder. He looked up in the sky and saw lights and then the vague outline of a black helicopter landing on his lawn.

"Oh, for Pete's sake," he said, releasing the jewelry box.

The helicopter was one of the larger models, the kind used as *Marine 1*, the helicopter the president flew in. A side door opened, and Ed Stanley stepped out onto the wet ground, ducking and holding his hat with one hand to keep it from blowing away as the rotors on the massive aircraft continued to turn. As Ed walked quickly to the house, Tommy's motion detectors turned on the floodlights. He held the mudroom door open for the older man, who stepped lightly over the threshold and took his hat off to shake the rain from it.

"I hope you don't mind a surprise visit," Ed said, smiling warmly. "I would have called, but I'm not sure how secure your phones are."

"Would you like a cup of coffee?" Tommy said as Otto gave the man a once-over with his nose, wagging his tail in approval. Arlo ignored the visitor, which Tommy had come to understand was Arlo's way of showing approval.

"No, no thanks," Stanley said.

"You're sure?" Dani said.

"Yes, yes. So listen, I got the names you sent me," he said to Dani. "Great work. We're running them now."

"That was fast," Dani said. "I didn't expect such quick results."

"I was already in the area," Stanley said. "We're up and running on the other list you gave me too. Actually, I thought you might be interested in joining me." He gestured over his shoulder toward the helicopter.

"For a ride?" Tommy asked.

"Just a little one. I've set up a meeting." Stanley looked at his watch. "I can get you back here in an hour. Do you mind? It's important." He held out his arm, extended toward the back door.

Tommy looked at Dani, who nodded.

"I'll get your coat," he said.

In the helicopter, Stanley brought them up to date. His people had continued surveillance on St. Adrian's from the air, and they'd intercepted a handful of unsecured texts and voice messages. His technicians had been unable to breach the firewalls protecting the school's computer network so far, but according to the intelligence they had been able to gather and analyze, something was indeed planned for Christmas Eve.

"We've also learned that the gathering at St. Adrian's is a reunion of sorts," Stanley said. "A fund-raiser, basically. Just like every other prep school has, only this one is a celebration of the 'New Millennium.'"

"What do you think that means?" Tommy asked. He and Dani had discussed the discovery Helen Trumble had made, that the *Vademecum* had been consecrated within a thousand-year design that apparently applied to both sides of the question. He was following Dani's lead, letting her disclose what she thought Ed Stanley needed to know.

"We're not sure," Stanley said. "I was hoping you could tell me."

"It's not that complicated," Dani said. "It's been a thousand years since the Druids first sailed from England. We can't be as precise as we'd like to be, but we know the first millennium is coming to a close."

As the helicopter descended, Tommy saw the terminal for Westchester County Airport, and then a building marked Duncan Aviation and another home to Panorama Flight Services. They flew low over a row of private jets and touched down at the southwest corner of the airfield, where a large motor home with darkly tinted windows was parked. They exited the helicopter and crossed to the RV. The rain was falling again, dappling the broad shallow puddles on the tarmac.

In the RV, Dani and Tommy were introduced to four men, a diminutive Russian named Konstantin, a young smiling Chinese man named Guangli, a frail-looking Frenchman named Lucien, and an overweight Egyptian named Abd-al-Rashid. Last names were not offered. Tommy thought it unlikely that even the first names were genuine.

"I'll be brief, because time is limited," Ed Stanley said. "Gentlemen, Dani—we have been given Code 1A clearance. Dani, Tommy, as outsiders, I know you're new to this sort of thing, and you probably need an explanation. The five of us here represent five different zones in the world. We all have people under us who work as operatives. Code 1A simply means that any . . ." He searched for the word. "Any *rules* that may or may not be broken as we pursue our different tasks will not be prosecuted by our respective governments. I should probably add that politically, some of us at this table are not necessarily allies or even friends. But as Konstantin was telling me—maybe I should let him speak for himself. Konstantin?"

"The devil is everybody's enemy," the Russian said. "So we will join forces to defeat him. And later, business as usual."

"Dajjal," the Egyptian said, "will not prevail. He cannot be allowed to gain footing in this world. This, we all agree on."

"We've divided the list of the names you gave us," Ed Stanley continued, winding the stem on his wristwatch. "Our friends here each have four, and I have five. We are grateful to you. You have done a great thing. Does anybody have any questions?"

"What did the angels look like?" Lucien asked. "I've wanted to see one my entire life."

"Too beautiful for words," Tommy said. "It almost hurt to look at them directly. Sort of like looking at the sun."

"Can you make contact with them?" the Frenchman asked.

"We don't make contact with them," Tommy said. "They contact us. They bring us messages."

The table fell silent.

"I have a question," Dani said. "What will you do with the boys when you capture them? What will happen to them?"

Ed Stanley and the others exchanged glances.

"Dani, you have to understand something," Stanley said. "Our goal is to stop them. That's absolute. We'll try to take them without a struggle if we can, but we have to assume they're no different from the suicide bombers we've been dealing with in Iraq and Afghanistan. If someone is intent on destroying the whole world and themselves with it, you can't quite walk up to them and say, 'You're under arrest.' Do you understand that?"

"I do," Dani said, but Tommy could tell she was very uncomfortable with the rules of engagement Stanley was laying out. Shoot on sight. He didn't like it much either but . . .

"This is our business. We're professionals, and we're good at what we do. The priority can't vary," Stanley said. "We can't leave it up to individual operatives to make judgment calls on a case-by-case basis, subjectively. That's not what we teach. One crack in the collective resolve can compromise the entire mission. Do you understand?"

"I understand," Dani said. "I don't like it, but I understand."

"Good," Stanley said. "Then let's get you back home."

"Before you take us home," Dani said, "I need to know why you're lying."

"What do you mean?" Ed Stanley said, incredulous.

"I know you're lying," Dani said. "That's what I do. That's my business, and I'm good at it. I evaluate people. And I know you're lying."

"You know that," Stanley said. "If this is some sort of women's intuition thing—"

"Stop right there," Dani said sharply. "So far I've been respectful of you because you're my grandfather's friend and because of what you've accomplished. If you're not prepared to be respectful of us, we're done. You'll get no further cooperation from us."

Tommy knew he had to back Dani's play, even though he wasn't sure what they were going to do without Stanley's help. "Should I call a cab?" he asked her.

"Wait," Stanley said. "Wait."

"We're waiting," Dani said.

"Just what is it you think I'm lying about?" Stanley asked.

"Peter Guryakin," Dani said. "You came to us with a story about how he'd been part of a Soviet biological warfare program, until he lost favor at the Kremlin. You said he'd dropped out of sight, and that you were looking for him, and you came to us because you wanted to know what he was doing visiting his alma mater."

"All that's true," Stanley said.

"I'm sure it is," Dani said. "That's what the most accomplished liars do. They tell you just enough of the truth to satisfy you, hoping you won't keep looking for the rest of the truth. What's the rest of it?"

Stanley didn't answer.

"Why don't you call the cab?" Dani said to Tommy. "This is a waste of time."

"Wait," Ed Stanley said. He turned to the Russian. "Konstantin, I don't suppose you need to run to the snack bar for a few minutes?"

"I had a Snickers," he said, holding his ground.

"Well," Stanley said, "you would have found out soon enough anyway." He turned to Dani again. "You've heard of DARPA?"

"I have," she said. "Though I'm not sure what it stands for. Defense . . ."

"Defense Advanced Research Program Agency," Tommy said.

"Project," Stanley corrected him. "Not program. But yes. It's the agency responsible for all defense-related research."

"Guryakin didn't disappear after he lost favor with the Kremlin." Dani suddenly realized. "He worked for you. For DARPA."

"Yes," Ed Stanley said.

"Doing what?"

"A number of things, actually," Stanley said.

"Such as?"

"Let me guess," Tommy said. "He developed Provivilan, as a weapon. For the US government."

"No," Stanley said. "Not exactly. When we brought him in, after we'd had a chance to debrief him, we had him working on antidotes for some of the things the Russians were doing. Antidotes and immunological pro-phylactics. If we were going to send our soldiers into an area that had been contaminated with a nerve agent or a biological toxin, we needed to protect them. Gas masks and Hazmat suits aren't the answer. They weren't the answer during World War I, and they certainly aren't the answer now. The answer now is immunization. And biological resistance."

"But what?" Dani said. "Something went wrong."

"Something went quite wrong," Stanley said.

The Russian sneered.

"Somebody stole the work Peter Guryakin was doing. Someone who was working with him."

"Who?"

"His son," Tommy said, before Stanley had a chance. "He brought his kid in, and his kid stole it."

The Frenchman appeared perplexed, so Tommy explained it to him.

"St. Adrian's is known as a place where world leaders can very safely and discreetly send their sons to be educated," Tommy said. "Has been for generations. Apparently what nobody figured out is that they teach the sons to spy on the fathers."

"Andrei stole his father's work and brought it to Linz," Stanley said. "We have people inside Linz. We've been keeping an eye on them."

"So why weren't your people able to stop them?" Tommy asked.

"I bet I can answer that," Dani said. "They didn't have anybody who could get close enough to Andrei Guryakin. They needed somebody Andrei could trust. So they sent the father in after the son. The father would have been the only person the boy thought he could count on not to betray him."

The big Russian leaned back in his chair and folded his arms across his chest.

"That's not exactly what happened," Ed Stanley said. "But close enough."

"So where is Peter Guryakin?" Dani asked.

"He's dead," Stanley said. "We found his body two days ago in a motel outside of Las Vegas. It was made to look like a suicide. But it wasn't."

Tommy looked at Dani to see if she was satisfied.

"Why do I think there's more?" she asked.

"Because there is more," Stanley said. "As I said already, your grandfather told me no one could fool you. I'll tell him he was right the next time I see him."

"He's going to be at my sister's for Christmas," Dani said. "Maybe you'll get the chance. What's the rest of the story?"

"The program Peter Guryakin was with, or rather, the project he was working on, started out at Defense Sciences Office but was moved over to the Strategic Technology Office. Do you know the difference?"

"The distinction is one the Americans like to make, to convince themselves they're not as bad as everyone else," the Russian said. "Defense means defensive. Strategic means offensive. The Americans like to believe they only kill people when it's necessary to protect the rest of the world."

"Konstantin is entitled to his opinion," Ed Stanley said. "But what he's saying is essentially correct. What began as a biological defense program developed into a strategic—an offensive program. Something that wouldn't just protect our soldiers but actually enhance their performance."

"The super-soldier pill," Guangli said. "We heard you were working on that."

"That isn't what we call it," Stanley said. "But essentially, yes. The compound Peter Guryakin was originally tasked to develop had the effect of both suppressing a soldier's response to nerve agents and stimulating the chromaffin cells of the adrenal medulla."

"He genetically engineered the virus that manufactures the drug," Dani guessed.

Stanley nodded.

"Creating a soldier hyped up on adrenaline who doesn't feel anything," she said. "And I'm assuming by that, you mean he won't feel empathy for his enemies. He'll be merciless."

"That's always been the toughest part of fighting a war," Tommy said. "Trying to convince your own people the enemy isn't human. Usually it takes years of propaganda. Now it comes in a pill."

"There are two versions of the drug," Stanley said. "There's the blue version, which you've discovered. That's the one that takes years to have any effect. And then there's the red version. Which has a more rapid effect."

"Instant homicidal insanity," Tommy said. "Accompanied by feats of superhuman strength."

"The program was discontinued," Ed Stanley said. "We tried a variety of dosages, but we learned we couldn't control the results. Or perhaps *contain* is a better word."

"But Peter Guryakin gave the red version to his son," Dani said.

"Not voluntarily," Ed Stanley said. "But yes. We think that may be what happened. Somebody figured out he was still working for us."

"And the red version is what they're dumping in the water," Dani said.

"Now do you understand why this was given Code 1A clearance?" Ed Stanley said.

"I have one last question," Dani said. "The red version—how long does it take to wear off?"

"Well, you see, that's the problem. It doesn't, really," Stanley said. "As long as the virus is alive, it produces the drug. In theory, the body's immune system would eventually kill the virus, perhaps in a week or two. But the drug proved to be thanatogenic before we could reach that stage."

"Thanatogenic?" Tommy said.

"It means death-producing," Dani said. "The government likes to use elevated diction to palliate words that make people uncomfortable. The drug was fatal."

"Yes," Stanley said.

"But it wasn't the drug itself that killed anybody."

"No."

"You tested it on people, didn't you?"

"Yes."

"And the people you tested it on either killed somebody, or they had to be killed to stop them."

Ed Stanley didn't have an answer.

"One other thing—you erased my medical examiner's files, didn't you? You knew we were getting too close. You've been monitoring us, and you deleted his files. And then you had someone follow me to see where I was going."

"Yes," Stanley said.

"Can we get that ride home now?" Tommy said.

In the helicopter, he had a question for Dani. "How did you know?"

"That he was lying?"

"Yeah," Tommy said. "I mean, I know you've been trained and all that, but how did you know? He seemed pretty convincing to me."

"I wish I had a fancier explanation," Dani said. "I told you my grandfather Howard used to be a judge, didn't I?"

"You did."

"He spent his whole life listening to testimony and figuring out when he thought people were lying."

"So he taught you?"

"Sort of. He plays poker with Ed Stanley. He said every time Stanley bluffs he starts to wind the stem on his wristwatch. He doesn't even know he's doing that. I was wondering about the story he told us about Guryakin, but I didn't know for sure until I saw him do that."

"Remind me not to play poker with your grandfather," Tommy said.

33.

December 23

Quinn was in his office on the Linz campus in Wilton, working late. He was waiting for the other buildings to empty, and in particular, Building C.

The first thing he did after logging in at his office was use the modified thumb drive containing the "mirror program" his friend at Anonymous had sent him the night before to find out who was monitoring his activity. He was not surprised to learn that Andrei Guryakin himself was his watcher. The mirror program worked beautifully, pinging back to Quinn the passwords and access codes Guryakin had stored. A quick scan of the numbers told Quinn what he wanted to know. Guryakin changed his passwords once a week, a standard security procedure, but he did so every Monday morning, usually between seven and eight. It meant that the passwords Quinn had accessed, sixteen in all, were still likely to work.

He spent the day answering e-mails, taking calls, and dealing with the pain in his head. It was getting worse, clearly. He wanted to "look busy," in the likelihood that Guryakin was monitoring him. At the same time, Quinn monitored Guryakin's activities, including his backlogs for the last month. By midmorning Quinn knew that Guryakin arrived every day before dawn, at five o'clock, and often worked until midnight.

He also learned that while Guryakin's on-campus movements were unpredictable, one off-campus activity was quite predictable. According to his corporate credit card activity, Guryakin spent every Wednesday evening at a motel outside of Bridgeport, after which his card was billed $129 for the room and $500.00 for something called Western Connecticut Entertainment Services. It was the only day of the week that Guryakin left work at the normal time, according to the gate logs. Using his GPhone, Quinn sent a text to Detective Casey, asking him if he could find out what Western Connecticut Entertainment Services was. A few minutes later Casey got back to him.

ESCORT SERVICE. BUSTED FOR PROSTITUTION 3 TIMES IN LAST 12 MO. CAUTION ADVISED.

By four o'clock the pounding in Quinn's head was more than he could bear. Perhaps it was because he'd been focusing on the computer screen all day. He had access to more powerful painkillers, but he was worried that anything strong enough to numb the pain would hinder his lucidity, so he took three ibuprofen—which was like trying to put out a volcano with a cup of tap water. He turned off the lights and lay down on the floor with his head under his desk, wrapping his scarf around his head to cover his eyes and block the light. At six thirty he felt better. He couldn't be certain if he'd fallen asleep or blacked out.

He logged off the system and left his office. He drove his rental car out of the garage, using his flash drive to open the automated gate. If Guryakin was still monitoring him, it would appear that he'd gone home for the evening. He parked in a wooded area down the street, crossed back over the road, and cut across campus on foot, pulling his hat down low over his eyes and staying out of the light so no surveillance cameras could pick him up. Turning his coat collar up, keeping his head down, he entered Building C.

There was a uniformed guard at the security desk.

"Illena Nemkova," Quinn said.

The guard frowned. "She doesn't work here anymore."

"You're quite right. Dr. Guryakin wanted me to look at her files. He said if I had any trouble getting access that you should call him," Quinn said with a pleasant smile.

The guard held up a finger, telling Quinn to wait, then made two phone calls, the first probably to Guryakin's office and the second to his cell phone. As Quinn suspected, both calls went to voice mail, Guryakin no doubt unwilling to be interrupted in the middle of a transaction with Western Connecticut Entertainment Services.

The guard eyed Quinn suspiciously.

"I've got the pass code," Quinn added, holding up his thumb drive.

"All yours," the guard said.

On the elevator Quinn used his GPhone to dial the number for the campus's central switchboard and asked to speak to reception in Building C. He waited for the guard to answer and then, knowing the guard was distracted, plugged his debugged flash drive into the USB port and used the ninth of Guryakin's sixteen passcodes to take the elevator to the basement.

Just as the elevator reached the bottom, Quinn felt a sudden, sharp pain in the back of his skull that nearly dropped him to his knees. He pressed the button to keep the doors closed and waited for the attack to subside, praying that the pain wouldn't cause him to black out or have a seizure.

For a moment he considered waiting for a better time. But there might not be a better time.

The pain abated, changing from agonizing to merely unbearable. He lifted his finger from the button, and the elevator doors opened.

He stepped out and into a small glassed-in, dimly lit lobby. There was a caution sign on the far wall.

WARNING

AUTHORIZED PERSONNEL ONLY BEYOND THIS AREA.

BIOSAFETY LEVEL 4

He moved a chair to block the elevator doors to keep them from closing, then crossed quickly to an access control station near the lab entrance,
where he encountered another USB port. He plugged his thumb drive in
again, grateful that there wasn't a retina scan or voice recognition lock to
get past.

Once the doors opened, he removed his thumb drive and entered a
locker room, where researchers and technicians could change into surgical scrubs. He moved forward through a double airlock and entered
a work area with a half dozen desks and computer stations, all of them
unoccupied. Nothing here was of interest to him. He crossed the room
quickly to another door with another Access Restricted sign molded to
it. When he used the thumb drive to enter, he found a second set of air
locks, and beyond that, a room filled with pressure suits for entering the
lab properly.

He donned a suit, attached the temporary oxygen bottle (noting he
had fifteen minutes of breathable air), then stepped into the ultraviolet
room. There he activated a bank of decontamination lights on a timer. If
he had been concerned about bringing microbes into the lab, he would
have raised his arms and rotated, but he saw no need to bother. Instead, he
waited. The ultraviolet lights shut off after a minute, and he moved into a
chemical decontamination room. Nozzles on the wall there showered him
with bleach, then blasted him with jets of hot air to dry him off. He'd once
heard a BSL4 technician call the process "going through the car wash." The
term seemed completely apropos.

Finally the doors opened to the BSL4 lab itself.

Quinn detached the portable oxygen bottle and attached his pressure
suit to the lab's air supply via a yellow oxygen tube coiling down from
the ceiling. He had to stop again, his head throbbing anew. This time he
needed to brace himself against a centrifuge to keep from falling. He closed
his eyes, and when he opened them again, objects seemed to be swimming and floating. He squeezed his eyes and slowed his breathing. The

throbbing lessened, and when he opened his eyes after a moment, he was able to focus. He had to hurry because he knew he was running out of time, in every sense of the word.

At the far end of the room Quinn saw a glass wall, and beyond it an octopus-like array of surgical arms similar to the surgical robot "DaVinci" that he'd briefly trained on in medical school. Beyond the robot he saw, through a glass door, a rack of test tubes inside an industrial freezer unit. The Doomsday Molecule. It had to be.

He went to the robot's operation console and turned it on. A message window on the LCD screen asked him to insert his thumb drive. When he did, the screen flashed the words ACCESS DENIED.

He tried manually entering one of Guryakin's access codes, then another. He tried again and again, until he'd entered all sixteen.

ACCESS DENIED

Quinn took a deep breath. He wondered, *What would Tommy do if he were here?* He'd probably just throw something through the window, Quinn thought, and then laughed as he realized that was actually a very good idea.

The heaviest thing he could find was a tank containing liquid bleach under pressure, to be used in emergencies when immediate localized decontamination was required. He lifted the tank over his shoulder, aimed the blunt end at the glass, and rammed the window as hard as he could.

A crack appeared in the Plexiglas, and simultaneously a piercing alarm sounded.

He had perhaps a minute. Maybe less. Company was on the way.

He rammed the glass again. The second blow cracked it even further, and the third blow brought it crashing down. Tommy would have escaped unscathed somehow, but Quinn wasn't Tommy, and he wasn't able to get out of the way of the glass fast enough to avoid a shard that ripped into his suit and pierced his thigh.

It hurt, but it didn't matter.

He pulled the shard of glass from his leg, cast it aside, ignored the bleeding, and climbed through the broken window, then used the tank again to break the glass door to the freezer. He removed the rack of test tubes, emptied the contents of each onto a sterile tray, set the tray on the floor, and was about to hit it with the bleach when he stopped. He had to be sure that this was the Doomsday Molecule.

He took the tray back through the broken window. The alarms made his head throb. He found an electron microscope and quickly prepared a slide, ripping off his gloves because they made his movements clumsy and time-consuming.

The virus he saw most closely resembled the rotavirus, looking a bit like a dimpled golf ball with hairs, except that the hairs were moving. It was an ugly thing, and it was alive.

He took the sample and the tray, placed both in a sink, and then emptied the bleach tank into the sink. When he finished, he made another slide and inserted it into the microscope. This time, the golf ball had collapsed like a month-old jack-o'-lantern, and the filaments that had been motile before were still.

It was dead.

Quinn smiled. He'd killed it. The Doomsday Molecule was dead.

He stepped back and noticed that his right shoe had filled with some sort of liquid that made a squishing sound when he walked. The bleach, probably. He ripped the pressure suit off and saw that the bleach was red. Not bleach. Blood.

He took a moment to collect his thoughts, then sent Dani a text: VIRUS LOCATED AND DESTROYED.

He stumbled out of the BSL4 lab, back the way he came. Back through the car wash. He made it as far as the locker room before he had to stop, his head pounding.

He leaned against the wall to brace himself, and instead slid to the floor.

Well, this certainly isn't good, Quinn thought. *You appear to be dying. You've got to tell Dani and Tommy what you've learned. Think!*

He found his phone and dialed 911. When the dispatcher answered, he gave her his name and location and said he'd accidentally stabbed himself in the leg with a piece of glass.

"Yes," he repeated. "Linz Pharmazeutika campus in Wilton. Building C. Yes. It's the first building on your right after the gate. I will do my best to meet you in the lobby."

He struggled to his feet and kept going, realizing that now he was only seeing out of his left eye and had no depth perception. All he could do was keep going for as long as he had the power to move. The vision in his left eye was getting dimmer.

At the elevator, he kicked the chair aside and allowed the elevator doors to close, pressing a button marked G. When it reached the ground floor, he kept the elevator doors closed by pressing the button to override the automatic opening. He tried to think. He heard someone pounding on the doors. His head throbbed. More pounding. He saw the tip of a crowbar trying to pry the elevator doors apart, but he kept his thumb on the button. He waited as long as he could. *Just keep moving. One foot in front of the other, for as long as you can.*

He allowed the doors to open.

"Put your hands in the air!" someone shouted. It was the security guard, and he was aiming his weapon at a spot between Quinn's eyes.

"What's all the excitement?" Quinn asked. He realized three other security guards had their guns drawn and pointed at him. "I'm unarmed."

"Shoot him," a voice said. He recognized the voice as Guryakin's.

Then someone shouted, "Wait!"

When Quinn looked up, he saw the lights of an ambulance flashing in front of the building and a pair of EMTs pounding on the door.

He turned to Guryakin.

"Checkmate," he said.

Then the pain in his head increased, and the room started to spin and whirl.

Quinn's legs gave way as everything went black, and he felt himself falling.

34.

December 23

Cassandra looked out the window of the stateroom. The door was locked. Had she been locked in her own stateroom, she might have made her way down from the balcony, but here, her only escape option was through a twelve-inch porthole. And supposing she made it through that, there was nothing but a fifty-foot drop to the sea. In the distance she saw the tender carrying the crew. Bauer had sent them away as she'd asked, even though she was pretty sure he'd changed his mind regarding his romantic plans for the evening. If nothing else, it seemed apparent now that he didn't want witnesses.

Worse, he'd taken her phone and thrown it overboard, leaving her without Henry's wise counsel or any way to call or signal for help.

She searched the drawers of the room, the closets, the bathroom, looking for anything she might use to defend herself, signal for help, or aid in escape. With a match or a candle, a can of hairspray could be turned into a makeshift flamethrower, or at least that's how it worked in one of the movies she'd made. There was nothing, not even a lamp she could pull the wiring from and strip away the insulation from the ends to fashion a crude Taser to electrocute the first person to walk through the door. That had worked in a different movie. In the movies she was good at playing the resourceful damsel in distress. In real life, it wasn't so easy.

It suddenly occurred to her that a piece of glass could be fashioned into a knife with an edge sharp enough to cut someone's throat. She hadn't done that in a movie—that one, she thought up all on her own.

The glass in the porthole was too thick to break, but there was a mirror in the bathroom. She was glad she'd decided to wear her Jimmy Choos instead of flats—the heel was the only thing she could find hard enough to break the mirror.

She had the shoe in her hand and was about to strike the mirror with her shoe when the intercom by the door beeped, and she heard a voice.

"Cassandra, this is Udo. You don't have to press any buttons. Just speak and I'll hear you."

"What do you want?" she asked.

"Only to say good-bye," Bauer said. "I had thought I would have you taken off the boat at the next port of call and put in jail for trying to steal from me, but Vito has convinced me that at this point in the campaign, we can't afford the publicity that would bring. Apparently I've misjudged you. It's sad, because for a while I was even considering sharing my wealth with you. You didn't have to steal it. You could have had anything you could ever possibly have wanted. I don't know who put you up to this, and I don't really care. At any rate, Vito's going to handle it."

"Handle it?" Cassandra said. "You think—you don't know! You're not in on it!"

"What is it that I don't know?"

"You don't know what that drug is going to do. You think all it's going to do is make you rich. You've been duped. Just like every other stooge they've duped for the last thousand years."

"I haven't the slightest idea what you're talking about," Bauer said. "Nor am I interested in finding out. Vito will handle it."

"He's going to kill me—you understand that, don't you?"

There was a long pause.

"Well, yes, I suppose he will," Bauer said. "The captain of a ship is an absolute ruler, both judge and jury. I've made my decision. What the people who work for me do is not my concern, as long as they help me attain my goals."

"He doesn't work for you," Cassandra said. "You work for him. And you don't even know it."

But the intercom was dead.

She returned to the bathroom and closed the door behind her, then covered the mirror with a towel to avoid being stabbed by any flying pieces. She struck the mirror once. Nothing happened. She struck it again and the mirror shattered, several large pieces clattering loudly to the tiled floor. She lowered the towel carefully, catching several long shards in it. One was perfect for her needs, about twelve inches long and two inches wide, with a sharp point at one end. She wrapped the wide end in a washcloth to give it a grip that wouldn't cut her.

She heard footsteps in the hall and moved to the door, turning the lights off to give her as much advantage as possible. When she heard a key turning in the lock, she pressed her back against the wall next to the door and raised the piece of mirror in her right hand, high above her head. She held her breath. She calculated that the mirror might break if she rammed it against the skull, and decided that her best shot would be to plunge it into Vito's eye and hope she could push it in far enough to dice his brain.

The door opened.

Someone said, "Cass?"

She brought the glass shard down with all her might—then stopped herself just in time.

"Laurent?"

"There you are," he said. "Come on. I've got a boat waiting."

"What happened to your accent?"

"Don't worry—they taught me a bunch of different accents at Langley."

"You're CIA?"

He held out his hand to her. "Matthew Shorter," he said.

She shook his hand.

"We'll have plenty of time to get to know each other on the Zodiac. This way. Leave your shoes. High heels and inflatables don't go together."

He stuck his head out into the corridor to make sure no one was coming, then beckoned to her to follow. They were amidships, headed aft, when she stopped.

"What's wrong?"

"We can't go," she said.

"What?"

"There's something in his safe."

"We can't open his safe," Shorter said. "I tried. You tried—"

"We don't have to open it," Cassandra said. "I just have to make sure nobody ever sees what's in it."

"Cass . . ."

"You can go without me if you want," she said.

He looked at her, pleading. "Just so you know, I'm not armed," he said. "They are."

"We don't have to be armed," she said. "Are you coming?"

"I'll give you five minutes," he said. "Then we're leaving."

She led him down a gangway, having memorized the way when Bauer gave her the initial tour. At the bottom of the stairs, they turned to starboard until she came to the door to the galley.

"This is no time to be thinking of snacks," he said.

"Look in there," she told him, pointing. "I need a potato."

She climbed up on top of an eight-burner range.

"What?"

"Just do it. Get me a potato. A big one."

She reached behind the range as far as she could until she found what she was looking for, a rubber hose about an inch in diameter, leading from the stove to the propane supply.

But her arm was too short to grab hold of it. She looked for something to hook it with, a ladle perhaps, or a set of tongs. Her gaze fell on the kitchen knives. During the tour, Bauer boasted to her that his chefs used only the sharpest knives, made by a German company, Wusthof, that had once made the finest military swords and bayonets.

Cassandra grabbed the one with the longest blade, a serrated bread knife, and returned to the stove. She blew out the pilot lights first, then reached behind the stove and used the knife to saw through the hose. After a moment of sawing, she heard a hissing sound. She kept sawing until the hose was severed.

"All I could find was a sweet potato," the CIA agent said when he returned. "What do I smell?"

"Propane," Cassandra said, taking the sweet potato from him and placing it in the microwave next to the stove. She set the timer for twenty minutes.

"That's more time than we need," she told her new friend. "For the first eight minutes or so, it's going to cook." She closed all the doors to the galley. "Then it's going to catch fire and ignite. The propane tank on a ship this size has got to be at least five hundred pounds. A ten-pound tank is big enough to blow up a house."

"How do you know this stuff?"

"I grew up on boats," she said. "My mom dated a guy who made a living blowing up people's boats for the insurance money and making it look like an accident. Let's go."

They moved quickly to the fantail and the helicopter landing pad. She was at the top of the spiral staircase leading down to the inflatable Zodiac, the CIA man halfway down ahead of her, when she heard footsteps behind her. She turned.

"Where do you think you're going?" Vito said.

"I have no—" she began.

Someone grabbed her forcefully from behind, pulling her by the hair with one hand and closing the other around her throat.

"I've got her!" Matthew Shorter said, but now he was using his French accent again. "Mr. Bauer thought she'd try to make a run for the boat and sent me here to wait. Go get him. Quickly!"

"But—" Vito said, confused.

"Go get him!" Laurent said, yanking hard on Cassandra's hair. "I'm sure he'll want to do this one himself. If I don't do her first. Go!"

The first mate ran to find Bauer.

"Sorry about the hair," Shorter said, releasing Cassandra. "I had to make it look real. You okay?"

"I'm fine," she said, following him down the stairs.

She raced down the staircase to the boat platform. Next to the Zodiac, a pair of Jet Skis hung from davits. Shorter told her to move to the bow, then loaded a pair of red five-gallon gas tanks into the Zodiac behind her. He untied the inflatable from the docking cleat and pushed off.

He let the Zodiac drift free and then started the sixty-horse outboard motor. He revved the throttle and sped away from the ship, glancing over his shoulder as he tried to put as much distance as possible between them and the ship before the propane ignited. "Minorca might be closer, but Sardinia will be easier to find," he shouted above the engine noise. "Just stay low and try—"

Suddenly, a surprised expression came over his face as he sat up straight, then fell to one side and out of the boat. In an instant he was gone, but Cass realized he'd been shot only when the next bullet ricocheted off the motor and pierced one of the flotation compartments on the port side of the Zodiac, deflating it with a hiss. She looked up and saw Bauer, his face contorted in fury, shooting at her from the fantail with Vito next to him. She lunged and reached for the throttle, turning the motor as far as it would go as a second shot missed. The third shot deflated another flotation chamber at the bow; the rubberized fabric flapped as the air escaped. The Zodiac began to take on water, riding forward but slower now, half submerged and foundering.

As she reached for a life preserver, she turned to see Bauer taking aim again. She was well within range of the rifle. There was nothing she could do but wave. He lowered the gun and waved good-bye. Then he took aim once more.

All at once, a colossal explosion rocked the night, a ball of flame lighting the sea as it burst from amidships. The *Freiheit* split into two separate pieces. Cassandra watched, but only long enough to see an oil slick spreading toward her, the oil on fire, about to engulf her.

She took a deep breath and dived from the Zodiac before the flames could reach her. The five-gallon gas cans from the raft detonated as she swam below the surface. She stayed under the water and swam as far as she could, and then farther, her lungs aching, until she had to surface . . . but then she swam still farther before bursting to the surface to gasp for breath.

The flames were behind her. She turned in time to see the last of the *Freiheit* disappearing into the depths.

Silence and darkness returned. Treading water, she looked around but saw nothing to hang on to, no sign of the life preserver that had been almost within her grasp. She swam toward where the ship had been, hoping to find some bit of floating debris big enough to support her. She was, by her best estimate, about a hundred miles from land.

It also occurred to her, as she stilled her thoughts and breathed deeply beneath the Mediterranean night sky and had time to thoroughly assess the situation, that there was also a great white shark somewhere in the vicinity.

What would Tommy do? she thought, and immediately knew the answer. He would pray.

"Lord," she said out loud, "I hope you don't mind if I go off the script. Usually I have people writing things for me to say, but just now I'm at a loss for words. But you've helped me turn my life around in so many other ways. So if you could just give me a little help here, I'll figure out how to repay you."

She swam, alone in the night, in the middle of the sea. She turned 360 degrees, her eyes getting used to the deep but somehow peaceful darkness.

Suddenly she saw something floating and swam to it. She would have been grateful for a piece of wood or a garbage bag she could inflate, but God had done her one better.

It was one of the Jet Skis.

35.

December 24

Two hundred miles east-northeast of Moscow, outside the town of Ostashkov in the Tver administrative district, two men waited in a white 2004 Lada Laika 210S, a boxy sedan of little distinction, remarkable only for the tinted windows, an after-market addition. Down the street, a large woman wearing a heavy wool coat and a fox-fur hat pushed a collapsible shopping cart full of food, her laden breath forming clouds ahead of her as she made her way home in the cold. The two men were parked where they could keep watch on a modest dacha owned by a minor Communist party member just down the road from the Monastery of the Sign and the Cloister at Zhitnyi. One of the two men carried, in a kit inside his coat pocket, a syringe containing propofol, a powerful, fast-acting sedative that had earned the nickname "milk of amnesia" for its hypnotic properties. The other man had served in Afghanistan as a sniper during the years the Soviet Union had attempted to occupy and subdue that beleaguered country; he carried a rifle loaded with a tranquilizer dart containing the same sedative, at a dosage strong enough to stop a charging grizzly bear. One of the men was in his early twenties, and the other was approaching fifty. Both men were also armed with more conventional weapons.

In that area of the Tver Oblast, Lakes Sterzh, Vselug, Peno, and Volga all drained into the Upper Volga Reservoir, above a dam built in 1843. The water contained pike, perch, and a bronze-colored species of bream unique to the region, making the town of Ostashkov a popular summer vacation spot. But now it was winter, and the Lada's heater was not enough to counter the temperature outside the car, a brisk nineteen degrees below zero. On a hill behind them, the two men in the car noted a squat concrete bunker, left over from the Second World War, and beside it a plaque commemorating the men who'd died fighting Adolf Hitler.

"He's moving," the younger man said, lowering his binoculars. The older man put the Lada in gear and followed the target, who was driving a black Volvo onto route P89, headed in the direction of the dam. The surfaces of the lakes and reservoirs in the region were frozen solid, but at the dam there was an overflow sluice where free water poured down the stoneworks into the Volga, and from there to the Moscow Sea, a 125-square-mile reservoir supplying potable drinking water to the Russian capital, Moscow.

Knowing the target's destination, the driver of the Lada stayed well back while his partner made a phone call to an accomplice waiting up ahead to tell him the target was approaching and to be ready.

The target, unaware he was being followed, patted the small box on the car seat next to him.

The target was a seventeen-year-old boy.

≈≈≈

During the entire twelve-hour, 300-mile bus ride from Lahore, Pakistan, to Uttarkashi, a town and district of the Garhwal division of the state of Uttarakhand on the border of India and Tibet, the boy in the front seat of the bus across the aisle from the driver only let go of the bag he was carrying once. This was at the border crossing, where he explained to the customs official that the box in his bag contained the ashes of his dead pet, and that he'd made a promise to the animal, a small dog named Yoshi, that he'd bring his ashes to the headwaters of the Ganges. The customs official could not understand why anyone would make such a fuss over a filthy dog, but the boy explained that he'd been living in the United States, where people felt about their dogs the way people in India felt about their cows.

The last two-thirds of the trip followed dirt roads that made everything in the bus rattle and shake as they climbed up into the foothills of the Himalayas. The boy saw girls carrying bales of clean laundry on the side of the road and old men driving donkeys pulling two-wheeled carts. Occasionally herds of goats or sheep blocked the road, and the driver explained that you could tell the difference because the tails of goats went up but the tails of sheep hung down, and sheep were too stupid to get out of the way of a moving vehicle. The boy might have been interested or amused if he were here as a tourist, but he was traveling to dump the contents of the box in his bag into the Bhagirathi River, which flowed out of the Gangotri Himanada, the glacier considered to be the true source of the sacred river of the Ganges, with 400 million people living in its basin.

When the bus finally stopped in the middle of the village, in the shadow of the Varun Parvat, beneath the shade of a large sacred fig tree, the boy stepped from the bus onto a surface of frozen mud. There was a light dusting of snow on the ground, making the village of sixteen thousand look cleaner than it was. The driver proclaimed loudly to the disembarking passengers that they should visit the Manikarnika Ghat, a set of steps leading down to the river where cleansing cremations were performed, named after the place where the god Shiva lost his earring while dancing.

The boy scoffed and headed off on foot to his assigned destination, a footbridge across the Bhagirathi made from rope and planks at the western end of village, where a bend in the river carried the water northward toward National Highway 34. At an elevation of 4,436 feet above sea level, the air was thin, and he was soon out of breath. He passed the Mahidanda headquarters, where a battalion of border police was stationed. He felt his spirits rising as he approached the completion of his task.

The boy did not notice that he was being followed by a man and a woman, both in their early forties. The two of them had boarded the bus with him in Lahore. Their mission, too, was approaching completion.

***

The Rio Tietê, or River of Truth, flowed down from the mountains in southern Brazil in the state of Sao Paolo, and reached a place only fourteen miles from the sea before being turned inland again by the Serra do Mar; then it meandered to the northwest until it ran into a reservoir formed by the Souza Dias Dam at a place called Três Lagoas in Mato Grosso do Sul. From there the water flowed nearly four hundred miles to the southeast and the city of Sao Paolo, with a population over twenty million. The artificial lake behind the Souza Dias Dam contained over eight hundred cubic miles of water.

In the parking area in front of the Hotel dos Gaúchos, in the center of Três Lagoas, a young man wearing only athletic shorts, running shoes, and a T-shirt—for here in the Southern Hemisphere it was approaching the dog days of summer—put a small cloth bag containing a wooden box in the basket behind the seat of his motor scooter, a Planet Blue Aprilia Sportcity 250, and headed for a place called Cachoeira de Menina, or Little Girl Falls. He'd been told he would find a small weir above the falls, with a gangway that would lead him to a place where he could pour the contents of his box into the River of Truth. He liked the sound of that, and the irony.

Behind him, keeping a discrete distance, was a second motorcyclist, a girl with beautiful long black hair, clad as well in shorts and a T-shirt, riding a more powerful Honda CVR 450R. The girl knew exactly how beautiful she was, and also knew exactly how to use her beauty to distract men—or in this case, a boy from St. Adrian's Academy. On the back of her motorcycle was a picnic basket containing sandwiches and chips and a thermos of ice-cold mango lemonade. Concealed beneath the sandwiches was a Glock 9 automatic pistol and a syringe loaded with propofol, as well as a pair of plastic flex-cuffs. The girl had trained from the age of six in the art of *krav maga*, a self-defense system taught by the Israeli Special Forces. As the child whose father was Mossad and whose mother worked for Shin Bet, and with six younger brothers, she knew how to take care of herself. She doubted she'd need to use the Glock. She doubted she'd need to use her beauty either, but she was glad she had both available. She'd been told the boy she was following might or might not be on a drug designed to stimulate adrenaline and amplify his hostility. She hoped he was because she looked forward to fighting him.

⸻⟞⟊⟌⸻

Standing on the balcony of the Spice Beach Hotel in the town of Bukoba, Tanzania, Qwesi was glad he'd brought his purple-and-red St. Adrian's sweatshirt with him because even though he was within a single degree of the equator, Bokuba's elevation above sea level meant the temperature at night had been dropping into the fifties. Down the street, a Pentecostal church was celebrating Christmas; the sound of familiar carols, played on African instruments and accompanied by African drums, drifted toward him through the darkening sky. A dozen small short-haired dogs with curling tails scavenged in the street below.

He stared across the array of thatched-palm beach umbrellas to the shape of Musira Island, the outline losing form as darkness descended on Lake Victoria. Below him, a boy who'd been fishing all afternoon for tilapia on the guano-covered rocks was finally calling it a day.

Qwesi sat on the edge of his bed and laced up a pair of hiking boots, then headed for his rented black Land Rover, parked in the shadows behind the hotel. There were no streetlamps or floodlights, and only a few dim bulbs burned in the nearby windows, making it so dark that it was difficult to find the keyhole to insert his key. He started the vehicle and followed signs in English to route B9, passing a group of boys using sticks to drive their cows down from the grassy slopes of Mt. Kashura for the night. The high beams of the Rover illuminated groups of women with broad aluminum pans balanced on their heads and men in flannel shirts walking home, weary after a long day of work, for even the day of Christmas Eve was a workday for Christians and non-Christians alike. At a roundabout at the edge of town, three boys, none older than ten, stepped in front of the Rover and tried to sell him small plastic bags of potable drinking water. If they only knew. He'd been born in the same country as they, but when Qwesi was ten his parents, who had money and power, had already sent him abroad to study at St. Adrian's Academy for Boys.

It would be another thirty miles on the red dirt of the B9 to the town of Kyaka, where the Kyaka Bridge spanned the Kagera River. Qwesi had been told to look for the ruins of a church that had been destroyed by troops belonging to Idi Amin, the brutal former dictator of nearby Uganda. Qwesi's father, one of Amin's generals and a close advisor, had led the raid that destroyed the church. The Kagera flowed back into Lake Victoria, the source of the Nile River, which flowed north for 4,130 miles before reaching Cairo and the Mediterranean.

The driving was rough, with potholes and ruts to maneuver around. Qwesi was careful as he drove to check in his rearview mirror to make sure he wasn't being followed. When he was five miles from Bukoba, he relaxed, knowing that in the absolute blackness of the African night he would have seen the headlights of anyone trying to follow him.

Just to be certain, he stopped the Rover, got out, and trained a pair of night-vision goggles on the road behind him. He saw nothing moving.

He got back in and drove, unaware of the man atop his car, dressed in black from head to toe, holding on to the roof rack, his black rubber-soled shoes wedged beneath the cross-piece to keep him from bouncing.

Similar covert pursuits transpired in cities and towns around the world, in Shanghai and Mexico City, Sydney and Caracas, Paris and Oslo. Operatives on the ground, controlled by Ed Stanley, coordinated their efforts with aerial intelligence assets providing falcon views of their targets. At the same time there were others close at hand, representatives of the Curatoriat, who had been fighting pagans for a thousand years and were no strangers to covert activities themselves. They'd had a head start, had the same targets but different objectives, and an imperative to reach those targets first.

In East Salem, New York, Reese Stratton-Mallins had asked Dani if he could try one more time to reach his brother by using the sensory deprivation tank in Tommy's media room. It was the day of Christmas Eve, and he found himself unable to quiet his thoughts any other way.

In the tank, he applied the breathing technique Tommy had taught him, a process Tommy said he used to go through before every game when he needed to focus his mind and become singular of purpose. Soon—or perhaps not soon, for there was no way to accurately gauge the passage of time—Reese found himself swimming in a sea of memories, remembering Christmases with his brother when their parents were still alive, eating delicious bread pudding and mince pie and roast goose stuffed with chestnuts, and going to church, and singing, and opening presents. He remembered attending school with Edmond, both of them smiling when the teacher said something funny, jokes nobody but the two of them got.

Slowly he realized that what he was seeing was no longer a memory. It was happening now.

In London, Edmond Stratton-Mallins left his flat and headed for the Underground. There he boarded a Piccadilly Line train for Heathrow Airport. At the Oxford Circus Station he saw carolers dressed in elaborate

Dickensian costumes singing to raise money for charity, their music sheets illuminated by handheld candles. He saw families traveling with children to spend Christmas Eve with relatives, and people carrying large shopping bags with purchases from Harrods and Debenhams and Fenwick and Harvey Nichols. In one station, as the doors to the train opened to let on passengers, he even saw a man dressed as Santa Claus arguing loudly about devolution and the monarchy to no one in particular in a thick Scottish brogue, a drunken slur to his speech.

At the airport he hailed a cab and asked the driver to take him to the village of Runnymede—the very place, he'd learned in elementary school, where the Magna Carta had been signed. Between Heathrow and Windsor Castle, two miles farther west, a series of reservoirs had been excavated shortly before the Second World War, including the Queen Mother, Wraysbury, Queen Mary, King George VI, and Staines Reservoirs, from which the metropolis of Greater London drew its drinking water via the Staines aqueduct. Edmond's destination was the canal where the Thames Water and Power Company took river water to fill the reservoirs at Hythe End, above the Bell Weir Lock.

As the A308 led along the shore of the Staines Reservoir, he saw flocks of pochard and gooseander, and recalled how his father had loved bird watching. He had tried to teach Edmond and Reese how to identify birds just by hearing their calls. Seeing the ducks only made Edmond feel sadder, but not because he missed his father—he did, but there was nothing he could do about that. No, who he missed was Reese, more intensely than he ever had missed anyone in his entire life. The two had never spent this much time apart; they'd never been so far from one another, an entire ocean away. And the more Edmond thought about Reese, the less he wanted to carry out his task.

Dr. Ghieri had talked about unity and loyalty and solidarity, and how St. Adrian's was the world's best hope for the future, but there was no solidarity, no loyalty, no unity greater than the bond between identical twins.

244

Stepping up from the Underground at Heathrow, it occurred to Edmond that he could, if he had a mind to, use a credit card, buy a ticket to New York, and be with his brother by Christmas morning, assuming he could find him. Before, he'd known that if he disobeyed Dr. Ghieri, somebody would hurt Reese. The threat was implied, never explicit, but it was clear.

But now he knew Reese was safe. The image of his brother inside the giant egg had become a recurring waking dream, a guarantee, almost, that Reese was beyond harm's reach. He had the image again. Edmond had spent a lot of time in the past few days considering the things he knew Reese was feeling. Edmond thought Dr. Ghieri was one of the smartest people he'd ever met, but Reese thought the school psychologist was evil, and now Edmond wasn't so sure. What kind of man, Reese wanted to know, would threaten to harm those who refused to obey him? What kind of man led by fear and bullying, promising to give you everything if you agreed with him, but to take away everything if you didn't? What kind of seeker of truth refused to entertain any truths other than the ones he already knew?

Edmond knew Reese, if he were there, he would disapprove. *Turn around*, he could hear him saying. *Go back. You don't know what you're doing.*

Edmond decided to compromise. When he reached the weir at Hythe End, he'd dump the ashes into the canal, then head straight for Heathrow and catch the first flight to Kennedy, and from there he'd take a cab back to East Salem and find his brother. Somehow he'd find him, and they'd be together for Christmas morning. That was the only thing he wanted, a fact he knew with greater and greater certainty as the taxi drove past houses filled with festively decorated trees and families settling down to spend the holiday together, past churches where couples and families and single people were all entering to worship. Edmond had never understood how important it was to be with his brother. And he would be with him, soon enough.

Two miles west of Hythe End, in the town of Old Windsor in a pub called The Bells of Ouzeley, an assassin named Alfredo Guzman finished a meal of "farm-assured chicken" and brussels sprouts grilled in balsamic vinegar. He paid his bill, left a gratuity in addition to the VAT, and took a cab back to the Beaumont House on Burfield Road, where he told the cab driver to wait. He went to his room and retrieved a case from the closet.

Guzman set the case on the bed and opened it. Of the several weapons inside, he chose a Beretta BU9 9x19-millimeter Nano, an absurdly small but powerful pocket pistol that would be good at close range, if he needed it, and wouldn't alter the hang of his new Burberry, a bonded leather Nappa field coat in olive green that made him feel a bit like a Gestapo officer. He made a mental note to take the coat off before he did the job. For the killing, he selected a seven-inch Swedish hunting knife with a serrated edge. Dr. Ghieri had told him to enjoy himself, but he'd also asked Guzman to bring back proof that the job had been completed, and the serrated edge would help if he needed to cut through ligaments or cartilage or bone.

"The boy has dishonored his selection," Ghieri had said. "I'd like something to show the next boy who thinks he can betray us." The head would make the best impression on Ghieri, but settling for a hand was the more practical solution.

Guzman wanted to make a good impression on Ghieri. After Wharton was disposed of, Guzman had every reason to think he was next in line to become headmaster at St. Adrian's, but now it appeared that someone else was vying for Ghieri's favor. Marko. A mere boy. Ghieri's little pet! Guzman had been given an opportunity to show Ghieri what he could do. He intended to make the most of it.

When he got back in the cab, the driver pointed out that it had started to snow. It looked like they might just get a white Christmas after all.

"Going home to family, then?" the driver asked cheerfully. The man had a Yorkshire accent but an Indian name.

"No," Guzman said. "Just meeting a friend."

"Good for you," the driver said. "It's not a night anybody should be alone."

"No," Guzman agreed with a smile. "It certainly isn't."

36.

December 24

Lucius Mills pushed the wheelchair bearing Tommy's father, Arnie. The lobby at High Ridge Manor was filled with Christmas decorations, including a twelve-foot-tall, perfectly symmetrical spruce trimmed with lights, tinsel, and ornaments made by local elementary school children. There were boxes under the tree filled with goodies sent by the local high school students—things to eat and things to play with, Rubik's cubes and jigsaw puzzles to keep the recipients mentally sharp. Three elderly residents, two of them also in wheelchairs, and all three dressed in their Christmas sweaters and pins, waited by the window for their families to come to pick them up.

Tommy needed to see his dad. Lucius had explained on the phone that Arnie had had only a few moments of partial lucidity since arriving at the nursing home. He had been sleeping a lot and was quite likely unaware of the approaching holiday. But Tommy needed to see him anyway.

When he did, the sight made Tommy's heart ache.

Arnie was wearing pajamas beneath his robe. He held his head lower now, and both hands trembled from the Parkinsonism that accompanied Lewy body dementia. Ten years ago doctors would have mistaken the disease for Alzheimer's. Tommy had mistaken it for forgetfulness, at the onset.

First it was a meal at a local restaurant where his dad left a tip equal to the size of the bill, apparently unable to calculate what 20 percent would be. Then Arnie, who'd run a nursery and landscaping business all his life, inadvertently placed the same order twice with their Halloween pumpkin supplier, and when Tommy said it looked like they were going to have to eat five hundred pumpkins, Arnie said, "That's a lot of pumpkin pie," but he wasn't joking. His mental functioning just wasn't what it should have been.

They were watching a basketball game between the Celtics and the Lakers when Arnie complained that they were playing too fast. Tommy realized his father's vision wasn't impaired, but his ability to process visual information was.

When Tommy saw his father's gait changing, his steps getting shorter and more hesitant, he brought him in for tests. The doctors performed tests for a specific protein, finding clumps of them in Arnie's brain stem. As the disease advanced, the protein clumps would eventually be found in the temporal region, making it hard for Arnie to form new memories. The doctor said the older man could expect light-headedness, a woozy feeling when he tried to move, difficulty concentrating, and then palsy, urinary incontinence, and eventually, nightmares and hallucinations.

And now things had gone from expectation to reality.

Tommy took a knee and leaned in so his father could see him. "Hey, Pops—how ya doin'?"

His father did not seem to recognize him.

"It's me. Your son, Tommy."

"Santa Claus was here," his father said.

"Was he?" Tommy looked at Lucius, who nodded.

"He came yesterday to visit," Lucius said. "They have the Christmas party early for people who won't be here on Christmas Eve."

"Santa was here," Arnie repeated.

"He's going to be pretty busy tonight," Tommy said. "That's why I was stopping by, Papa. Because I'm not going to be able to have you home for Christmas Eve. There's just a lot going on that I can't explain right now, but it's safer if you stay here."

Tommy had worried that his father would feel let down, but the news did not appear to register.

"Evelyn was here too," Arnie said. "I spoke to her."

Evelyn was Tommy's mother, who'd died in a car accident when Tommy was in the eighth grade.

"What did she say?" Tommy asked.

"She said she was sorry," Arnie said.

"What did you tell her?"

Arnie blew a loud raspberry with his lips. Tommy couldn't help but smile.

"I'm a lucky man," Arnie said. "Lucky, lucky, lucky."

"So am I," Tommy said. He took the jewelry box from his pocket and opened it to show his father the diamond ring. "This is the ring I'm going to give Dani Harris. I've been having a little trouble finding the right moment. Do you remember Dani Harris? The girl who was homecoming queen when I was homecoming king?"

Lucius leaned over to get a better view and whistled his approval.

"Did Santa Claus bring that?" Arnie asked.

Tommy's heart sank again. He was too late; this news—the most exciting news he'd had since he'd been a number one NFL draft pick—was something he was not going to be able to share with his father.

"I'm good to stay the night, Tommy, if you need me," Lucius said.

"No way, Lucius," Tommy said, straightening up. "You've done too much already. Go home to your family."

"My sister's kids are going to jump all over me," Lucius said. "Either I'm getting too old or they're getting too big. Thanks, Tommy. I appreciate it."

"This is for you," Tommy said, handing his father's caregiver a new GPhone, which Lucius received with thanks. Tommy then gave his father a GTab, essentially a larger tablet version of the phone, preloaded with all of Arnie's favorite books, movies, and songs, and plenty of games designed for kids four through ten, simple enough for Arnie to figure out intuitively. Lucius agreed to stay long enough to help Arnie get started on it.

"Just show him the Paint program," Tommy told his friend. "Maybe he can paint pictures."

Tommy kissed his father on the forehead and wished him a Merry Christmas.

"Merry Christmas to you," Arnie said, the way he might address a stranger.

"I'll check in tomorrow," Tommy said.

"I'm a lucky man," Arnie said. "Lucky lucky lucky lucky lucky. Lucky lucky lucky lucky lucky."

Tommy wanted to stay longer, but he needed to get home before darkness fell and things started crawling out from under the rocks.

It was still raining—even harder than before—as he sprinted to the Jeep. He'd been hoping for a white Christmas, he always did, but it was lucky that the temperature was unseasonably warm—if it were below freezing, they'd have been buried in snow. *No white Christmas this year*, he thought. But it was certainly going to be a very, very wet one.

He smiled, picturing Santa Claus carrying an umbrella.

He started the Jeep, turned on the headlights, and turned the windshield wipers to high. Suddenly he was struck by a powerful sense of déjà vu. As the raindrops splattered against the hood of his car, he remembered how many of Dani's dreams had involved water. The night they'd had the same identical nightmare, that dream had been about a flood. Now it was December 24th, Christmas Eve, and it was pouring.

He'd been telling himself all day not to read ominous portent into every little thing that happened, but those two things were incontrovertibly true.

He and Dani had both dreamed of water.

And it never rained on Christmas Eve.

37.

December 24

4:12 p.m. EST

"Reese? It's Dani. Can you hear me?"

"Maybe he's sleeping," Helen Trumble said. "Should we wake him?"

Dani was Skyping with the new Curator from Great Britain, her laptop open on the coffee table.

"No," Dani said. She and Ruth were kneeling beside the sensory deprivation tank, the lid propped open, the lights low in Tommy's expansive man cave. Reese's twinstincts had grown stronger each time. Time, however, was running short.

Something new was happening. When Dani turned the microphone on, she'd heard noises coming from inside, words she'd been unable to make out. If Reese was sleeping, he was talking in his sleep, but she didn't think he was sleeping; rather, he was more likely in a transitional state between sleep and wakefulness, not quite lucid but not quite dreaming either, a time when sleepers had what psychologists called "hypnagogic dreams," dreams that incorporated external stimuli into the dream experience. A dreamer, hearing someone mowing the lawn outside, might dream he was riding a motorcycle. If that was happening now, Dani had an idea.

"Let me try something," she said to the girl on her computer screen before turning to Tommy's aunt. "Ruth, would you mind turning the lights all the way off? Thank you."

Ruth moved to the wall switch and lowered the dimmer, then returned to the tank.

"Reese," Dani whispered. "This is Dani. I don't want you to wake up, but I just want you to tell me if you can hear me and understand what I'm saying."

"I can hear you, Dr. Harris," the boy said.

"That's good," she said. Hearing him say her last name meant he was at least partially conscious. "Keep your eyes closed, but tell me what you see."

"It's snowing."

"Where is it snowing?"

"England. It's snowing in England. It's beautiful."

"Can you see your brother?"

"No," Reese said.

"Is he there?"

"Yes, but I can't see him. I can see what he sees."

"As if you're looking through his eyes?"

"Yes."

"What do you see?"

"Water. Airplanes."

The files they'd stolen from Ghieri's computer had given them not only the names of the boys tasked to poison the world's water supply, but the latitudes and longitudes marking the spots where they were to commit the deed. Edmond was supposed to go to the King George VI reservoir, near Heathrow. The fact that Reese was "seeing" airplanes meant his brother must be close.

"That's good," Dani said. "Stay with it. It's snowing. What else?"

"I'm walking."

"Where are you walking?"

"On a street. Along a canal."

"In Hythe End?"

"Yes."

"Are you alone?"

"No."

"No?"

"Someone is up ahead."

"Who's up ahead?"

"A man."

"Are there two men?"

"No," Reese said. "Just one."

"Are you sure?" Dani asked.

"Yes."

Dani switched off the microphone, then spoke into her laptop's webcam. "How many men did you send?"

"Two," Helen Trumble said.

"Are they in position?"

"They say they are."

"Why does Edmond see only one?"

"I don't know."

"Could one of your men be behind him, in case he tries to run?"

"Possibly," the English girl said.

"Can you call your men?"

"Are you saying I should risk spooking the boy?"

"Negative," Dani said. "Stand by."

She turned the tank microphone back on. "How many men do you see?"

"I only see one."

"What does he look like?"

"He's young," Reese said. "He has black hair and dark skin."

Dani looked at her computer screen. Helen shook her head to say the description did not fit either of the two men she'd sent.

"Reese, tell your brother he needs to turn around. Tell him to turn around, right now, and run."

"He won't."

Dani tried to keep her voice calm. "He needs to turn and run. You need to tell him—"

"I'm telling him. Wait."

"Wait?"

"They know each other."

"How?"

"From school. They know each other from school."

"Can you hear what they're saying?"

"'Greetings from Dr. Ghieri.' 'What are you doing here?'"

"Tell your brother he's in great danger," Dani said.

"He won't listen."

"Reese—"

"No!" Reese suddenly called out. "No, no, no—run!"

"Reese—wake up! Wake up right now!"

"No—run! Please!"

"Reese—wake up!" Dani opened the lid and shook the boy until he opened his eyes and looked at her.

"He shot him, Dani," Reese said, his face a mask of horror. "He shot him!"

38.

December 24

6:07 p.m. EST

They were in the kitchen, checking their weapons and ammunition supplies and finalizing their defenses, when the intercom sounded. Reese was trying to act a lot braver than he really was, Tommy thought, but then the boy sat up straight in his chair, startled by the sound.

"Relax," Tommy said, putting a hand on Reese's shoulder. "I don't think those cave weasels are going to ring the doorbell when they come caroling."

"Ordinarily, I would have little use for the great American love affair with the gun," Reese said, "but tonight I think I'll make an exception."

Tommy smiled at his Aunt Ruth, at Reese, and then finally at Dani. He walked to the intercom panel and pressed a button.

"Fort Gunderson," he said. "Whom shall I say is attacking?"

"Hey! Anybody home?"

It was Detective Casey, and apparently he was on foot. Tommy drove to the end of the driveway, wipers slapping the rain from his windshield. A large puddle had formed in his driveway. Tommy was glad he'd installed a snorkel-style air intake on the Jeep for driving through high water, though he doubted he'd need it.

"It's ridiculous out here," Detective Casey said, climbing into the Jeep. "They're saying this is more rain than anything on record."

"And the ground is still frozen," Tommy added. "The water has nowhere to go."

Casey was dressed in a full-length VisGuard lime-green reversible duty police raincoat, his hood up against the downpour, the brim of his Red Sox cap dripping, old-fashioned black rubber galoshes on his feet.

"Where's your car?" Tommy asked.

"I had to hoof it," Casey said. "The road's washed out downhill from here."

"I came from the other direction earlier," Tommy said, recalling the drive home from seeing his dad. He reversed direction and shifted into first. "I crossed a place where the water was almost to the top of my wheels."

"Most of the roads heading out of the city are closed. The Merritt, the Saw Mill, the Sprain, the Taconic, the Hutch . . . there's more on the way too. A big front moving in off the North Atlantic. Nor'easter. I was coming out to warn you."

"You could have just called," Tommy said.

"Tonight's the night, right?" Casey said. "I thought maybe you could use some help."

"According to everything we've learned, yeah," Tommy said. "We can use an extra hand."

"I got two and you can have 'em both. I wanted to tell you, we got another call from the school about Wharton," Casey said. "Guy said last they knew, Wharton was headed to your place. They're doing everything they can to tie you up with this."

"Who called?"

"Ghieri."

"Figures," Tommy said.

"*Habeas corpus*, far as I'm concerned," Casey said. "No body, no charges. And there ain't gonna be a body. My guy in Rhode Island made sure of that. I told Ghieri his headmaster probably just went on a vacation and didn't tell anybody. Thought the guy was gonna blow a gasket. Assuming those guys even have gaskets. You hear from Quinn?"

"He's not answering his phone," Tommy said. "Cass either."

"So what's going on?" Casey asked.

"Tell you inside," Tommy said.

Casey hung his raincoat up in the mudroom and then stopped in the kitchen doorway, surprised by the arsenal laid out in front of him.

"It looks like you're expecting company," he said.

Aunt Ruth's weapons collection covered the food island in the middle of the kitchen. She'd been training Reese in how to use one of the shotguns.

"Just pretend you're Prince Charles's third son and you're out in the yard shooting grouse in your snazzy Barbour raincoat," she said.

"For me to pretend to be a royal, you'd have to stick a straw in my ear and suck out two-thirds of my brain," Reese said, closing one eye to sight down the barrel. "And Barbour may possibly be the worst raincoat ever made. On a day like this you'd be soaked to the bone in five minutes. The only people who still buy them are Americans. And royals."

When Tommy asked Ruth how the training had gone, she said, "He'll do all right when the time comes." Then she added, "When this is over, I want to make a big fire in your fire pit and burn these things into charcoal. I've had it with guns."

"When this is over," Tommy said, "I'll help you."

They had four shotguns available to them, as well as nine hunting rifles, two Uzi automatic pistols, the Ares "Shrike" light machine gun with its M203 grenade launcher, a dozen sidearms in a variety of sizes and calibers, and a pair of Barnett Ghost 400 CarbonLite deer hunting crossbows with 185-pound draws, capable of firing bolts at 400 feet per second, each with an illuminating scope and a dozen carbon bolts with razor-sharp big-game tips. Tommy had ordered another dozen Helios 9000 floodlights online and set them up in a circle around his house to shine in all directions.

The plan had been for Tommy to watch the northern quarter of his property, Ruth the east, Reese the west, and Dani the south. Now that Casey had joined them, Tommy asked Casey to take the south quadrant, which would leave Dani free to monitor the security cameras.

"So what exactly are we shooting?" Casey asked, examining one of the hunting rifles and raising it to gaze out the window through the scope.

"Cave weasels," Tommy said.

"Creatures from hell," Ruth said. "Literally. They evolved in caves. They don't like light."

"We think they're mesonychids," Tommy said. "Like giant moles that were once thought to be extinct."

"Giant nasty moles," Dani said. "With claws and fangs. But flesh and blood. Or something close. They can be shot."

"They absorb light, so they're hard to see without floodlights," Tommy said. "They've been waiting outside the walls for the last four nights."

"Waiting for what?"

"For tonight," Tommy said. "I assume."

"How many are we talking about?" Casey asked.

"Let's find out," Tommy said. While Dani manned the ground control station for the drone, flying the aircraft in slow, steady circles above the house, Tommy turned the floodlights on. It took a moment for them to power up, and then the woods surrounding his property were filled with light.

"See anything?" he asked Dani.

"Not on infrared."

"Switch to night vision."

Dani did, and an army of black shadows popped up on screen, too many to count. They were closing in on the perimeter.

"Well, that's not good," Tommy said, leaning over her shoulder.

"Reminds me of the Alamo," Casey said. "A little bit. Just the good parts."

"What were the good parts?" Tommy asked.

"There weren't any good parts?"

"Not that I'm aware of," Tommy said. "Stations, everyone. Don't wait until you see the whites of their eyes. If it moves, shoot it."

39.

December 24

6:12 p.m. EST

"You did good," Quinn heard someone say.

He opened his eyes. A man with long shaggy hair, a diamond stud earring in one ear, and a chain around his neck, just visible inside his leather jacket, leaned over him, seated on his right.

On his left an EMT, a young Asian woman, was listening to his heartbeat through a stethoscope. Quinn realized he was in an ambulance. His head was a furnace of pain that throbbed with every beat of his heart. Yet the man in the leather jacket was smiling.

"Charlie?" Quinn said.

"How ya feelin'?" the angel asked.

"I've been better."

"That was a brave thing you did."

Quinn searched his chest with his hand, feeling for blood. "Have I been shot?"

"Almost," Charlie said. "The ambulance got there just in time."

"Where are they taking me?"

"Northern Westchester Hospital," Charlie said.

"Can they—"

Charlie shook his head.

"They can't hear us," he said. "Or see me."

Quinn felt relieved. "I'm ready now," he said.

"What do you mean?"

"You've come to take me, right? I'm ready to go."

"You might be ready, but we're not," Charlie said.

"What?" Quinn said.

"It's not your time, Quinn."

"It's not?"

"No," Charlie said. "You have more to do here."

"Okay," Quinn said. "I'll see how long I can last, but right now, I'm not buying any green bananas, if you know what I mean."

"I know what you mean," Charlie said. "But I also know you're not going to need that midgrade infiltrating multiform glioblastoma of the pons reticular formation anymore."

Charlie reached down and put his hand under the back of Quinn's neck, cradling his head. His hand felt warm and soothing, and then, as if it were nothing more than dirty water in a sink, Quinn felt the pain drain out of him and into the angel's hand.

Charlie raised his hand, fist closed, to show Quinn, and then he squeezed, the way someone might crumble a fortune cookie. When he opened his hand, nothing more than a bit of dust fell from it, desiccated and harmless. Quinn realized the pain in his head was gone.

"Don't try to get up," Charlie said. "You should still spend the night in the hospital, recuperating, but tomorrow you should be good to go."

For the first time in a long time—for the first time he could remember, in fact—Quinn didn't know what to say.

"Thank you," he whispered finally.

"I'm not the one you need to thank," Charlie said. "But on his behalf, you're welcome. And thank you. And oh—I almost forgot. If you're still awake tonight, turn on the local news."

Quinn closed his eyes. When he opened them again, Charlie was gone.

The EMT took the stethoscope from her ears and handed them to her partner, a young African American man, who took his turn listening.

"I thought you said he was arrhythmic," the man said.

"He was," his partner said.

"Well, he's not now."

"I know. That's what I'm saying," she replied. "Seems like he's stabilized."

"Keep the paddles ready," the male EMT said, "but I don't think we're going to need them."

"I would have bet anything he'd be DOA," the woman said.

"You would have lost," Quinn said. "I'm hungry. Have you got anything to eat?"

40.

December 24

6:17 p.m. EST

The Gevaudan beasts were undeterred by the electrified fence. A few drew back from it when they touched it and felt the electricity, but they were trampled by the beasts storming in behind them.

"They're pushing through the wire!" Tommy said. "Bluetooth and conference call everybody, like we practiced."

He took a deep breath as everyone scattered; they'd rehearsed for this as much as they could, short of firing live rounds. With the drone in the air above them providing intelligence, at least they commanded the high ground. While Tommy was on his boat on Lake Atticus getting water samples, Dani had practiced with the drone so that now she was nearly as good at flying it as Tommy or Reese. Even so, the Gevaudan outnumbered them a hundred to one.

"Any sign of them?" Tommy asked.

"Nothing yet," Dani said. She knew he wasn't talking about the beasts, of course, but rather Ben and Charlie. The angels had promised to be there when they needed them, and as far as Tommy could see, they needed them now. "Fingers are crossed. And hands are folded."

The alarm sounded again.

"Incoming!" Dani called out. "Fences down!"

Tommy fired his weapon before seeing what he was shooting at, knowing only the height and range without picking out his targets visually. The shapes became clearer in the driving rain as the beasts approached. He hit one, then another, then another, using a sandbag he'd placed atop his Viking barbecue grill to bolster his aim.

"Ruth—to your left!" he heard Dani yell over the GPhone link. Tommy heard Detective Casey shout from around the corner of the house and then fire his shotgun.

Tommy killed two more, if *killed* was the word—it presumed they were alive in the first place. They had animation and corporeal form, but they knew only darkness, and they did not know God, so how was that life? He popped another magazine into the Ares and fired a burst to his left, and then he fired a grenade to his right, the explosion lighting up the sky.

When he turned, he saw that one of the creatures had reached a floodlight. It lifted the extension cord and bit it in half. That creature electrocuted itself, but there were more right behind it. Too many more, Tommy realized. They came on and on, swarming from all directions like angry bees.

"Pull in—pull in!" Dani shouted over the link. They'd planned for this too; a last stand from inside the house, using the walls as shelter for as long as the walls stood.

Tommy emptied the Ares, ejected the clip, reloaded, and emptied the gun again.

"Tommy! Didn't you hear me? Pull in! Pull in!" Dani shouted again.

He fired the shotgun at point-blank range, blowing the head off one of the creatures. Two more took its place.

Tommy turned to retreat and found another standing right in front of him.

41.

December 24

Dani's heart caught in her throat as she saw Tommy surrounded. He raised his shotgun again. She closed her eyes, unwilling to watch.

Help him, Lord, she prayed. *Send him—*

A huge explosion rocked the ground. There was a second explosion, and then a third.

"What was that?" Tommy's voice asked over the headset.

"I don't know," Dani said. "It's not us."

She heard the sound of machine-gun fire, tracers arcing across Tommy's property from all directions. A burst of static came from the GPhone and then . . .

"Thought maybe you folks could use a little help," said a voice. A familiar voice.

"Ed?" Dani said. "How'd you get on this line? How did you know—"

"We need you to stay inside until we're done," Stanley said brusquely. "If we have to use missiles, we may not be able to limit collateral damage."

Dani switched monitor views in time to see Tommy grab one of the Helios 9000s and point it up into the sky, illuminating the black outlines of

266

a dozen drones far larger than the Orison passing overhead, firing missiles and machine guns.

"Didn't see you coming," Tommy said.

"No one does," Stanley replied. "That's the point."

Dani had Tommy and the others take shelter in the windows and doorways of the house. They kept shooting, but the CIA drones took the larger part of the battle now.

As the gunfire slackened, Tommy joined Dani in the kitchen. She'd had the Orison 6 fly high above the battlefield, keeping the camera aimed at the house, giving them a bird's-eye view of the battle. As the drone climbed, she saw the Gevaudan beasts retreating, defeated and decimated.

Out the window, the fallen body of one of the Gevaudan dissolved in the rain, as if it had been made of smoke or ash.

Casey, Ruth, and Reese met them in the kitchen just as a Skype call from Ed Stanley came in.

"Are you all right?" Stanley said.

"We're good," Dani said. "Your timing couldn't have been better."

"Speaking of timing," Stanley said. "We had people at the coordinates you gave us for the boys, from the file Tommy got off Ghieri's computer. But somebody got there ahead of us."

"Who?" Dani asked.

"Not sure," Stanley said. "We'll have some time to look at the surveillance footage from the drones we had on scene. It looks like somebody shot them with tranquilizer darts, like on a National Geographic special. I thought maybe you could tell me. You're the ones who wanted to take them alive."

"We did what we had to do," Dani said. "Those things out there in the woods, I don't care. But the boys Ghieri sent out with his little packages— they're just boys. They didn't ask for this, and they don't know what they're doing. They've been manipulated, and they're victims. I'm not going to allow them to be killed. It's that simple."

"And that's exactly what Ghieri was counting on," Ed Stanley said.

"That's why they used children. They knew that somebody was going to be too . . . sentimental to take them out. According to my sources, six of them were able to poison the water supplies they targeted before you were able to subdue them. Six."

"I understand that," Dani said. "According to my sources, you killed one of the boys."

She exchanged glances with Reese.

"If you're talking about Hythe End near Heathrow, yes. We took out the target. And he was one of the six who got through. Both your defenses and ours."

"He wasn't a target," Dani said. "A target is a piece of paper with a bull's-eye on it. He was a human being. His name was Edmond Stratton-Mallins."

"I'm sorry," Stanley said. "It couldn't be helped."

"Is there anything else you need?" Dani said.

"There's a party at St. Adrian's Academy tonight," Stanley said. "We're going to be flying over it to take some pictures. I suggest you keep your little paper airplane out of the way."

He logged off, and Dani did the same.

"Did he just insult my drone?" Tommy said. He was holding the drone's control module and watching it on the screen. "Speaking of which, I think you ought to see this."

"What is it?" Dani asked, coming to Tommy's side.

"Charlie and Ben said they'd be here when we needed them, right?"

"I guess we didn't need them," she said.

Tommy shook his head. "This was too easy," he said. "This was just a screen pass."

"A what?"

"A screen pass," he repeated. "The quarterback fakes a play, and the offensive line lets the defense through without much of a fight. And just when the linemen are about to tackle the passer, he lobs it over their heads to a running back. A guy who's been pretending to be a blocker."

"A feint, you mean," Dani said.

"Exactly. It's one of the oldest strategies known to warfare. I've seen it a thousand times."

"On a football field. Hitler thought Normandy was a feint," Dani said. "And he was wrong. Normandy was the real thing."

"These beasts attacking the house were a feint," Tommy repeated. "If it wasn't a feint, how do you explain this?"

He showed her the controller for the drone, which was still flying at fifteen thousand feet, surveying the town. The view was from the infrared camera; she saw a blue haze on the ground and above Bull's Rock Hill. Tommy froze the frame, then played back a portion he'd just recorded at thirty times slower than real time.

A chill ran down Dani's spine. "Dear God," she said. "Oh, dear God."

The air above Bull's Rock Hill, and the ground around it, was teeming with demons, fallen angels far larger and stronger and far more evil than the beasts they'd just driven from Tommy's property.

"That's it," he said. "That's the real battle." He put his raincoat on, then took the shotgun he'd been using and a backpack full of shells.

"Where do you think you're going?" Dani asked.

"Bull's Rock Hill," Tommy said.

"The road's out," she reminded him.

"I'm not taking the road."

"What are you going to do?" Dani asked him.

"Attack," Tommy said.

"Tommy—wait."

He stopped.

"So you're going to singlehandedly attack a thousand demons, armed with nothing but a shotgun, even though you fought one single demon in your own driveway and couldn't defeat it?" Dani said.

"Well, it sounds really stupid when you put it that way," Tommy said.

"That's because it is really stupid."

"They'll be there if I need them," he said. "Ben and Charlie."

He tried to smile, but she saw the fear on his face.

"Dani, I know this is right," he told her. "This is faith. Sometimes it makes total sense, and sometimes it flies in the face of common sense, but for me, it's simple. We've located the enemy. We attack the enemy. And we attack with faith."

"I'm coming with you," Reese said.

"You can't," Tommy said. "Someone has to stay here—"

"If you're about to say 'and protect the womenfolk,' I'm going to punch you in the face," Dani said. "We womenfolk can protect ourselves."

"Hey," Detective Casey said. "What am I? Chopped liver?"

"You're okay with this?" Tommy said, looking first to Reese, then at Dani.

"I'm okay with this," Dani said. "I trust you. Just make sure you come back."

Tommy ran across the courtyard to the garage bay where the ATV was parked, the driving rain impossibly falling even harder than it had earlier. He pushed the key into the ignition, pressed the starter button, waited for Reese to take a seat on the cargo rack behind him, then sped out into the rain, pausing briefly in the driveway to mount one of the Helios 9000 spotlights to the front gear rack.

"Hold on tight," he called over his shoulder. "If I hit a bump, you might be airborne. We both might be airborne."

Half a mile down the road he found Detective Casey's car, tipping precariously where the water had eroded away the road beneath the passenger's side wheels. He turned off the pavement and headed cross-country, following paths and trails he'd run hundreds of times in high school. As he sped, it seemed as if the night was growing brighter.

"Tommy," Reese said. "Stop for a second."

"No stopping," Tommy shouted. "We don't have time."

"Well, then at least slow down," Reese said. "I really think you're going to want to see this."

He slowed the ATV to a walking pace and turned around to look behind him. What he saw took his breath away. He heard a voice in his ear. It sounded like Dani's.

He realized he was still wearing the Bluetooth earpiece. As Dani spoke, the drone flew low overhead.

"Tommy," she said. "I'm right above you."

"I wish you were. I wish you were here to see this."

"See what?"

He hesitated, wondering how to put into words the glorious sight before his eyes. A sky filled with angels, shining white, too many to count, following him into battle.

"Tommy?" Dani said. "See what?"

"Lord, please let her see," Tommy prayed. "Let Dani see your glory too."

42.

December 24

6:28 p.m. EST

From the rain-soaked commons in the center of East Salem; from the steps of the church where white paper luminaries were being positioned in preparation for the midnight service; from the town's grand estates and horse farms, where CEOs and financiers and investment bankers were gathered around their elegant and expensively appointed dinner tables with their families; from the upper-middle-class homes of Willow Pond Estates and the more humble dwellings on Lake Kendall's shores, festooned with outdoor Christmas lights, inflatable lawn Santas, and snowmen reduced by the rain and the warm temperatures to clumps of slush; from multiple vantage points, the battle between good and evil was—partly—visible. Anyone gazing into the night in the direction of Bull's Rock Hill would have seen a spectacular display of lightning, accompanied by a raucous symphony of thunder that shook the rafters and echoed from the hillsides, with gusts of wind that made the strings of white LED holiday lights on the trees downtown toss and sway like pom-poms. Onlookers might have thought they were witnessing an extreme weather event, a storm of the sort that came along once every thousand years. According to the Channel 12 weatherman, that was what was happening: a collision of weather systems, a mass of warm, damp tropical air moving north, meeting a nor'easter heading inland and a winter storm moving south from Canada.

But the weatherman was wrong.

Tommy told Reese to hold on tight, then jumped a shallow ravine where the runoff had eroded the gravel and skidded to a stop in the mud. He and Reese dismounted from the ATV just short of the bull-shaped outcropping that gave Bull's Rock Hill its name.

"Put these in your pockets," Tommy said, handing Reese two boxes of shotgun shells, then a Mossberg 590-A1 shotgun with a 14-inch barrel. "These are police model riot guns. They don't have a lot of range, but anything you point at within a hundred feet or so, you're going to hit. You've got one in the chamber and eight in the magazine. So keep track, if you can, because after that, you're going to have to reload."

"I'll just pretend I'm Prince Charles, shooting grouse," Reese said. "Really ugly grouse."

Above and ahead of him, Tommy saw Satan's army, black and deformed spirits crowding the sky, preparing to mount their attack, while opposed to them were God's angels, themselves divided into three groups. The main part held the central position while smaller groups of angels split off to either side, flanking the enemy. Tommy shone his flashlight into the sky, his bright beam forming a cone of light in the falling rain.

"Is this it, then?" Reese asked.

"Is this what?"

"*It*," Reese said. "The final battle. I've read Revelation, you know. Wharton and Ghieri could very well be the False Prophet and the False Teacher that Scripture talks about. I suppose you've thought of this."

"I won't pretend I haven't," Tommy said. "But Scripture didn't mention the False Prophet turning up dead in my fishing pond. There's a lot that doesn't fit. Scripture also says Satan, in his drive to replace God, is going to win some battles before losing the final one."

"Indeed," Reese said, following Tommy as he moved toward Bull's Rock Hill. "Which do you suppose this one is? One he loses, or one he wins?"

"Would it change what we do if we knew?"

"I don't suppose it would."

Tommy watched as the Lord's shining white angels, so perfect in form, their flaming swords held high, easily repulsed the demons' first attack, slaughtering them in great numbers. The air around him seemed to sizzle, as if charged with an electrical excitation he could feel in his teeth, and the night smelled of sulfur and rust, a scorched metallic kind of stench. The demons, as they fell, dissolved into nothingness, their faces masks of agony and despair as they paid for the choices they'd made.

To Tommy's right, an angel chased down a fleeing demon and swung him by the tail before dashing him against the rocks. Above him, a smaller angel dispatched a demon three times his size with four quick blows before the black thing could raise an arm in self-defense.

These creatures had no loyalty to each other. They were all fighting as individuals, while angels working in pairs or teams closed off their escape routes.

All at once an angel dived straight at him, sword raised high above his head. Tommy ducked reflexively as the heavenly being swooped over him. Tommy turned and saw the angel cut down a Gevaudan beast that had been approaching Tommy from behind. A half dozen other beasts rushed toward him as well.

"Here we go!" Tommy shouted to Reese. "Behind you!"

He dodged the first beast coming at him, turned and blasted it, then swung the barrel of the shotgun as he pumped and shot a second creature in the throat. A third knocked Tommy down, but he took the blow and rolled with it, grabbing the thing by its oily fur and throwing it off him, where Reese shot it dead.

Tommy repaid the favor by destroying a beast racing up on Reese from behind. The air began to reek of noxious fumes, as if the beasts had already begun to decay.

Reese shot three more in quick succession, including one that turned and ran.

Tommy raised the barrel of his gun, only to see two of the creatures stepping aside to make way for a demon of another kind entirely, a beast three times larger than any of the noxious cave weasels they had yet encountered. The monster rose up on its hind legs, spread its arms wide to display its might, and roared into the night, snarling at Tommy and Reese, eyes wild with fury. His breath smelled like the bottom of a garbage can.

Tommy smiled at Reese, who nodded.

"Welcome to the twenty-first century, Einstein," Tommy said, and then both men fired three quick blasts each directly into the beast's head. The lifeless carcass tumbled backward into the weeds; the other beasts turned and ran. Angels from above swooped down and caught all of them; the last fell, struck down with a single slash of a blade.

The battle above was now a rout, the main body of demons reduced to a few score, huddled together, at last attuned to the virtues of fighting as one, but too late.

A flight of angels circled the trembling cluster, flying faster and faster, closer and closer. There was no forgiveness here, no redemption, no repentance—just the full measure of God's wrath. One of the angels swooped out from the ranks, severing a demon from the larger group and cutting it in half. The other demons whimpered, cowering behind each other. Another angel dived down, piercing the cluster, leaving a half dozen slain demons in his path. The demons scattered, but the angels followed quickly behind them to finish the battle Satan had started. A battle the Great Deceiver had now lost.

Tommy felt awe, and then an afterglow as the awe slowly faded, leaving a sense of wonder. What he'd seen was far more magnificent than anything he could have imagined. As the images dissipated in the night, he suddenly heard a gurgling noise behind him.

He spun around and saw that someone was standing behind Reese, pressing a knife to the boy's throat. Tommy shone his flashlight on the pair. Amos Kasden, or rather his twin brother, Marko, was threatening to slice into Reese's carotid artery.

"Let him go," Tommy said.

"Throw your weapon over the cliff," Marko commanded.

Tommy complied.

"Now that one," Marko said, pointing at the weapon that had fallen out of Reese's hands. Tommy picked up the second shotgun and flung it out into the night.

"Now let go of him," Tommy said. "Your fight is with me."

"My fight is with both of you," Marko said. Unlike Amos, who'd been adopted at a young age, Marko retained a strong Russian accent.

Tommy wondered how long the boy had spent in Russian orphanages, or perhaps prisons. He was breathing rapidly, not because he was out of breath, but because, Tommy guessed, he was amped up, with a manic sneer and a crazed look in his eyes. He'd taken the red version of the drug, the so-called "super-soldier pill," Tommy had no doubt. He'd tried to subdue a kid on angel dust once when he'd tried to break up a bar fight after a game against the Steelers in Pittsburgh. He'd seen the kid on angel dust toss off two massive defensive linemen as easily as if they'd been Girl Scouts selling cookies. He suspected he had even less of a chance against Marko.

"I'm the one who killed your brother," Tommy said.

"If you didn't, I would have," Marko said. "He was a little pissant. He thought small."

"So you got the brains in the family?" Tommy said, smirking. "It didn't exactly help you pick the winning side here, did it?"

"This is the trash talk thing American athletes do?" Marko said, tightening his grip. Reese looked like he was about to pass out from the pressure on his neck.

"Yeah, but I'm terrible at it," Tommy said. "Let him go. Show me what you've got."

Marko threw Reese aside, lifting him clear off the ground and tossing him ten feet before he landed and rolled, clutching at his throat and gasping for air on the ground where he lay.

Tommy took a step back, glancing to the left and to the right.

"You want to run?" Marko said, coming toward him. "I know you're fast, football man. But you already know you can't outrun me."

Tommy had once been the fastest linebacker and one of the fastest players, period, in the NFL. But on the day his Mustang had caught fire, he had chased someone through the woods, and whoever it was had gotten away. He'd wondered, as he watched his car burn, if he'd lost more than a step since his prime. Now he knew who he'd been chasing. Marko was right—he couldn't outrun him. He took another step back, but Marko closed on him.

"You really think you need that knife, Marko?" Tommy said. "I got nothing, and you've got a knife. Come on—man to man. And I can wait until you grow into one, if you want."

He stepped back again as Marko stepped closer. Two more steps and Tommy would have his back to the cliff's edge, with nowhere to retreat.

Marko tossed the knife to the side.

"After I tear you apart, I think I'll feed the pieces to your friend until he chokes," Marko said.

"You'll have to catch me first," Tommy said. From the time he'd started playing youth football, he'd realized that if you faked one way and went the other, you were less likely to get hit or hurt or blocked, and more likely to be successful. It had become virtually second nature to him, until commentators said he had the best feints and fakes in the game. It had also been his experience that the more hyped up and overexcited an opponent was, the more likely he was to fall for a false step.

He took a sudden step to his right, planted his right leg, then reversed direction and jittered quickly left, throwing in a spin move, just because he could. Marko lunged at him with great force and incredible speed, arms outstretched, ready to crush Tommy like a peanut shell, until his arms closed around nothing, and then he couldn't stop himself. He rushed out over the edge of the precipice and into thin air.

Tommy had ridden his motorcycle off the same cliff at ninety miles an hour, clearing the rocks at the water's edge below by almost half a football field. More to the point, there'd been an angel waiting to catch him and break his fall. Marko wasn't moving at ninety miles an hour, and he most certainly didn't have an angel to break his fall.

Tommy peered over the edge of the cliff to the rocks below, where he saw a body lying at an angle that told him the neck was broken. But that wasn't good enough.

He crossed to where Reese had managed to sit up. Reese was coughing and holding his throat.

"You okay?"

"I will be," Reese said. "What happened?"

"He tripped," Tommy said. "I'll be right back."

He clambered down to the bottom of the cliff along a trail he'd climbed a dozen times as a boy, but never at night, and never in the pouring rain. When he reached the body, he rolled it over and shone a flashlight in Marko's still startled eyes. The pupils didn't dilate. He felt for a pulse. Nothing. He held the flashlight perpendicular to Marko's mouth to illuminate any steam that might be coming from his lungs. Nothing. He searched the boy's pockets, hoping to find a thumb drive or perhaps a bottle of pills they could analyze, but he found only a small key chain attached to a rubber dog. In that moment Marko became human again to him. Not the drug-addled, brainwashed fiend he'd thought him to be but, as Dani had said, just a kid. A boy with a rubber dog in his pocket.

Tommy wanted to cry for the loss of that little boy.

He put the key chain in Marko's hand and closed his fingers around it, then climbed quickly back to the top of the cliff.

"Is he dead?" Reese asked.

"He's dead enough," Tommy said, catching his breath. The wind had died away. Tommy stood atop the rock in the downpour and looked down to the lake below and the town of East Salem beyond the lake—or where the town should have been.

There was no sign of it. Not a single light shone in the darkness.

There was a burst of static over his Bluetooth earpiece.

"Tommy! Tommy!" Dani shouted in his ear. "Answer me! A ou ay?"

"You're breaking up," he said. "Can you repeat that?"

"Are you okay?"

"I'm okay," he said. "Reese is too. What happened to the town? I can't see it."

"All the power's out. There are trees down everywhere. Your generator came on, so we've got power. Guess how much rain we've had in the last six hours?"

"A lot."

"Ten inches. I'm glad you're okay."

"I'm glad you're okay," Tommy said. "Did you see it?"

"We saw it," Dani said. "In infrared images, but we saw it."

"Hang on a second . . ."

Tommy stopped to listen. A civil defense siren mounted atop a tower on the roof of the fire department sounded whenever there was bad weather, but the alarm Tommy heard now was different, an air horn giving three long blares, then three short, in a pattern that repeated; three long, three short, three long, three short.

As a member of the volunteer fire department, Tommy had been taught what that alarm meant. Indeed, every school child who grew up in East Salem had been taught what to do if they ever heard that pattern—evacuate and seek higher ground.

The dam holding back Lake Atticus was about to give.

"You hearing what I'm hearing?" Dani asked.

"I heard," Tommy said.

"What does it mean?"

"It means evacuate," Tommy said. "Immediately. The town. Not you—you're okay."

"I'm coming to find you."

"No. Wait where you are," Tommy said.

"Tommy," Dani said, in a tone of voice that would brook no debate. "My place is with you. Whatever happens. And don't get all sexist on me—your place is with me. Fifty-fifty, side by side."

"Agreed. But not tonight. Tonight you need to—"

He stopped talking, because the earpiece had gone silent.

Tommy kicked the ATV into gear and headed down the mountain.

43.

December 24

He used the extra floodlight to show the way, retracing the path he'd taken, which worked fine until he suddenly found the way forward blocked by a raging stream of water that had completely dissolved the road—a river twenty feet across and too deep and too fast to ford.

"That wasn't there before," Reese said. "How deep is it?"

"Two feet," Tommy said. "Maybe three. Too deep to drive across."

"We could wade it," Reese said. "You could carry me on your back."

"Are you unable to walk?"

"I'm *able* to. But it looks really cold."

"We don't have time to walk."

"What are we gonna do?"

Tommy had to think. He could try an alternate route, but it would mean a detour of several miles, and for all he knew, that way could be blocked too. There wasn't time. He had to get across.

He saw a spot to his right where the pavement had buckled, creating an uplift of asphalt and a kind of ramp several yards across. He eyed the angle of the uplift and the width of the newly formed river, calculating. Dani had once commented that he possessed a remarkable "physical intelligence," and it was true; all his life, he'd be able to physically execute anything he could mentally visualize.

"What are you thinking?" Reese said.

"I think I could jump it on the Grizzly," Tommy said. "I just don't know if I could make it with both of us on it."

"So go," Reese said. "I can walk back."

"Are you sure?"

"After what we've been through tonight? You think *this* is going to stop me?"

"Take this," Tommy said, handing Reese his flashlight and his phone. Reese examined the phone briefly.

"You mind if I make a video of you jumping the stream that I could put on YouTube?"

"That would be awesome," Tommy said.

He turned the ATV around and raced up the hill. He'd once gotten the Grizzly up to 65 mph on dry pavement, on level ground. This was downhill; he should be able to go even faster.

He took a deep breath, then opened the throttle to full with his thumb and gunned it, heading straight for the buckled pavement. He had no idea how fast he was going when he hit it, but the ATV launched into the air, just as he'd planned. He leaned back and pulled on the steering bar to raise the front wheels but stayed forward enough, knees bent, to remain centered above the airborne vehicle. *Alive*, he thought thankfully, and then the back wheels hit, hard enough to bounce him completely out of the seat, his legs lifting high above his head behind him. He clung to the handlebars, managing to pull himself back down as the ATV bounced twice more before settling to a stop.

He turned around and saw he'd cleared the rivulet by twenty feet. Reese waved to him.

Part of him thought that if the private detective thing didn't work out, a new career as a stuntman was waiting for him.

The warning horn, three longs and three shorts in a repeating pattern, required as many members of the volunteer fire department as were available to meet at the service road leading to the dam, the rendezvous point laid out in their disaster preparedness training. As he gunned the ATV past his driveway, he came to a more formidable roadblock—Dani, standing in front of his Jeep, between the headlights, her arms crossed against her chest.

She raised a hand to shield her eyes from the beam of the ATV's floodlight.

Tommy hit the brakes and slid sideways, skidding to a stop next to her. He turned off the light.

"Where's Reese?"

"He wanted to walk," Tommy said. "He didn't like the way I drive. He'll be here in maybe twenty minutes."

"I said I'm coming with you," she said. "Tonight. Thick or thin. You and me."

He'd wanted only for her to be safe, but he understood. They would be together, through anything, always.

"I'll drive," he said, moving the ATV off the road and parking it. He grabbed the floodlight and ran around to the other side of the Jeep. He climbed in and threw the light into the back.

"What have you heard?" he said, turning on his high beams and shifting from second to third as he sped away.

"The National Guard is on the way," Dani said. "The roads are bad all around Westchester. They're trying to get everybody out of town but . . ."

She didn't have to say more. If the dam gave, the town would be destroyed. After what had gone wrong in New Orleans during Hurricane Katrina, the Army Corps of Engineers had examined and certified that the earthworks, built in 1897, would hold up to the most severe storms and associated flooding, but they couldn't possibly have prepared for this sort of assault from the elements.

"Everyone at the house is okay?"

"They're okay. Casey said he'd call if he learns anything. I got a text from Quinn. He destroyed the virus."

"Where is he?"

"I don't know. I can't reach him."

"Nuts," Tommy said, braking suddenly.

The road in front of them was gone, another washout, but this time there wasn't a ramp for Tommy to jump the stream, and he wouldn't have made it in the Jeep anyway. The raging water here was a hundred feet across. There was water everywhere he looked, the whole world saturated, with nowhere for it to go, and it was still falling from the sky.

"What do we do?" Dani asked.

"Plan B," he said, backing up and reversing direction.

"What's Plan B?"

"It's what you do after Plan A fails," he said. "Or as my dad liked to say, 'Use common sense and make something up.'"

A quarter mile up the road, he turned into the parking lot at the Pastures, roared past the darkened clubhouse, and skidded onto the first fairway, which sloped down toward the lake. The Jeep's knobby tires left deep grooves in the spongy turf as he navigated past sand traps filled with standing water.

"They're not going to like that," he said, looking over his shoulder at the ruts he'd made before turning right and leaving the golf course to crash through the brush and maul his way through the fence that separated the Pastures from Gardener Farm. He skewed his way through a small apple orchard and slowed as he approached a flooded field.

"Hang on," he told Dani. "I don't know how far this will get us."

He shifted into second gear and stomped on the gas as he hit the water, spraying a rooster tail behind them as he plowed forward, fast at first, then slower and slower as the water deepened.

"Where are you going?" Dani said. "The road—"

She stopped talking then as the Jeep's headlights fell on the Boston Whaler Tommy had left moored to the dock after getting the lake water samples Quinn had requested. The boat was now floating almost level to the front porch of the Gardener home.

The Jeep's engine coughed, sputtered, and died as the water rose above the air intake. They were fifty yards short of their goal.

"Come on!" Tommy said. He reached in the backseat and grabbed the floodlight. He tucked it under one arm and jumped from the vehicle. The water was waist deep.

"Yowza, that's cold," Dani shrieked.

"Try not to think about it," Tommy said, taking her by the hand to make sure she didn't trip and fall.

"How can I not think about how cold it is?" she said. "I'm waist deep in a giant bucket of ice water."

"You should try peeling onions."

"What?"

"Peel onions," Tommy said. "That'll make your ice water. Sorry. That's from a Marx Brothers movie."

"That's terrible."

"Have you noticed how screaming at each other like this actually makes you feel warmer?"

"I noticed."

By the time they reached the Whaler, they were both shivering. He lifted her up over the transom, handed her the floodlight, then climbed aboard.

While Dani cast off, Tommy started the engines. He reversed slowly, backing the boat out from the trees and into the open water.

"Grab on to something!" he shouted, and pushed the throttle to full. The three massive 300-horsepower engines kicked the craft forward with enough force to knock Dani off her feet and back into the seats.

The hardtop canopy over their heads and the windshield in front of them provided minimal shelter from the rain, but enough of a windbreak that if they shouted, they could hear each other.

"Plan B seems to be working," Dani yelled. "What now?"

"Plan C," Tommy shouted back. "Obviously."

"Which is . . . ?"

"Why are you looking at me?" Tommy said. "I came up with Plan B. It's your turn."

"I'll tell you the second I think of something," Dani said.

Tommy turned the volume on his marine radio to ten and dialed in channel 16, the emergency distress frequency. Ahead, where the earthworks held back the water, he saw a single orange flasher—and closer to the road, the flashing lights of a police car. He turned on the floodlight on the bow and aimed it as far forward as possible.

He held the microphone to his mouth. "Mayday, Mayday! Whoever's on the dam—I've got a boat on the water," he said. "What have you got? Come back."

"We have maybe five minutes to failure," someone said. "That you, Tommy?"

"Who've I got?"

"DeGidio," the radio said. "Turn around. Get to shore. We can't fill it. It won't hold."

"Fill what?"

"There's a gap. The earthworks is breached," DeGidio said. "We're trying to slow it down, but it's just getting wider."

"What about the overflow sluice?"

"Already full capacity. There's a flood sluice at the bottom, but we can't open it. Something's blocking it."

"Did you send a diver?"

"No time," Frank said.

As Tommy approached the dam, he saw what Frank was talking about. There was a weak spot at the top of the earthworks, a gap, and water was pouring through it over the lip of the dam. Frank and two utility company workers were trying to throw sandbags into the gap, but the water just flowed around and over them.

"Get to your car!" Tommy shouted. Dani turned the floodlight and shone it where the men were working frantically to save the town. Tommy turned on his ship-to-ship hailing speakers and repeated his suggestion. "Get to your car—I'm going to plug the hole!"

Frank DeGidio made an X over his head with his arms to tell Tommy to back off, that it was no use, but Tommy ignored him. Fifty yards from the breach, he turned the boat to starboard and then circled back, bringing the Boston Whaler around slowly until it was parallel to the dam before inching forward into the current, using his bow thrusters to position the boat more precisely, drifting sideways toward the gap. The force of the water took the Whaler the rest of the way, wedging the 37' long, 13,500 pound craft in the gap to temporarily plug the hole. It was only after he'd done it that he stopped to think that had he misjudged the distance or the current or the size of the gap, the current would have pushed him over the dam, either bow first or stern first. That would not have ended well.

"Go, go, go!" Tommy told the three men, waving his arms frantically. "Dani, go with them!"

"What are you going to do?" she asked.

"I'm going to hold the boat here as long as I can," he said.

"Then I'm staying." The look on her face told him there would be no further discussion.

He waved Frank DeGidio off and angled the floodlight up to light the way, then watched as Frank and the others reached the squad car and headed toward higher ground, their taillights disappearing in the rain.

He moved aft and saw where the floodwaters coursed behind the boat, then ran forward to the bow, where the same thing was true. They'd plugged the hole in the dam, but now there was no way off the boat. Sooner or later, perhaps in only a few minutes, the dam would give. They'd bought the people in the town below some time, but failure remained inevitable.

Dani was a step behind him; Tommy grabbed two lifejackets and handed her one.

"I'm glad I'm here," she told him. "I wouldn't want to be anywhere else."

"I can't say I'm glad you're here, but I'm glad you're here. You'd better put this on," he said.

"Ya think?" she told him, taking the lifejacket from him and helping him tighten the straps on his own. Then she grabbed him and pulled him close.

"Tommy Gunderson," she said, "you're the most amazing man I have ever met in my entire life. It just blows me away, day after day. You're funny and smart and handsome as all get-out, but none of that matters compared to how pure your heart is, and I love you the way I have never loved anybody. Will you marry me?"

"What?" he said.

"Will you marry me?" she said.

"No, I heard you," he said, at a loss for words. "It's just . . . You have no idea."

"Don't say no or I'll throw you off this boat."

He fished in his pocket and found the ring he'd been carrying with him for the last four days, the blue velvet box soggy enough to crumble in his hand.

"I'll marry you if you'll marry me," he said. "I got you a ring."

He opened the box, squeezing the soggy lid until it fell from the hinges, but the ring shone brightly. She reached into her pocket and produced a similar box.

"I got you one too," she said, opening it to reveal a band of broad silver with two small diamonds set into it side by side, a ring that was clearly masculine and, Tommy thought, more precious than the cost of its components. "I went to Gruen's."

He put it on. It fit. Dani's ring fit her as well.

"That guy can keep a secret. You know, technically, as the captain of this boat, I'm legally empowered to marry us right now. If you want."

The boat shifted beneath them, lurching a foot closer to the edge.

"I was sort of hoping we could have a big wedding in a church," Dani said.

"So was I," Tommy said, thinking that if they made it out alive, that was exactly what he wanted. "So it's a date?"

"It's a date."

She kissed him, and he kissed her back, and the earth moved under their feet, or rather, under the boat.

Tommy opened his eyes and saw that the dam was collapsing.

44.

December 24

Tommy leapt for the controls, gunned the engines, and turned the wheel hard to port, his propellers churning mightily against the current. But as the water poured over the top of the dam, the Whaler, moving full speed ahead, only held its place, pulling slowly forward at first but losing ground as the speed of the water flow increased.

He pushed hard against the throttle.

"Come on!" he shouted at the boat. "Gimme more!"

The engines strained. The boat inched forward. For a second he believed he'd reached escape velocity. Then the big boat moved backward again. He didn't dare turn the wheel in any direction except straight against the flow, but he was losing ground.

He pointed to Dani to buckle her seat belt as he fought to stay above the brim.

"Hold on to something!" he yelled, but he realized as he shouted that it was pointless. They were going over the dam, as were the contents of Lake Atticus. It took him just a split second to decide that if he was taking a "Nantucket sleighride," he'd rather go facing forward. "Are you buckled in?" he shouted.

"I'm good—go for it—I trust you!"

He swung hard about and launched the Whaler into the darkness.

The boat fell out from underneath him—only his hands on the wheel saved him from flying straight up in the air. It was 120 feet from the lip of the dam to the catchment area below, but to Tommy, it felt like he was weightless for a full minute, everything in slow motion, water all around him, water below him and above him and to every side. The boat accelerated and pitched forward, yawing right and rolling such that it finally landed tilting thirty degrees to starboard, the bow completely submerged, the deck and cockpit awash before the unsinkable Whaler lived up to its name and righted itself.

He looked over at Dani, whose eyes were open wider than he would have ever thought possible.

"You okay?"

She gave him a thumbs-up, pushing her wet hair away from her face.

As the decks cleared of water, Tommy heard the automatic bilge pumps kick in and wondered how much water they'd taken on, though the cabin hatch was closed. Judging from how the boat rode, it appeared that the hull had maintained its integrity, but now they were riding the flood, moving fast.

"Watch out!" Dani shouted.

Tommy turned the wheel to avoid hitting what appeared to be a small floating house, or perhaps a garage, grateful he still had engine power. He throttled all the way back, carried along by the force of the water, short of the leading edge of the flood, keeping only enough power to maneuver as the wall of water picked up speed, destroying everything in its path.

Up ahead he saw a large building, lights aglow in the darkness.

"Look!"

He pointed at it just as the mass of water poured over the stone walls surrounding St. Adrian's Academy and arced through the air. A million tons of water landed on the main building, crushing it into pebbles. The dormitories, the new science building, the art museum, all fell before the power of the raging waters.

But now he felt himself falling again. Dani grabbed hold of his arm and held tight as the earth itself gave way—as the weight of the water pressed down on the campus of St. Adrian's and the hollow caverns beneath it.

A split second later, the place where the school had stood turned into a colossal waterfall.

The boat lurched beneath his feet as they went over the falls. He lost his footing and felt himself falling overboard—then Dani grabbed him and held on to him. They circled once in a whirlpool before spinning out again. Tommy got to his feet and worked his way back to the steering wheel.

"The town!" Dani shouted. "It's below the school."

"Get on the radio," he said, handing Dani the microphone. "See if you can—"

He stopped.

"See if I can what?" Dani asked him. She shook his arm. "Tommy—see if I can what?"

"Never mind," he said, his voice relaxed now. He regained control of the boat, then tapped Dani on the shoulder and pointed. "Look."

She turned. Below the cliff where the campus had once stood, a pair of angels were holding their wings out wide to divert the flood. Charlie and Ben. They'd promised to be there when they were needed, and here they were now, fully revealed in holy raiment, their forms shimmering with a golden light where they stood above the waters. The town below the school was safe.

Tommy wrapped his arm around Dani's shoulders. She put her arms around him and held him close.

"That's Plan C," she said. Then out of the corner of her eye she caught sight of something flying above them. Tommy looked up and saw the drone.

"Tommy and Dani. You okay?"

It was Reese's voice, coming over Tommy's Bluetooth earpiece.

"We're fine," Tommy said, giving the drone a thumbs-up. "Is anybody there hurt?"

"The school is gone," Reese replied. "Who's on the boat with you?"

"Who's what?" Tommy asked.

"Behind you."

Tommy turned to see Adolf Ghieri holding Dani by the throat.

45.

December 24

The fiend was decaying from the inside out, his spiritual corruption eating away at him like a cancer. He looked older, sicker, paler, but Tommy knew the demon still possessed a power superior to his own. The rain dripped off his bald skull. He was dressed in what had been formal wear, his bow tie unknotted at his neck. He'd been attending the gala at St. Adrian's, Tommy realized. The fund-raiser. Ghieri had been inside the main building when the water came, and now . . . he was here.

The monster held Dani toward the rear of the boat, her hands pulling at his arm but unable to move it.

"Let her go," Tommy said.

"Or what? You're not in charge here," Ghieri said.

"So you'd rather fight girls than me?" Tommy said. "I was going to ask you if it made you feel like a big man, but I keep forgetting—you're not human. That would constitute a major upgrade."

Ghieri tightened his grip around Dani's throat. "You feeling strong, little man?" he said. "Would you like to know what true power really is? Invite me in. This body is no longer useful to me. I need a new one. Invite me in, or this woman you cherish dies in my hands. Invite me in and I'll let her go."

"Don't do it!" Dani said before Ghieri tightened his grip to silence her.

With no one at the helm, the boat drifted in the current, spinning like a leaf in a stream. Tommy grabbed the console to steady himself, his hand only a foot away from the emergency flare pistol attached to the console by a plastic bracket.

"Come on—what's the matter? You afraid of me?" Tommy said. His only thought was to get Ghieri to attack him, not Dani. Perhaps she would have a chance to escape.

"You challenge me?" Ghieri said. "Are you as mentally defective as all the other humans I've known?"

"Do you own a television?" Tommy asked.

"Do I what?"

"Do you own a television?" he repeated. "Because I'm guessing you must have seen me play football. Maybe I can't defeat you, but you know I can hurt you."

"Like the boy you killed on the field?" Ghieri said.

Tommy tried not to react. Tried . . . and failed.

"Dwight Sikes," Ghieri said. "Remember how you felt when you cracked his skull open? You exalted in it. You raised your arms to the sky and danced. Remember? You belong with me. Invite me in. I'm giving you the chance to join the winning side."

"How is it that you've lived a thousand times longer than I have, but I'm so much smarter than you?" Tommy said. "You were thrown out of heaven because Satan thought he was smarter than God, and now you're so stupid, something that should be obvious escapes you completely."

He moved his hand closer to the flare pistol.

"You have absolutely no idea what I can do," Ghieri said.

"And you have no idea what God can do," Tommy said. "That's what you don't get. Dani and I aren't afraid to die. It just means we'll meet Jesus a little sooner than we expected. You don't get to meet him at all. You blew that one a long time ago."

"Your faith is pathetic."

"My faith is intact."

"You want to test it?" Ghieri said. "I've been breaking men more pious than you for a thousand years."

"Yeah," Tommy said, "but did they have one of these?"

He grabbed the flare pistol and fired it at Ghieri from fifteen feet away.

Ghieri caught the burning missile in his left hand, snatching the potassium nitrate and magnesium projectile in midair. He examined it for a moment, then popped it into his mouth as casually as if he were eating a grape and swallowed.

The demon took a step toward Tommy.

"All righty then," Tommy said. "So much for Plan D."

Ghieri snarled and threw Dani aside. "This is where the villain tells the victim to say his prayers," he said. "And you'll see just how much good they'll do you."

He stepped closer, reached out, and put a finger to Tommy's chest, pressing hard against Tommy's sternum.

Tommy had no illusions about Ghieri's strength. He knew that if the fiend wanted to, he could tear a hole in his chest and pull his heart directly out of him.

"It's rude to point," Tommy said.

"Are you supposing your angel friends will step in to help you?" Ghieri said. "Last I checked, they were busy holding back the floodwaters."

The demon pressed harder against Tommy's chest. Tommy wanted to cry out from the pain, but he held his tongue, and his ground, defiant. He would not give the demon what he wanted.

"Do you know how your friend Abigail Gardener died?" Ghieri asked. "We sucked the life out of her. She was crushed, like a submarine at the bottom of the sea. But maybe you're one of those humans who responds well to *pressure*."

He laid a finger on Tommy's lips, and suddenly Tommy felt himself unable to breathe. He felt like an elephant was sitting on his chest, squeezed from all directions; his head felt like it might implode, his eyes like they might burst from his head.

There was a sudden crack, and the finger lifted from his lips. Ghieri was wobbling on his feet.

Tommy saw Dani standing behind him, holding the fire extinguisher she'd used to smack the demon on the side of his head.

"Leave him alone!" she shouted.

"I forgot," Ghieri said, sneering. "You *love* each other. That's going to make this even more pleasurable."

The demon got to his feet, and once more his finger pushed on Tommy's chest. This time Tommy screamed and almost fell to his knees.

"Let go of him!" he heard Dani shout.

"Stay back," Tommy said through gritted teeth. "Leave him—"

He looked up just in time to see Dani grab Ghieri by the shoulder and spin him around to face her.

"I told you to let go of him," she said. She pulled her hand out from behind her back.

"What's that?" Ghieri asked. "A pocketknife?"

"It's more than a pocketknife," Dani said. "It's a Swiss Army knife."

Tommy had seen a knife very similar to the one she was holding once before—in Charlie's hands.

"That's a special knife," he said. "Where did you get it?"

"Someone must have given it to me without telling me," Dani said. "I found it in my coat pocket."

"What's so special about it?" Ghieri scoffed.

"Well," Dani said. "It has attachments." She gave the knife a squeeze.

Nothing happened.

Ghieri took another step toward her.

"I said, *it has attachments*," she repeated, louder now.

"Say please," Tommy suggested.

"Please."

Suddenly the knife became a blade of pure fire, though the flames did not scorch her hand. Ghieri stepped back, but too late. Dani jumped toward him, raised the fiery sword high above her head with both hands, and speared the demon clean through the heart.

The demon's face registered his shock as he fell backward, grasping the flames with both hands. Dani twisted the sword, put one foot on Ghieri's chest, and pushed him over the gunwale and into the water.

And then, just as suddenly, all she held was a Swiss Army knife.

Tommy had slumped to the deck. She ran to his side and held him close, kissing him, grateful to find him safe and whole.

"Are you okay?" she asked.

"I will be," Tommy said, sitting up and rubbing his chest. "It's like getting the wind knocked out of you, except a thousand times worse."

"Just rest for a second," she told him.

"Can I see that? The knife?" he asked her. Dani handed it to him. It seemed quite ordinary now.

"We're going to need that back."

He turned to see Ben and Charlie standing by the cockpit.

"You sure?" Tommy asked, smiling. "I'd take good care of it."

"I'm sure you would," Charlie said, "but this was just a loan."

"We know how much you like gadgets," Ben said.

The angel held his hands out to form a basket.

Tommy sighed. "Oh well." He tossed the knife to Charlie.

"Wait—Ghieri said—" Dani began, but the angels were gone before she could ask them a question.

Tommy took her in his arms and kissed her. When they broke the embrace, though, she wasn't smiling.

"What's wrong?" Tommy asked. "We won. Ghieri's gone. He's not coming back."

Dani shook her head.

"We didn't win," she said.

46.

December 24

9:39 p.m. EST

Dani said she needed to think. Tommy wanted to help her, but without knowing exactly what was bothering her, he didn't know what to do. He focused on practical matters, on the boat, and on getting them back on solid ground.

The city lights of Stamford glowing in the sky downstream told him they were approaching the ocean and open water. The floodwaters had joined with the Georgetown River, causing it to overflow its banks, where the people and the businesses were accustomed to periodic flooding and were prepared for it. There was too much debris in the water, and it was still too dark to safely turn the boat around and head upstream, so he went with the strong current, riding the high water as they passed beneath Interstate 95, which paralleled the shoreline.

He dialed the radio to the local NPR station, which reported that the only structures seriously damaged by the floods had been the school and the research campus for Linz Pharmazeutika, where the building closest to the river, Building C, was completely destroyed. He called Ruth to check in. She didn't have good news. She hadn't heard a word from either Quinn or Cassandra.

Tommy managed to raise Frank DeGidio on a police frequency to make sure he was okay.

"Any casualties?"

"They're still trying to count. There were a number of people at St. Adrian's for some sort of celebration. That place was wiped out."

"How about in town?"

"None in East Salem," DeGidio said. "They're calling it a miracle. The whole lake spills down the valley and nobody gets hurt. We thought we had one but turns out we were wrong—you remember that kid who killed that girl?"

"Amos Kasden?"

"Yeah," DeGidio said. "Apparently the floodwaters disinterred his grave, because we found his body washed up near the school. Anyway, looks like East Salem got lucky."

"Looks like," Tommy said. Amos Kasden had been cremated, but no matter.

"You'll never guess what they found at the bottom of Lake Atticus after all the water drained out," DeGidio said. "Some guys went up there to survey the damage."

"A Harley Fat Boy and a Night Rod," Tommy said. "And the 2004 Honda CRV George Gardener drove into the water when he disappeared."

"How'd you know?"

"Just a guess."

"Okay, wise guy—guess what else? Guess what was clogging the floodgates at the bottom of the dam?"

"What?"

"A 1968 Mustang Boss. Wasn't that the car you sank in the lake when you were racing Gerry Roebling on the ice in high school?"

"Do you really think I'd do something that lame?" Tommy said. It had been a stupid prank in high school, a dare that made him drive his car out onto the ice and then fall through, but it had been part of God's plan, even then. If his car hadn't blocked the sluice, the rain might not have overwhelmed the dam. He'd been playing his part, even in high school, when he had no idea of what was to come. The wonder of it all astonished him.

"Yes, you would," Frank said. "Thank you."

"For what?"

"For saving my life back there," DeGidio said. "I'm gonna make sure people know what you did for the town."

"If you don't mind, I'd rather you didn't," Tommy said. "I've really had it with the whole fame thing. Right now, the less attention I get, the better."

"Okay. I gotcha. Merry Christmas, Tommy," Frank said.

"You too. Merry Christmas," Tommy said, and hung up.

"Maybe not so merry," Dani said.

"Dani—talk to me. Tell me what's bothering you."

"We failed," she said, turning to face him. "Look."

She held up a small plastic case. It was Quinn's case, containing the water samples taken from Tommy's pond and from Lake Atticus, as well as the reagents Quinn had devised to test for the presence of the endocrine disrupting agent. The Doomsday Molecule. That name felt right to Dani now. It was a simple test. Take a water sample, add the EDA reagent, and if the water turned red, it meant the water was contaminated.

"Watch." She took a water sample from the bottom of the boat, Lake Atticus water, and added the reagent. It turned red.

"We were too late," she said. "Ed Stanley was right. It's already happened. It's already spreading."

"We did the right thing," Tommy said. "We just have to figure out what to do next."

"What would that be?" she said. "We can't clean up all the water in the world. After all this. After everything we did . . ."

"Dani—"

"After Charlie and Ben . . . I don't understand. We couldn't let them kill all those boys. How could we fail? How? How could we fail?"

"I don't know," Tommy said. "I don't have an answer."

"No Plan E?"

"No Plan E," Tommy said.

The rain had stopped. Tommy gazed toward the sea and realized they'd drifted into Bowden Harbor. To his left he saw a single star in the sky. He recalled the stories of the star of Bethlehem, but the star of Bethlehem had risen in the east. It was the North Star he saw, unless the axis of the earth had changed.

He dumped the water sample Dani had given him overboard, then leaned down to rinse out the test tube. He raised the test tube up to look at the city lights through it. The water was clear. Just curious, he poured some of the EDA reagent into it. The water remained clear. He dumped the contents overboard.

"At least the water here isn't contaminated," he said.

"Well, this is saltwater," Dani said. She could hear the despair in her own voice, and she didn't like the sound of it. She sighed. "Nobody drinks saltwater."

Then, in an instant, she had an epiphany.

"What did you say?" she asked Tommy.

"I said the water here isn't contaminated."

"And what did I say?"

"You said it's saltwater, and nobody drinks saltwater."

"Banerjee thought Carl must have drowned in saltwater, but he didn't," Dani said. "I remember that when he was eating, he used way too much salt. I wanted to tell him it wasn't good for him."

She reached into the plastic case for a fresh test tube and handed one to Tommy.

"Fill this with saltwater," she told him.

She filled the second test tube from the water in the bottom of the boat and added the EDA reagent. It turned red. She added saltwater to it. It turned clear again. She repeated the experiment and got the same results. She started to laugh.

"Tommy," she exclaimed, "I could be crazy, but—it's too obvious. It's so obvious they wouldn't even think about it."

"What is?"

"Salt," she said. "The antidote is salt." She laughed in full now, no reason to hold back. "They tested the drug in fresh water. They wouldn't test it in saltwater, because nobody drinks saltwater."

"Still not following you," he said.

"Quinn said they had to modify the drug right before the release because the side effects were so extreme that nobody would keep taking it. He said it takes a few months to build up in the body before it has any effect. All drinking water recycles through the oceans. Even if you put the drug in fresh water, eventually the salt in the oceans would nullify it. We didn't fail. I mean, we did, but God didn't."

"What about the red version they developed at DARPA?" Tommy said.

"The blue version recombines with molecular metabolites already in the water to feed the virus," Dani said. "The red version is just the concentrated virus. It's the same thing once you dilute it in a large reservoir."

She turned to see the stars shining on the Atlantic. She took Tommy's hand.

"'God was moving over the face of the waters,'" Dani said. "Isn't that how Genesis starts?"

"It sure is."

"There's a lot of salt in the ocean," Dani said. "God took care of it. A long time ago."

"I have a better one," Tommy said. "'Have salt in yourselves, and be at peace with one another.' Mark chapter 9, if I recall."

He saw a place to bring the boat in and steered for it. As he did, he started to laugh.

"What's so funny?" Dani asked him.

"I was just thinking of how hard we tried to stop the dam from breaking," he said. "If we'd been successful, the school would still be there. We failed. But God wanted us to fail. It's just . . ."

"What?"

"The word is overused, but all I can think is, it's just awesome."

47.

December 25

On the island of Sardinia, at a place called Porto Palmas just up the coast from the village of Argentera, a young shepherd boy was moving his flock along the dirt road that hugged the shoreline. His mother had asked him to bring the sheep out for the day and then hurry home because she had a special Christmas breakfast waiting for him, and presents under the tree as well. It was quite early in the morning, and so he was surprised when he saw a woman—a beautiful woman, at that—emerging from the sea. This was not a time of day when people usually went swimming, nor was this a part of the island commonly visited by tourists. On top of which, it was Christmas morning.

The most surprising thing of all, though, was that he recognized the woman. It was the famous American actress, the one who had dated Alberto, the soccer player. He froze where he stood, watching as she stepped up from the sea and crossed the beach and then the sea grass.

She paused and turned to look back in the direction from which she'd come. He followed her gaze and saw something submerged just beneath the surface of the water, a Jet Ski that had grounded itself on the reef, and beyond that, unless his eyes were playing tricks on him, the dorsal fin of a large shark.

"Io ti conosco," the boy said. *"Lei è Cassandra Morton."*

"Hello," she said cheerfully. She gave him a dazzling smile. "Do you know where I can find a phone?"

"È possibile utilizzare il mio cellular," the boy said, reaching into his pocket and handing her his own cell phone. *"Io amo i tuoi film."*

"Thank you," she said, dialing the operator number and then, as it rang, turning to wave good-bye to the shark that had been following her all night. After starting the Jet Ski, she'd circled back to where the *Freiheit* had sunk, on the chance that Laurent—that CIA operative Matthew Shorter—was still alive, but she was alone on the sea, so she located the North Star in the sky and then steered a course to the east. It had been a long night, but she never doubted she'd make it to land. When the operator answered, she asked to speak to anyone who spoke English. A few minutes later, from a remote beach in Sardinia, she heard the phone ringing at Tommy Gunderson's house, but then the call went to voice mail, so she left a message before handing the boy his phone back.

At the airport, she called her agent in Hollywood collect, woke him up, and had him buy her a one-way ticket home, first class. She was in the waiting area when she saw the news on the television. A terrible rain had caused a dam to burst in the town of East Salem, New York, she could understand, even though the newscast was in Italian. She borrowed a phone from a fan who wanted an autograph and called Tommy again, but again could only leave a message—she surmised that the flood had probably knocked out the landlines, and she didn't know his cell phone number—and then it was time to board.

In the lobby of Northern Westchester Hospital, in the town of Mt. Kisco, just as the sun was rising in the east, the woman at the reception desk rose from her chair and walked quickly to catch up to the man who was trying to escape. He was dressed in a hospital-issued Johnny that opened in the back, though he'd managed to somehow secure a pair of pajama bottoms.

"Excuse me, sir—you have to wait," she said, touching him on the arm to stop him. "You have to be discharged."

Quinn McKellen turned to face her. "I'm sorry," he said. "I don't want you to get into trouble, but I'm fine."

"Sir," the woman insisted, "you have to be discharged. Patients can't just leave."

"I'm a doctor," Quinn said. "I'm a patient, and a doctor. I just looked at my MRI. I had a midgrade infiltrating multiform glioblastoma of the pons reticular formation, but I don't anymore. There's really no reason for me to stay."

"Sir "

"Please," he said. "You have all my insurance information if it's the bill you're worried about."

"Yes, sir," she said. "But you have to be released. By a doctor."

"I am a doctor," he said. "I can release myself."

"Really?"

"Really," he said. He looked at her name tag. "Ellen, it's Christmas morning, and I'm fine, and I don't want to spend it in a hospital if I don't have to. I have . . ." He almost said *family*, but his real family was far away. "People. I have people I need to be with. I promise you I'll check back with you tomorrow, and if they hold you responsible for letting me go, I will assure them I escaped and you did everything you could to deter me."

A cab driver got out of his cab in front of the hospital's main entrance and held the door open for Quinn. The woman looked down and saw that Quinn was stocking-footed.

"You don't have any shoes," she said.

"I'm not walking," he said, getting into the cab.

The television in Tommy's kitchen was tuned to the news. They were calling it the Miracle on 769th Street, which was approximately where East Salem would have ranked if the cross street numbers of Manhattan kept going. Miracle because after the dam holding back the waters of Lake Atticus had broken, the town of East Salem, New York, fifty miles north of the city, had been miraculously spared when the saturated ground under St. Adrian's Academy for Boys gave way and collapsed, the landslide leaving behind a stone escarpment that diverted the path of the water, sparing the town and the thousands of residents who hadn't had time to evacuate. Known casualties included a group of St. Adrian's alumni who'd returned to campus for a holiday party, believed to number close to a hundred. The names had not been released, pending notification of next of kin, but according to a Detective Phillip Casey, one of the first to arrive on the scene, it was believed that both headmaster John Adams Wharton and school psychologist Adolf Ghieri had perished in the flood. The only other known victim was a research chemist named Andrei Guryakin who'd been working late in the basement of Building C, on the Linz Pharmazeutika campus, on the banks of the Georgetown River.

The cab Dani and Tommy took back to his house had been forced to detour several times where trees or downed power lines blocked the roads, making a trip that would ordinarily take forty-five minutes take twice as long. They'd passed dozens of utility company crews already hard at work. More good news awaited Tommy when he got home shortly before noon. Ruth told him the landlines were already working and that Cassandra had called and left two messages, one that she was safe, and a second message sometime later saying she'd heard about the flood and worried that everyone was okay. He sent her a text saying everything was fine.

At the airport they met Cassandra at the baggage area. She ran to Tommy and Dani and Ruth and Reese and hugged each one, saying she'd been so worried that they'd gotten caught in the flood, but somehow had had faith that they were going to be okay. She pointed out her one piece of luggage to Tommy, a large suitcase she'd purchased and filled with Christmas presents.

"I hope you like things made out of coral," she said. "And salami. There's not a lot to buy in Sardinia at the airport."

"They make things out of coral and salami?" Tommy said.

"You know what I mean," Cassandra said. "I would have asked Henry to recommend places to shop, but I lost the phone you gave me."

"Don't worry about it," Tommy said. "Who's Henry?"

"From the phone," Cassandra said.

"Henry from the phone?"

"The personal assistance voice," Cassandra said. "Like the one they have for iPhones."

"I'm not sure what you're talking about," Tommy said. "GPhones don't have personal assistance avatars."

"Well, of course they do," Cassandra said. "I've been talking to him for the last—" She looked from face to face until she realized they weren't playing a trick on her. "Then who have I been talking to?"

"I don't know," Tommy said. "But if angels can take the form of bikers and Native Americans, I don't see why one couldn't be present as a phone avatar."

Cassandra opened her eyes wide and then smiled.

Dani held out her left hand, where a large diamond glittered on her finger.

"Oh my goodness," Cassandra said. "Tell me how he proposed."

"Long story," Dani said.

As they left the baggage area and headed for the one where the flight from London would off-load its cargo, Dani saw someone she knew. Ed Stanley was at the luggage carousel, waiting for them, wearing the same camel hair overcoat and Borsalino hat. He dragged behind him a small black suitcase on rollers.

"I'm guessing this isn't a coincidence," Dani said.

"No, it's not," Ed Stanley said. "Well, in a way it is. I'm flying back to Montana in an hour, from a different terminal, but I told my men I wanted them to keep an eye on you to make sure you were safe. They told me you were here."

"Did you come to say good-bye?" Dani asked. She'd sent him a brief e-mail earlier in the day, telling him what they'd learned about the threat, or lack thereof, to the world's drinking water.

"I suppose I did," Stanley said. "And to apologize. Our people at DARPA confirmed your results. I'm sorry I didn't trust you. I should have. And I'm sorry about the boy."

"His name is Edmond Stratton-Mallins," Dani said.

"Yes," Stanley said. "Edmond. I'm sorry that the result was so . . ."

"Thanatogenic?"

"We made a mistake," Stanley said. "I'm sorry."

"You're sorry for killing Edmond?"

"Yes."

"Why don't you tell him yourself, then?" Dani said.

Stanley turned, and Dani pointed to the escalator and to a boy coming down it, identical to the brother who waited for him at the bottom, their faces beaming with pure joy.

"I don't understand," Ed Stanley said.

"The person you killed was named Alfredo Guzman," Dani said. "I wanted you to think you'd killed Edmond. Guzman had been sent to assassinate Edmond. So yeah, you got the bad guy, but don't let it go to your head—you still made a mistake. But I think you can be forgiven for it."

Edmond, who had taken the same flight from Heathrow that Cassandra was on after changing planes, reached the bottom, and the two brothers jumped into a hug and pressed their heads together.

"Nothing is ever going to come between us again," Reese told Edmond. "We can add people to our lives without subtracting each other."

"I know," Edmond said. "I have to explain—they told me if I didn't do what they said, they were going to kill you. I couldn't let them hurt you. I'm really confused right now. About so many things."

Dani smiled and squeezed his shoulder. "It's all right, Edmond," she said. "We're going to help you. You and the other boys as well."

She'd spent some time already making arrangements to bring all of the Selected back to the United States, where she would work with them and counsel them and, with God's help, restore them to their former selves.

"It might take time, but we're going to bring you back."

"Thank you," Edmond said. "I've heard a lot about you."

"How could you have heard a lot about me?" Dani asked.

Edmond looked at his brother.

"Don't worry," Reese said. "They'll get it eventually."

Passengers were using their cell phones to take pictures of Cassandra the second she stepped beyond the security area. Tommy put his right arm around Dani and pulled her close to him.

"As soon as somebody gets Cass and me in the same picture, they're going to sell it to the tabloids, and the tabloids are going to say there are rumors that we're getting back together," Tommy told Dani. "It's not that I care what the tabloids say, but if I get my picture taken with anyone, I want it to be with you."

"'Mystery Woman Breaks Up Tom-Sandra Reunion,'" Dani said. "I can live with that."

When they got back to the house, Quinn was there. He told Dani and Tommy and the others what Charlie had done.

"The doctors have given me the all-clear too," he added. "And I don't need a second opinion."

Otto and Arlo were curled up together in front of the fireplace. Detective Casey had gone home to his own wife and family. Ruth told Dani her sister had called to check in, and that their grandfather had arrived safely. She had a message for Tommy as well—a lawyer had called to say he represented the estate of George Gardener, who, the lawyer said, had recently added a codicil to his will, leaving the Gardener Farm and everything on it to Tommy. The will was entirely valid, signed and witnessed. Tommy looked at Dani.

"It would make a nice halfway house for all those boys," she said. "Once they rebuild the dam and the lake fills up again. Though we might want to move the paintings to a more secure location."

"I was thinking the same thing," Tommy said. "Anybody else call?"

"Yes," Ruth said. "An Agent Cooney called from the FBI. Detective Casey spoke to him. They've closed the files on Dr. Wharton."

"All right, then," Tommy agreed.

Ruth had supper waiting, but Tommy told Dani they had one more stop to make.

He'd called ahead. His father was waiting in a wheelchair in the lobby at High Ridge Manor. A nurse, a pleasant woman of about fifty, was waiting with him. Arnie was drawing pictures on the GTab Tommy had given him, pictures of trees.

"How's he doing?" Tommy asked.

"Oh, he's been real good," the nurse said. "He watched a movie last night on that thing you gave him."

"Oh yeah?" Tommy said, taking a knee in front of his dad. "What movie?"

"Well, I don't really know," the nurse said. "Some movie where angels and demons were fighting each other in the sky. It was quite exciting."

"You saw that, Papa?" Tommy said.

Dani knelt down beside him.

"Dad," Tommy said. "I want you to meet somebody. This is Dani. Remember me telling you about her?"

"Dani," Tommy's father said, looking right at her.

"Pleased to finally meet you," Dani said.

"We're getting married, Papa," Tommy said.

"Really?" Arnie said. "Who to?"

"To each other," Tommy said. "Now I'm going to take you home for Christmas dinner."

"Well, isn't that just corn on the cob?" Arnie said.

Arnie smiled all the way back to Tommy's house, commenting only, as they drove through the center of East Salem, that the church bells were beautiful.

"They don't work, Dad," Tommy said. "They haven't for years."

"Yes, they do," Arnie said. "Roll the window down."

Tommy stopped the car for a moment and got out. Dani joined him.

Arnie was right. The bells that hadn't chimed for years were ringing out from the church steeple in town.

After they'd gotten home and helped Arnie into the house, Tommy headed back out to put the car in the garage, and Dani followed him. In the car, she turned to him.

"Tommy," she said, her face close to his, their eyes locked on each other.

"Dani," he said.

"Before we go back inside, I want to tell you something."

"Shoot."

"I love you."

"I love you."

"I don't know if *normal* is the word I'm looking for," she said. "Things will probably never be 'normal' again. But at some point, very soon, I am looking forward to being alone with you. Somewhere quiet. Just us. No . . ."

"Distractions?"

"Yeah," Dani said. "No distractions."

"I want that too."

They kissed.

He backed the car around to move it into the garage. He pressed the opener and, as the garage door lifted, saw two figures waiting for him in the garage. Charlie and Ben stepped aside to give him room to park.

Charlie was admiring Tommy's Harley-Davidson Sportster, one of two remaining motorcycles.

Ben was grinning from ear to ear. "We just wanted to say good-bye," he said when they'd gotten out of the car.

"For now," Charlie added.

"We want you to be alone together without distractions too," Ben said.

"Thanks," Tommy said. "Can I ask you a favor?"

"What would you like?"

"Can we see you one more time?" he said. "The way you really look?"

Charlie and Ben stepped out into the courtyard and then, standing side by side, they spread their arms, and in an instant the night was filled with a brilliant light. The two angels, now towering over Dani and Tommy in their heavenly forms, rose into the air, smiled, and in a vortex of transcendent glory, vanished.

"Wow," Dani said. "Just wow."

Back in the house Reese, with his brother next to him, found Tommy in the kitchen.

"I was wondering if perhaps you'd want to play another game of foosball?" Reese said. "I was telling Edmond how lucky I was to beat you the last time. I was hoping maybe you could show us how the game is played."

"I'd be happy to," Tommy said.

Before exiting the room, Reese glanced over his shoulder at Dani, gave her a thumbs-up, and winked. When Dani laughed, Tommy asked her what was so funny.

"Nothing," she said. "Everything. I'm just . . ."

"You're just what?"

"Wow," she said. "Just wow."

READING GROUP GUIDE

1. Do you think there's an ongoing invisible war being waged between angels and demons?

2. The Bible mentions only two instances of multiple births, that of Jacob and Esau (Genesis 25) and Zarah and Perez (Genesis 38), but makes no mention of identical twins. What might explain this?

3. Do you think, as supported by anecdotal evidence, that identical twins have a way to communicate telepathically over long distances?

4. Sensory deprivation tanks have been used in health spas for relaxation purposes for the last 30-40 years. How do you think you would feel inside one, and why?

5. Detective Casey cites an incident of an angel running into a burning building to save two small children. Have you heard any similar stories?

6. Can you cite any incidents where angels have directly intervened in your life?

7. Which Hollywood actress can you think of who's the most like Cassandra Morton?

8. The East Salem Trilogy uses, for literary purposes, the idea of prophecies. What prophecies do you believe in? What's the difference between a false prophecy and a true prophecy?

9. *Final Tide* posits a fictitious coalition of Christians from within the governments of warring states who band together to fight the

common enemy—Satan. Do you think such a coalition would be possible in the real world?

10. The East Salem Trilogy plays with the idea of a super-drug that could make the whole world happy and live in peace. If such a drug existed, would you take it? Explain your answer.

11. Of the three books in the trilogy, which was your favorite, and why?

12. If you were writing a sequel or a new book featuring Tommy Gunderson and Dani Harris, what would it be about?

ACKNOWLEDGMENTS

Thank you to the readers of the East Salem novels. Thank you for taking this amazing journey with Dani Harris and Tommy Gunderson and all the characters in East Salem and beyond.

Thank you, O'Reilly, from Wiehl. And Roger Ailes, an intrepid leader, who took a chance on hiring a certain legal analyst. And Dianne Brandi, whose judgment is infallible. Thank you, Deirdre Imus, my sister from another mother.

Thanks to Pete's lovely wife, Jen, and their son, Jack for all their patience.

Thank you to the ceaselessly stunning team at Thomas Nelson! Daisy Hutton, vice-president and publisher, is wise well beyond her years; Ami McConnell, senior acquisitions editor, so honored to call her friend; Amanda Bostic, editorial director, brilliant; LB Norton, line editor, with the keenest of pens and sharpest of wits; Becky Monds, editor, keeps the whole team on track with a smile on her face; Jodi Hughes, the ever on-target associate editor; Kristen Vasgaard, a brilliant manager of packaging; Ruthie Dean, marketing and publicity specialist, always with new and better ideas; Laura Dickerson, marketing and publicity specialist, is inspired; Kerri Potts, marketing and publicity coordinator, and the inspiration behind my Facebook; and, of course, special thanks to my friend Katie Bond, director of marketing and publicity. We're so proud to be part of this team!

Special thanks to our book agents, Todd Shuster and Lane Zachary of the Zachary, Shuster, and Harmsworth Literary Agency. We couldn't have done this without your amazing vision.

And always, Mom and Dad, thank you.

All the mistakes are ours. All the credit is theirs. Thank you!

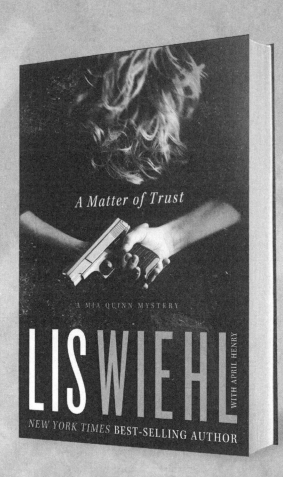

Two little girls,

frozen in black and white.

One picture worth killing for.

SNAPSHOT

LIS WIEHL

NEW YORK TIMES BEST-SELLING AUTHOR

Available January 2014

CONNECT WITH
LIS WIEHL

/liswiehl   @liswiehl

www.liswiehlbooks.com

9781595549464-C